An Integrative Approach to Counseling

MULTICULTURAL ASPECTS OF COUNSELING AND PSYCHOTHERAPY SERIES

SERIES EDITOR

Paul B. Pedersen, Ph.D.,
Professor Emeritus, Syracuse University
Visiting Professor, Department of Psychology, University of Hawaii

EDITORIAL BOARD

VOLUMES IN THIS SERIES

An Integrative Approach to Counseling

Bridging Chinese Thought, Evolutionary Theory, and Stress Management

Robert G. Santee

Chaminade University of Honolulu

Multicultural Aspects of Counseling and Psychotherapy Series 23

SAGE Publications
Los Angeles • London • New Delhi • Singapore

For information:

Sage Publications, Inc.
2455 Teller Road
Thousand Oaks,
  California 91320
E-mail: order@sagepub.com

Sage Publications India Pvt. Ltd.
B 1/I 1 Mohan Cooperative
  Industrial Area
Mathura Road, New Delhi 110 044
India

Sage Publications Ltd.
1 Oliver's Yard
55 City Road
London EC1Y 1SP
United Kingdom

Sage Publications Asia-Pacific Pte. Ltd.
33 Pekin Street #02-01
Far East Square
Singapore 048763

Printed in the United States of America

Library of Congress Cataloging-in-Publication Data

Santee, Robert G.
An integrative approach to counseling: Bridging Chinese thought, evolutionary theory, and stress management/Robert G. Santee.
    p. cm.—(Multicultural aspects of counseling and psychotherapy; 23)
Includes bibliographical references and index.
ISBN 978-1-4129-3980-5 (cloth)
ISBN 978-1-4129-3981-2 (pbk.)
    1. Cross-cultural counseling. 2. Evolutionary psychology.
3. Stress (Psychology) 4. Stress (Psychology)—Religious aspects. I. Title. II. Series.

BF636.7.C76S26 2007
158.'3—dc22   2007005960

This book is printed on acid-free paper.

07   08   09   10   11   10   9   8   7   6   5   4   3   2   1

Acquiring Editor:	Kassie Graves
Editorial Assistant:	Veronica Novak
Copy Editor:	Pam Suwinsky
Typesetter:	C&M Digitals (P) Ltd.
Proofreader:	Anne Rogers
Indexer:	Rick Hurd
Cover Designer:	Candice Harman
Marketing Associate:	Thomas Mankowski

Contents

Series Editor's Foreword

The Multicultural Aspects of Counseling and Psychotherapy (MACP) series has provided an "encyclopedic" coverage of the need to make each cultural context central rather than marginal to counseling and psychotherapy. This book by Robert G. Santee fits perfectly into that puzzle by demonstrating that counseling and psychotherapy has been around for thousands of years in a historical and seamless connection of each person adapting to her and/or his environment. As Santee explains it: "At its most basic, simple level all counseling or therapy begins from the perspective of helping people help themselves develop solutions relative to adapting to an environmental context. All counseling or therapy is about change. Clients enter counseling or therapy because, for whatever reason, their current behavior is, in some sense, compromising their ability to functionally adapt to their environment." Santee provides an application of a culturally diverse integrative approach to counseling with attention to familiar counseling concepts such areas as rapport, thinking, feeling, behaving, interpersonal relationships, and spirituality.

The goal of this text is to build a bridge between Western approaches and contrasting approaches described by Buddhism, Daoism, and Confucianism. This bridge of understanding will help the reader both to test the assumptions underlying conventional counseling and psychotherapy in its own ethnocentric perspective and to discover how these three Chinese perspectives provide a contrasting perspective for making counseling and therapy fit a diversified world environment. The metaphor Santee uses is the building of a "bamboo bridge," borrowing from the characteristics of bamboo to be both flexible and strong. This bridge, based on the Daoist approach of simplicity, commonality, and beginning points, and constructed with concepts from evolutionary theory, evolutionary psychology, and stress management, allows for the integration of non-Western approaches into Western counseling. The purpose of this bridge is enhancing and informing Western counseling, and increasing potential treatment modalities for clients.

In the original proposal for this book Santee clearly describes what he is attempting to do. "The primary goal for writing this book is to build a bridge between contemporary Western counseling and the ancient teachings of Confucianism, early Daoism, and Chan Buddhism relative to increasing cross-cultural understanding, both theoretical and practical, within the field of Western counseling. This bridge needs to be built as Western counseling is too narrow in scope, seeing counseling as merely one hundred or so years old while, in fact, the art of helping others functionally adapt to their environment (counseling) is over two thousand years old in the traditions of China."

This book is a critique of conventional counseling and psychotherapy with implicit cultural bias toward individualistic thinking and measuring all environments against a Euro-American context. The Santee book will broaden the reader's perspectives through an interdisciplinary and evolutionary and integrative framework that is grounded in historical fact. Santee provides an integrative approach to counseling that views the counseling context from the perspective of evolutionary theory, evolutionary psychology, chronic stress, and stress management. Challenging our assumptions will make the reader uncomfortable and even angry at times or at least frustrated by having to relearn what he or she thought they already knew! However, pretending that other worldviews are not important will not make them go away and ultimately the competent counselor and psychotherapist will be forced to reexamine their worldview and accept a more integrative approach in a new paradigm. Counseling and psychotherapy involves viewing problems and symptoms that bring clients to counselors as based in difficulties in adapting to various environmental contexts, which gives rise to chronic stress, which in turn gives rise to an overall sense of dissatisfaction or unhappiness. This being the case, a treatment approach is generated that focuses on discovering the adaptive problem and addressing it through stress management.

Our non-Western colleagues know much more about us than we know about them. This book will help the reader move beyond cultural encapsulation by the conventional literature about counseling and psychotherapy. This book will supplement the other books from a Euro-American perspective in your library. This book will provide a bridge between worldviews and identify common ground across cultures. This book does not provide easy answers. After reading this book you will have even more questions than you do at present but this book will help you sharpen those questions more skillfully. There are many teacher-friendly features in the Santee book. There are end of chapter exercises that allow the reader to put theory into practice, chapter tables that succinctly summarize the chapter narrative and a culturally diverse approach to living life that views continual change as the nature of reality.

Each book in the Multicultural Aspects of Counseling and Psychotherapy series seeks to "push the envelope" of conventional publications about counseling and psychotherapy with each book in the series providing a balance of critique on the one hand and positive action on the other. All books in the series take an optimistic approach rather than merely deconstructing conventional theories. All books define culture inclusively and broadly to include both between-group and within-group similarities and differences. The Santee book fits perfectly within that context, contributing to a world perspective of counseling and psychotherapy.

—Paul Pedersen

Acknowledgments

This book has its beginning point in Taipei at a conference on intercultural research. After my presentation, a gentleman walked up to me, introduced himself as Paul Pedersen, and said, "Would you like to write a book?" I cannot thank Paul enough for all of his support, encouragement, wisdom, expertise, and mentoring.

I want to thank my colleague Ron Becker for his reading of the manuscript, his comments, suggestions, and guidance. To my assistant Jan Martin, thank you for all of your help.

To Arthur Pomponio, formerly of Sage, I appreciate your guidance. To Kassie Graves, acquisitions editor, human services, at Sage, thank you for all of your encouragement, support, and expertise. To Kassie's assistant, Veronica Novak, thank you for your help. And to copy editor Pam Suwinsky, thank you for your expertise, guidance, suggestions, and very sharp eyes.

Sage Publications gratefully acknowledges the following reviewers:

Daniel Coleman, Portland State University, Graduate School of Social Work

Lisa Paler, College of New Rochelle

Vikki L. Vandiver, Portland State University, Graduate School of Social Work

Christinen Yeh, Teachers College, Columbia University

Doris F. Chang, New School for Social Research

Larisa Buhin, The Chicago School of Professional Psychology

Heather C. Trepal, The University of Texas at San Antonio

Jim Kotleba, Judson College

Mary Jane Anderson, Augusta State University

Paul Pedersen, University of Hawaii, Manoa

For my three purities

Cameron Tian Xi Kubo
Liliana Zhen Ai Kubo
Emma Hai An Santee

Introduction

To hold that which is still is easy

To plan for that which does not have omens is easy

To break that which is brittle is easy

To scatter that which is small is easy

Act before something arises

Govern/heal before there is disorder

A tree that you can wrap your arms around is produced from a sprout

A terrace nine levels high rises up from a clump of dirt

A thousand-mile journey begins with the first step

To act on something is to spoil it

To put limitations on something is to lose it

Therefore the naturally integrated person

*Does not interfere [*wu wei*], thus nothing is spoiled*

Does not put limitations, thus nothing is lost

In their interactions in the world people are nearly successful, yet they spoil them

Be attentive of the end as if it were the beginning, thus nothing is spoiled.[1]

—*Dao De Jing,* Chapter 64

These ancient—more than 2,000 years old—Chinese Daoist teachings for addressing challenges in one's environment suggest that one should engage the challenge at its earliest stages. Engage the challenge at its origins, when it is easiest to understand and resolve. For the Daoist, people appear to have a tendency, unfortunately, to view challenges from the perspective of endpoints, complexity, and differences. This can result in limited viewpoints, unnecessary interference with the natural course of events, and problematic results. These Daoist teachings understand this tendency and clearly show the seamless connection between endpoints, differences, and complexity back to beginning points, commonality, and simplicity. A return to where the challenge can be more easily seen, understood, and addressed.

Even though the challenge appears to be at an endpoint, different, and complex, in Daoist teachings the individual should try to determine its origins in order to resolve it. To accomplish this, the individual should always remain attentive, in the here and now, and focused on the challenge as if it were just beginning. Looking at the challenge from this perspective removes the limitations and barriers that are associated with endpoints, differences, and complexity. The seamless connection among all things is then clearly established.

The Challenge

Pedersen (1999) suggests that there appears to be a paradigm shift occurring in psychology today. This shift is moving toward a more integrative and culturally focused approach. He notes:

> We know that fundamental changes are taking place in the social sciences and particularly psychology. Some sort of paradigm shift is occurring. We know that these patterns of change are more than a continuation of historical patterns and represent a significantly different set of rules and patterns. There is still a great deal of disagreement about the basis of these fundamental changes but there is increased attention to the metaphor of "culture" or "multiculturalism" as the basis for understanding these changing rules. We do not know what impact the notion of culture or multiculturalism will have on traditional psychological theories. . . . Elements of analytical reductionism in psychology seem to be giving way to a more holistic, culturally inclusive and integrative approach which recognizes that people from all populations are both similar and different at the same time. (Pedersen, 1999, pp. 192, 197)

Norcross, Hedges, and Prochaska (2002) surveyed experts in the field of psychotherapy, with a Delphi Poll, in order to determine possible future trends in psychotherapy. In their analysis of 29 theoretical orientations, both multicultural psychotherapy (rated second) and theoretical integrative psychotherapy (sixth) placed in the top six theoretical orientations most likely to increase in use by the year 2010 (p. 318).

Corey (2005, p. 464) argues for the importance of developing an integrative approach to counseling and psychotherapy. He points out that no counseling theory and its derived techniques, in and of itself, is adequate to address the diversity of the current client population. He emphasizes the need to examine, learn from, and incorporate appropriate aspects of multiple theories and their techniques, within the framework of cultural factors, in order to better address the challenges faced by this diverse population of clients.

Walsh (2000) argues that the field of Western counseling and psychotherapy has not given adequate attention to the benefits of utilizing culturally diverse approaches, both in theory and practice, to assist in resolving psychological difficulties. He notes:

> There is growing evidence that Western psychotherapists may have significantly underestimated the psychologies and therapies of other cultures. This may be especially true for Asian therapies, which have often been dismissed as primitive superstitions despite the fact that some, but not all are highly sophisticated and effective systems. . . . Studying—or better yet, actually practicing—these techniques can provide both theoretical and practical benefits. Theoretical benefits include new perspectives on human nature, health, potential, and pathology. . . . On the practical side, Asian therapies are effective, simple, inexpensive, and often pleasurable. They can reduce stress, ameliorate multiple psychological and psychosomatic disorders, offer profound insights into the mind, accelerate mental and emotional development and foster latent capacities and potentials. Finally studying Asian systems has the healthy effect of unveiling and undermining ethnocentrism. (Walsh, 2000, p. 407)

Lee (1993) points out that when psychology texts examine the early history of psychology, they focus on the early Greek thinkers. There is no consideration for the contribution that early Chinese thought—for example, Confucianism and Daoism—may have made to psychological thinking. Lee acknowledges that Chinese thought presents significant challenges to the Western mind but, nonetheless argues that Western psychology by ignoring the Chinese contribution, is culturally biased.

Recently there have been attempts to analyze Chinese thought relative to its contribution to psychological understanding. Tweed and Lehman (2002) analyzed Socratic and Confucian approaches to learning relative to their influence in the modern classroom. In response to Tweed and Lehman, Gurung (2003) suggested that these two approaches to learning may not be as distinct as the authors suggest. Li (2003), also in response to Tweed and Lehman (2002), suggests that the authors did not adequately present the Confucian model of learning. In response, Tweed and Lehman (2003) addressed the concerns raised by Gurung and Li.

Nisbet (2003) compares and contrasts Western processes and Asian processes in the area of cognition. Early on he gives specific focus to Greek thinking and Chinese thinking. He notes that as much as there is a divergence between Western and Asian perspectives,

> a third view should be considered which is that the world may be in for convergence rather than continued divergence, but a convergence based not purely on Westernization but also on Easternization and on new cognitive forms based on the blending of social systems and values. (Nisbet, 2003, p. 224)

One of the earliest explorations of the possible relationship between Western psychotherapy and culturally diverse perspectives for healing occurs in the writings of Alan Watts. Watts (1961) examined the potential relationship between Western psychotherapy and Eastern liberation philosophies. He concluded that Western psychotherapy and Eastern liberation strategies do indeed share commonalities in their mutual concern with the process of changing behavior. He noted:

> If we look deeply into such ways of life as Buddhism and Taoism, Vedanta and Yoga, we do not find either philosophy or religion as these are understood in the West. We find something more nearly resembling psychotherapy. . . . The main resemblance between Eastern ways of life and Western psychotherapy is in the concern of both with bringing about changes of consciousness, changes in our ways of feeling our own existence and our relation to human society and the natural world. (Watts, 1961, p. 11)

More recently, non-Western healing methods have been examined relative to their integration into Western counseling and psychotherapy. Moodley and West (2005) offer for examination a wide range of psychotherapeutic healing methods from culturally diverse contexts. They argue that this examination is necessary because of the failure of Western counseling and psychotherapy to adequately address the needs of a culturally diverse population. This being the case, they propose that various culturally diverse approaches to healing be considered for integration into Western counseling and psychotherapy. Wong and Wong (2006) present numerous culturally diverse approaches to be considered for managing stress. They argue for the importance of contextually understanding stress and coping and not being limited to a Western paradigm.

The integration of Western psychotherapy and counseling with non-Western healing methods can be seen in the publication of numerous texts that integrate Buddhist mindfulness with Western psychotherapy. One of the earlier such texts was by Epstein (1995), in which he integrates mindfulness with Western psychodynamic theory in the hope of enhancing the Western approach to psychotherapy. Segal, Williams, and Teasdale (2002) integrate mindfulness with cognitive therapy in order to improve their approach to addressing issues with relapse relative to depression. McQuaid and Carmona (2004) integrate mindfulness and cognitive behavioral psychology in order to provide clients with new tools for addressing depression. Germer, Siegel, and Fulton (2005) present a series of articles that explore the relationship between mindfulness and Western psychology, the therapeutic relationship, and clinical applications. Hayes, Follette, and Linehan (2004) present a series of articles that attempt to expand the field of cognitive behavioral therapy by incorporating mindfulness and acceptance. Jeffery Brantley (2003) employs mindfulness and compassion in his integrative approach to addressing the problems of anxiety, fear, and panic.

Given the works of Corey (2005), Norcross, Hedges, and Prochaska (2002), Lee (1993), Moodley and West (2005), Pedersen (1999), Walsh (2000), Watts (1961), and Wong and Wong (2006), there are two fundamental problems, both rooted in cultural diversity, facing the counselor and psychotherapists in the 21st century. The first problem is that the Western paradigm in counseling and psychotherapy, with its focus on one theoretical approach, is inadequate in addressing the needs of a culturally diverse population. An integrative approach to counseling is clearly needed.

The second problem is that the Western paradigm in counseling and psychotherapy is ethnocentric. While exceptions have clearly been noted previously, in general, the Western paradigm by its own parameters restricts the field to only those approaches that are consistent with how it defines the helping profession. By definition it eliminates most non-Western approaches to healing by defining them as belonging in the domain of religion, philosophy, or superstition. This being the case, these non-Western approaches are believed to be categorically different from the field of psychology and are not be considered for the healing process.

The challenge is to find *commonality* between Western counseling and psychotherapy, on the one hand, and the non-Western approaches on the other hand. Once the commonality is established, theory and practice from non-Western approaches can be *integrated* for the purpose of informing, enhancing, and expanding the Western paradigm of counseling and psychotherapy. This being the case, it is necessary to build a bridge, if you will, between Western counseling and psychotherapy and non-Western approaches to allow for the transference of theory and technique. This bridge will allow for a solution to the previously noted problems of (1) the restrictive paradigm in Western counseling and psychotherapy and (2) the removal of ethnocentric bias.

The Bamboo Bridge

Given the importance of integrating non-Western teachings into Western counseling and psychotherapy, the Daoist teachings of beginning points, simplicity, and commonality can serve as a guide for the construction of the bridge. Table I.1 presents some of the ways that the bamboo bridge can serve as a metaphor for our task. The bridge consists of three components, which are discussed individually next.

Evolutionary Theory and Evolutionary Psychology

All human beings (commonality) are engaged in the process of addressing and solving challenges and demands (simplicity) relative to successfully adapting to various, continually changing environmental contexts (beginning points). All individuals, as part of their evolutionary heritage, have a series of essentially the same physical and psychological mechanisms that assist them in addressing and solving their problems relative to functionally adapting to the environment. The first component of the bridge is, in essence, evolutionary theory and evolutionary psychology.

Evolutionary theory and evolutionary psychology can bypass the restrictions created by the Western paradigm in psychology. By focusing on problems and their solutions relative to adapting to the environment, clear comparisons can be made between culturally diverse perspectives. Buss (2004) notes:

> Current disciplinary boundaries within psychology may be somewhat artificial. Evolutionary psychology cuts across these boundaries and suggests the field of psychology would be better organized around the adaptive problems that humans have faced over a long expanse of evolutionary history. (p. 371)

The Stress Response

The evolutionary process has wired all human beings (commonality) with mechanisms to perceive threats in the environment (beginning points) and to initiate massive physiological changes to assist them in addressing the threat by either fleeing, freezing, or fighting (simplicity). The combination and integration of these mechanisms are generally referred to as the *stress response* or *fight-or-flight response*.

McEwen (2002) indicates that the stress response (*allostasis*), in most cases, is a normal response to the challenges and/or threats of everyday living. It assists the human being in becoming aware of and solving adaptive problems by the physiological changes it causes in the body and the brain.

Table I.1   Bamboo Bridge

Characteristic	*Symbolism*
The inside of bamboo is empty.	Emptiness is symbolic of openness, potentiality, and freedom. There are no restrictions or limitations. There is no chronic stress. Practitioners of Western counseling/psychotherapy need to be open to culturally different ways of viewing existence. They need to suspend, at least temporarily, their own cultural restrictions and limitations. This suspension will allow them to explore and examine Chinese thought relative to its potentiality and usefulness in a counseling context.
Bamboo is flexible.	To be flexible is to be sensitive to environmental and contextual demands. Given the cultural diversity of clients, practitioners of Western counseling/ psychotherapy need to be flexible in their approach to assisting clients. Clients need to be flexible in addressing and solving their adaptive problems.
Bamboo is adaptable.	Western counseling/psychotherapy and Chinese thought are both about assisting people in functionally adapting to their various environmental contexts.
Bamboo is a simple grass.	Simplicity is a basic component of Daoist teachings. At the most simple level, life is about adapting to the environment.
Bamboo is common in many places throughout Asia.	Commonality is a basic component of Daoist teachings. Addressing, solving, and adapting to the demands of the environment is common to all people throughout the world. Stress is common to all people.
Bamboo is a fundamental beginning point for the use in and creation of bridges, houses, buildings, baskets, furniture, boats, roofs, floors, and many other utensils, handicrafts, and objects of art. Bamboo is a fundamental beginning point in diets as it is nutritious and provides fiber.	Beginning points are a basic component of Daoist teachings. All human beings begin with essentially the same physical and psychological mechanisms. All human behavior begins with attempting to address and solve various environmental demands.
Bamboo is associated with rooted, powerful, and sturdy growth.	Rooted, powerful, and sturdy growth requires the management/elimination of chronic stress.

This normal response turns off, if you will, once the challenge and/or threat has been addressed and/or solved.

McEwen (2002) notes, however, that if the stress response is activated, as it will be by any threat, but is unable to assist in resolving the problem, it will not turn off. This chronic activation of the stress response (*allostatic load*) compromises both the physical and psychological health of the individual. This being the case, psychological behavior such as chronic anxiety, depression, or hostility is not to be viewed as a disease or a diagnostic category. The chronic anxiety, depression, or hostility is a manifestation of a stress response that has not turned off. This psychological behavior, across cultures, must be seen as an attempt, albeit dysfunctional, by the human being to adapt to or solve the challenges and threats in his or her environment (Nesse & Williams, 1996). This being the case, the stress response, or more specifically the chronic activation of the stress response, is the second component of the bridge.

Stress Management

If it is the case that dysfunctional psychological behaviors, in any cultural context, are in fact the manifestation of the chronic activation of the stress response, and that the chronic activation of the stress response compromises both the physical and psychological health of the individual, then the various solutions offered by culturally diverse perspectives are fundamentally attempts at stress management. All culturally diverse perspectives (commonality) have solutions (simplicity) for turning off (beginning points) the chronic activation of the stress response. The third component of the bridge, albeit under many different names, is the theories, teachings, and techniques for turning off the chronic activation of the stress response. In other words, stress management.

This bamboo bridge between Western counseling and psychotherapy, on the one hand, and non-Western approaches, on the other hand, integrates Chinese thought (Daoist teachings) and Western thought (evolutionary theory and evolutionary psychology, stress response, and stress management) and establishes a common ground. Thus the first challenge of commonality has been met. The second challenge is to select a non-Western approach to integrate with, inform, enhance, and expand the Western paradigm for counseling and psychotherapy. The non-Western approach selected to address this challenge is that of Chinese thought.

Chinese Thought

Chinese thought was selected as the approach to integrate with the Western paradigm for three reasons. The first reason is that of history. During the beginning of the first millennium (CE), the teaching of Buddhism entered China from India. Over the course of approximately 500 years, Buddhism was integrated into the Chinese way of life. This of course required significant adaptations both for the teachings of Buddhism and the Chinese people. The entrance of Buddhism into China and its eventual assimilation is considered to be one of the major cross-cultural events in the recorded history of the world.

The second reason for the selection of Chinese thought is that Buddhism and the indigenous teachings of China—Daoism and Confucianism—during a time frame of 1,000 years, enhanced and informed each other. This cross-pollination, if you will, resulted in integrations that produced new schools of thought. It is this type of integration that informs the structure of this text.

Daoism and Buddhism integrated to produce Chan Buddhism (6th–8th century CE). Chan Buddhism is probably better known by its Japanese counterpart and pronunciation: Zen.

Daoism, Buddhism, and Confucianism were integrated with two different focuses. The Confucian focus resulted in the development of Neo-Confucianism (approximately 10th–12th century CE), with Daoism and Buddhism enhancing and informing it. The Daoist focus resulted in the development of the Complete Reality School of Daoism (10th–12th century CE) with Confucianism and Buddhism enhancing and informing it.

The third reason is that in addition to being a PhD in educational psychology, I am also trained in Chinese philosophy, holding a PhD in philosophy, and am able, with much pain, to read classical Chinese.

In China, a bridge was built allowing the assimilation of a culturally diverse perspective—Indian Buddhism—to inform, enhance, and expand the Chinese worldview. With a new bridge, our focus now is on utilizing Chinese culture, specifically the classical teachings of Buddhism, Daoism, and Confucianism, to inform, enhance, and expand Western counseling and psychotherapy.

How the Text Is Organized

This text is designed to provide the reader with an integrative and culturally diverse view of healing, with the ultimate goal of informing, enhancing, and expanding the Western paradigm of counseling and psychotherapy. In order for this to occur, it is necessary for the reader to have an in-depth, contextually based understanding of the teachings of Buddhism, Daoism, and Confucianism. Thus, there are a significant number of translations from the Chinese for each of these three teachings. It is only by reading the original classical teachings that the reader will be able to walk across the bridge. In the text itself are the pinyin or the romanization of the Mandarin pronunciation of important Chinese characters (words or concepts). The actual characters are found at the end of the chapters.

Part I, "Fundamental Principles and Concepts," provides an in-depth analysis of each of the three components of the bridge. Chapter 1 examines Buddhism, Daoism, and Confucianism in light of evolutionary theory and evolutionary psychology. Chapter 2 examines Buddhism, Daoism, and Confucianism in light of the stress response and chronic stress. Chapter 3 examines the stress management programs of Herbert Benson and Jon Kabat-Zinn. At the end of each chapter in Part I, there is a list of important terms and an exercise.

As the teachings of Buddhism, Daoism, and Confucianism are essentially stress management programs, they are examined individually in Part II. Part II, "Culturally Diverse Approaches to Managing Stress," presents the basic teachings of Buddhism, Daoism, and Confucianism in light of the topic of stress management. The three chapters in Part II are the core of this text and are quite extensive. Chapter 4 examines the teachings of early Buddhism, with a significant number of translations from Chinese Buddhist texts. Chapter 5 examines the teachings of the two fundamental texts of early Daoism: the *Dao De Jing* and the *Zhuang Zi*. Translations from the Chinese of these two texts are provided. Chapter 6 examines the teachings of Confucius, with translations from the Chinese of the *Lun Yu*. At the end of each chapter is a list of important terms and an exercise.

Part III, "Integration and Application of Culturally Diverse Approaches to Managing Stress," explores cultural assumptions and then integrates and applies the teachings/stress management programs of Buddhism, Daoism, and Confucianism to the areas of rapport, thinking, feeling, behaving, interpersonal relationships, and spirituality. Chapter 7 examines the cultural assumptions of Western thought with a focus on philosophy, religion, and science. These cultural assumptions are then contrasted with Chinese thought. Compared to the earlier chapters in this book, the remaining chapters are quite brief, as they seek to provide but a glimpse of integration and application. Chapter 8 examines rapport in light of the teachings/stress management programs of Buddhism, Daoism, and Confucianism. Chapter 9 examines thinking in light of these programs. Chapter 10 examines feeling; Chapter 11, behaving. Chapter 12 examines interpersonal relations, and Chapter 13 concludes the book with an examination of spirituality in light of the teachings/stress management programs of Buddhism, Daoism, and Confucianism.

The goal of this text is simply to provide the reader with the opportunity to view the culturally diverse perspectives of Buddhism, Daoism, and Confucianism in a context that will allow for the integration of these teachings into Western counseling and psychotherapy. This integration will, it is hoped, contribute to resolving the problems facing contemporary counseling and psychotherapy caused by its own ethnocentric perspective and the need to address cultural diversity. It is a move toward embracing a new paradigm. It is a bamboo bridge.

Note

1. The translation/interpretation of this chapter of the *Dao De Jing* is my own. The primary text utilized for this translation is the standard transmitted text with the Wang Bi commentary. This Chinese text can be found in Yang (1972). In addition, I also utilized Wang (1993).

References

Brantley, J. (2003*)*. *Calming your anxious mind: How mindfulness and compassion can free you from anxiety, fear, and panic.* Oakland, CA: New Harbinger.

Buss, D. M. (2004). *Evolutionary psychology.* Boston: Allyn & Bacon.

Corey, G. (2005). *Theory and practice of counseling.* Belmont, CA: Brooks/Cole.

Epstein, M. (1995). *Thoughts without a thinker.* New York: Basic Books.

Germer, C. K., Siegel, R. D., & Fulton, P. R. (Eds.). (2005). *Mindfulness and psychotherapy.* New York: Guilford.

Gurung, R. A. R. (2003). Comparing culture and individual learning tendencies. *American Psychologist, 58,* 145–146.

Hayes, S. C., Follette, V. M., & Linehan, M. M. (Eds.). (2004). *Mindfulness and acceptance.* New York: Guilford.

Lee, Y. T. (1993). Psychology needs no prejudice but the diversity of cultures. *American Psychologist, 48,* 1090–1091.

Li, J. (2003). The core of Confucian learning. *American Psychologist, 58,* 146–147.

McEwen, B. (2002). *The end of stress as we know it.* Washington, DC: Joseph Henry Press.

McQuaid, J. R., & Carmona, P. E. (2004). *Peaceful mind: Using mindfulness and cognitive behavioral psychology to overcome depression.* Oakland, CA: New Harbinger.

Moodley, R., & West, W. (2005). *Integrating traditional healing practices into counseling and psychotherapy.* Thousand Oaks, CA: Sage.

Nesse, R. M., & Williams, G. C. (1996). *Why we get sick: The new science of Darwinian medicine.* New York: Random House.

Nisbet, R. E. (2003). *The geography of thought: How Asians and Westerners think differently . . . and why.* New York: Free Press.

Norcross, J. C., Hedges, M., & Prochaska, J. O. (2002). The face of 2010: A Delphi Pole on the future of psychotherapy. *Professional Psychology: Research and Practice, 33*(3), 316–322.

Pedersen, P. (1999). The positive consequences of a culture-centered perspective. In P. Pedersen (Ed.), *Multiculturalism as a fourth force* (pp. 191–211). Philadelphia: Brunner/Mazel.

Segal, Z. V., Williams, J. M. G., & Teasdale, J. D. (2002). *Mindfulness-based cognitive therapy for depression.* New York: Guilford.

Tweed, R. G., & Lehman, D. R. (2002). Learning considered within a cultural context: Confucian and Socratic approaches. *American Psychologist, 57,* 89–99.

Tweed, R. G., & Lehman, D. R. (2003). Confucian and Socratic learning. *American Psychologist, 58,* 148–149.

Walsh, R. (2000). Asian psychotherapies. In R. J. Corsini & D. Wedding (Eds.), *Current psychotherapies* (pp. 407–444). Itasca, IL: F. E. Peacock.

Wang, K. (1993). *Lao zi dao de jing he shang gong zhang zhu.* Beijing: Zhong Hua Shu Ju.

Watts, A. W. (1961). *Psychotherapy East and West.* New York: Random House.

Wong, P. T. P., & Wong, L. C. J. (Eds.). (2006). *Handbook of multicultural perspectives on stress and coping.* New York: Springer.

Yang, J. L. (Zhu Bian). (1972). *Lao zi ben yi, Lao zi xin kao shu lue.* Taibei: Shi Jie Shu Ju.

PART I

Fundamental Principles and Concepts

The chapters in Part I introduce the three components of the bamboo bridge. The first chapter explores evolutionary theory and psychology. The second chapter examines stress and the stress response. The third chapter investigates stress management.

Chapter 1 views behavior as occurring as the result of the interaction between the human being and the environment as the human attempts to solve an adaptive problem presented by the environment. In this light, behavior is seen as functional insofar as it is attempting to solve a problem occurring in an environmental context. The environment is observed to be an ongoing, continually changing, interdependent, integrated process.

Buddhism, Daoism, and Confucianism are all analyzed from the perspective of providing solutions for specific problems occurring in such an environment. This is the first commonality between Western counseling and psychotherapy and the teachings of Buddhism, Daoism, and Confucianism.

Chapter 2 focuses on stress and the stress response. The issue of stress is viewed from the perspectives of Buddhism, Daoism, and Confucianism. The stress response is examined as an adaptive tool developed during the evolutionary process that is fundamental for the survival and the reproduction of human beings.

Normal stress (allostasis) and chronic stress (allostatic load) are explored. Chronic stress is postulated as being the fundamental problem, albeit in different terms, addressed by Buddhism, Daoism, and Confucianism. It is argued that the problem of chronic stress is what is addressed by counseling or therapy. This is the second commonality between Western counseling and psychotherapy and the teachings of Buddhism, Daoism, and Confucianism.

Chapter 3 looks at stress management and the solutions offered to address chronic stress relative to solving adaptive problems in the environment. This is the third commonality between Western counseling and psychotherapy and the teachings of Buddhism, Daoism, and Confucianism. Particular focus is given in this chapter to the integrated approaches of Herbert Benson (relaxation response) and Jon Kabat-Zinn (mindfulness).

Given the three commonalities, a bamboo bridge is established, allowing for the teachings of Buddhism, Daoism, and Confucianism to inform and enhance Western counseling and psychotherapy.

1

Evolutionary Theory and Evolutionary Psychology

Confucius said, "By their nature people are close
Through their practice they are distant."[1]

—*Lun Yu*, XVII-2

The perspective of evolutionary theory and evolutionary psychology provides a common ground for integrating Chinese thought into Western counseling and psychotherapy. Evolutionary theory was Darwin's (1979/1859) attempt to explain the process of change relative to living entities adapting to their environment, surviving and reproducing. Evolutionary psychology is the application of the fundamental principles of evolutionary theory (such as adaptation to the environment, natural selection, variation, continual change, survival, reproduction, and so on) to how human beings think, feel, behave and interact. Evolutionary psychology focuses on the relationship between human beings and their environment relative to addressing and solving *adaptive problems* for the purpose of survival, reproduction, and maintaining and perpetuating their gene pool (known as "inclusive fitness") (Buss, 2004; Hergenhahn, 1997). This focus eliminates artificially contrived boundaries both within the discipline of psychology and outside of the discipline, allowing for exploration, comparison, and integration from traditions long considered not relevant, such as Buddhism, Daoism, and Confucianism. (See Table 1.1.)

Table 1.1   Evolutionary Theory and Chinese Thought

Evolutionary Theory	Confucianism, Daoism, Buddhism
Human organisms have essentially the same physical and psychological mechanisms at birth.	At birth, people are essentially the same.
Differences in behavior arise as people interact with their environments, attempting to address problems in adapting to their various environmental contexts.	Differences in behavior arise as people engage with and react to the environment, attempting to address fundamental human problems.
The environment, which the human organism is part of, is a continually changing process.	Continual change is the fundamental nature of existence.
Human organisms are involved in an ongoing challenge of adapting to their environment for the purposes of survival, reproduction, and the maintenance of their gene pool.	People are involved in an ongoing process of developing and maintaining a harmonious relationship with the environment.

Regarding the field of psychology, Buss (2004) feels that it is fragmented because of artificial boundaries. These artificial boundaries create barriers to the progress of understanding human behavior. Arguing for a common ground as the best way to explore human behavior, he notes:

> From the perspective of evolutionary psychology, many traditional boundaries are not merely arbitrary but are misleading and detrimental to scientific progress. They imply boundaries that cleave mechanisms in arbitrary and unnatural ways. Studying human psychology via adaptive problems and their solutions provides a more natural means of "cleaving nature at its joints" and hence crossing current disciplinary boundaries. (Buss, 2004, p. 411)

Not only are disciplines in psychology divided from each other, there is division within the disciplines. McAdams and Pals (2006) argue that the field of personality psychology is fragmented and in need of a common ground for the purpose of developing a comprehensive, integrative framework for understanding personality. They argue:

> We contend that an integrative science of persons should be built around a first principle that enjoys the imprimatur of biological sciences. Personality theory begins with human nature, and from the standpoint of the

biological sciences, human nature is best couched in terms of human evolution. To the extent that the individual person is like all others, the deep similarity is likely to be a product of human evolution. . . . Over the course of human evolution, human beings have been designed by natural selection to engage in behaviors that ultimately make for the replication of the genes that determine their design. (McAdams & Pals, 2006, p. 206)

Confucius and Evolutionary Theory

The quote at the start of this chapter—from the *Lun Yu* (*Discussions and Sayings*), or as is it is more commonly known, the *Analects of Confucius* (551–479 BCE)—is clearly consistent with the Daoist focus regarding beginning points and endpoints, commonalities and differences, and simplicity and complexity. For Confucius, people at birth—their beginning points—are quite similar regarding their natural endowment. There is a definite, simple commonality here. Once individuals engage and react to their environment, they develop behaviors, some of which they continue to practice. The continual practice of these select behaviors leads to endpoints, differences, and complexity.

For Confucius, nature and practice (engaging and reacting to the environment) are not separate from each other. They are both part of the same contextual process. Hall and Ames (1987), discussing the quote presented at the beginning of the chapter, argue that, for Confucius, people's nature must be understood in its relationship to the environment.

The Chinese character *xing*[a], which is translated in the quote as "nature," consists of two radicals (a *radical* is the basic building block of Chinese characters; there are 214 radicals) or components. On the left-hand side is the radical *xin*[b], which is a drawing of a heart and means "heart/mind." For the early Chinese, thinking and feeling were intimately intertwined. On the right-hand side of the character is the radical *sheng*[c], which is a picture of a plant or grass growing out of the earth and has the meaning, depending on the context, of birth, growth, or life. The combination refers to the potential growth of the heart/mind or one's nature. For Confucius, this potential for the growth of thinking and feeling or one's nature is quite similar in all people. Growth must occur, however, in an environmental context. It is in the engagement with and the reaction to the environmental context that people begin to differ.

The Chinese character *xi*[d], which is translated in the quote as "practice," consists of two components. The top component of this character is the character *yu*[e], which is a picture of wings. The bottom part of the character is a modified version of the radical *zi*[f], which is a picture of a nose and has the meaning of self, origins, beginnings, and a starting point, as, for the Chinese, the nose sticks out and is a strong indicator of the beginning of the person.[2] The combination is suggestive of a baby bird beginning to flap its wings, and through the continual flapping or repetitive movement of its wings it eventually develops the behavior of flying.[3] Thus the meaning of repeating, practicing, and an eventual extension into custom or habit. This behavior of practicing and repeating that leads into custom or habit must be seen, of course, as occurring as a result of the interaction between one's nature and an environmental context.

The resulting behavior is explained in a 2nd-century BCE commentary to this quote. The Chinese intellectual tradition has been sustained, in part, through the tradition of commentaries on the classical texts. The *Zheng Yi* (Orthodox/Correct Meaning) commentary to this quotes states:

> This chapter says that the fully integrated person [*jun zi*^{g}] must be cautious regarding what they practice. Nature [*xing*^{a}] is that which a person is endowed with at birth and it is still. Having not interacted with the environment all people are similar. This is near. Having interacted with the environment, their practice [habit, custom] is taken as their nature. If people practice [*xi*^{d}] what is appropriate they become a fully integrated person [*jun zi*^{g}]. If people practice what is not appropriate they become a fragmented person [*xiao ren*^{h}] becoming far apart from each other.

It is clear from this commentary that there are two levels of separation or difference. These two levels of separation or difference must not, however, be seen as categorically distinct. They are very much integrated and are a result of the interaction of one's nature with the environment. One level is concerned with practice (habit or custom) in an environmental context, and the other level has to do with successful or unsuccessful adaptation to the environmental context.

The first level is when custom or habit tends to dominates over nature. Once people begin to interact with their environment, they focus on their habits or customs (practices) as their guiding principles. At this point their behaviors may or may not be different, due to their practices arising within their various environmental contexts.

The second level of difference refers to the integration or fragmentation of the person from his or her environmental context. People may differ as a result of their behavior (customs and habits), but as long as their behaviors are appropriate and thus allow them to successfully adapt to their environment, they will be considered fully integrated persons (*jun zi*^{g}). If the individual engages in inappropriate behavior, he or she will not be successful in the adaptation process and will clearly be separate from the environment. The commentary refers to this type of person as a "fragmented person" (*xiao ren*^{h}).

The *Lun Yu* and the Components of Evolutionary Theory

Nature and Behavior

It is interesting to point out that this quote and commentary are quite comparable to one of the components of evolutionary theory that indicates that people have a similar physical and psychological nature and that they behave differently or may behave differently as a result of the interaction between their nature and their different environmental contexts over the course of time. In fact, the quote is so close to evolutionary theory and scientific research that the United Nations Educational, Scientific and Cultural Organization (UNESCO) selected it along with only one other quote, from Darwin's *Descent of Man* (2004/1871), out of all the literature available to them, as part of its 1950 statement on race.[4] The UNESCO (1950) statement is clearly based in science, evolutionary theory in particular, and notes that the scientific evidence supports the approximately 2,500-year-old quote of Confucius that has been discussed in this chapter regarding the similarity (nature) and differences (practice) between the people of the world.

The Ongoing Process of Change

A second component of evolutionary theory is that everything in the environment or, maybe more appropriately, the environment itself, is a continual process of change. This includes the human beings that roam throughout the environment. Confucius was quite aware of this ongoing process of change.

> The Master [Confucius], standing above a river, said, "Its passing away is like this. Not stopping day or night." (*Lun Yu*, IX-17)

The nature of existence as an ongoing process of continual change is fundamental to classical Chinese thought. Confucius is not different regarding this point. This is one of the major areas, however, where mainstream Western thought and Chinese thought are clearly different. Mainstream Western thought finds change problematic and looks for an underlying, unchanging, eternal reality or truth behind the appearance. For the Chinese, reality is the process of change itself. As the preceding quote from Confucius did not elaborate on the meaning of *its*, commentators have provided explanations. The first commentary we discuss is from Zheng Xuan, a very famous commentator from 2nd century BCE.

> Zheng Xuan said, "Its continual passing away means the motions of the ordinary world are like a flowing river."

It is obvious from this commentary that Zheng Xuan felt Confucius was referring to the ordinary world or life itself as being engaged in a continual process of change and passing away. As a river continually changes and flows away, so does life itself. This changing and passing away is a normal part of existence.

Zhu Xi (1130–1200), the most famous of the Confucian thinkers after Confucius himself and Mencius (4th century BCE), also views the river as representing the changing and flowing process we call existence. Commenting on this quote from the *Lun Yu,* Zhu Xi states:

> It is the continual transformations of the sky and the earth (universe). Coming and going continuously without stopping a moment for a rest. It goes without saying, this is the essence of *dao*[i] itself. Is the universe not like a flowing river? As such Confucius pointed to the river because it was easy to see. He took the river as an example to guide those desiring to learn. Continually examine yourself and the world without a single thread being broken.

Zhu Xi not only links the quote to a description of the process of life itself but also ties it into a method for studying and learning. One should continuously (like a flowing river) investigate and examine oneself and the world wherein one lives. Everything, the entire process, needs to be seen as linked or threaded together and as such, the individual should not interrupt the investigation nor see himself or herself as disconnected from the process of life itself.

This continually changing, interrelated process is very consistent with the evolutionary view of how life unfolds. From an evolutionary perspective, nothing is constant or unchanging. Like the flowing river, all things change as time passes on.

Adaptation to the Environment

A third component of evolutionary theory is that of adaptation. Those organisms that are able to adapt to their environment have a greater probability of surviving, reproducing, maintaining, and perpetuating their gene pool (inclusive fitness). Adaptation is contingent upon variations in the genetic makeup of human beings incorporated through the process of natural selection. Those variations, expressed through functional behavior, which increased the probability of our distant ancestors adapting, surviving, reproducing, and maintaining their gene pool, were passed on to successive generations. They were continually, like Confucius's river, passed on because they worked. These variations allowed for ongoing adaptation, survival, reproduction, and sustaining of the gene pool. These physical and psychological mechanisms, genetic variations that humans possess at birth—what Confucius referred to as "nature"—and that are activated through interaction with the environment—what Confucius called "practice"—assist the individual in adapting to the environment.

While Confucius and his followers did not use the word *adaptation,* their use of the word *harmony* and what it entails appears to be fairly close to what Darwin (1979/1859, 2004/1871) meant by adaptation and all that it encompasses. Master You, one of Confucius's disciples, discussing the relationship between harmony (*he^j*) and contextually appropriate behavior (*li^k*) noted:

> In using *li^k*, harmony is valued. In the way of the early kings this was perfection. It is the starting point for things small and large. In situations that are problematic, understand harmony. Yet harmony that is not guided by *li^k*, simply will not work. (*Lun Yu,* I-12)

It is clear that Master You links harmony or adaptation to the environment with contextually appropriate behavior or *li^k*. Given any environmental challenge, large or small, the goal is to adapt in a harmonious manner. This adaptation, however, will not occur if the contextually appropriate behavior is not selected. To focus simply on harmony without considering contextually appropriate behavior results in problems and compromises in the adaptation to the environment.

The scholar Ma Rong (2nd century CE) understood this relationship between harmony and contextually appropriate behavior. In his commentary to the preceding quote he stated, "When people understand *li^k* and value harmony, then everything follows harmoniously. If *li^k* is not taken as a guide, things will be problematic."

Contextually appropriate behavior is functional insofar as it allows the individual to successfully adapt to or be in harmony with the environment. The individual must be aware, however, of the environmental challenges and select the contextually appropriate behavior to address the challenges. Thus harmony and contextually appropriate behavior or adaptation and functional behavior must be seen as linked to each other.

For Confucius, the person who is in harmony with the environment is the fully integrated person (*jun zi^g*), while the person who is not in harmony is the fragmented person (*xiao ren^h*). The fully integrated person is the person who practices what is appropriate for any given situation. The fragmented person does not practice what is appropriate for a given situation. There is a definite distinction between the fully integrated person and the fragmented person. In their behavior, they are simply not the same.

> Confucius said, "A fully integrated person [*jun zi^g*] is in harmony, and not the same as others. The fragmented person is the same as others and not in harmony." (*Lun Yu,* XIII-23)

The *Zheng Yi* (Orthodox/Correct Meaning) commentary to this quote examines what is, for all intents and purposes, the psychological difference between the fully integrated person and the fragmented person. The fully integrated person is psychologically whole, as his or her thoughts, feelings, and behaviors are oriented toward being in a harmonious relationship with the environment and the people who populate it. On the other hand, the fragmented person's thoughts, feelings, and behaviors are disconnected and disjointed. The fragmented person is not interested in being in a harmonious relationship with the environment or the people who populate it. This person is oriented toward obtaining a personal advantage over others. He is out for his own gain and profit. The fully integrated person and the fragmented person do not look at or act in the world in the same manner.

The *Zheng Yi* said:

> In this section of the chapter, the will and practice of the fully integrated person and the fragmented person in their interactions in their worlds are not the same. The fully integrated person's mind/heart is in harmony. Because of this he sees each thing differently. Thus it is said he is not the same as others. The fragmented person because of his habits is the same as others. Each interaction in the world is for his personal advantage. Thus it is said, he is not in harmony.

Fully integrated people in their actions are not trying to control the environment or the people who populate it. They are not trying to gain a benefit or advantage through their actions. Guided by appropriate contextual behavior (*li^k*), they are oriented to being in harmony with the environment and other people. In other words, they are focused on establishing relationships among themselves, their environments, and other people. This being the case, they are able to view and address each situation or individual as unique or different.

Fragmented people, on the other hand, look toward the environment and the people who populate it as potential sources of gain, benefit, or advantage. There is no focus on unique relationships. There are no real distinctions or differences in this perspective. Everything and everyone are the same: potential sources for gain, benefit, or advantage. In order to obtain the gain, benefit, or advantage, fragmented people believe and act in a manner that is directed toward controlling the environment and other people. This perspective separates or disconnects them from the environment and other people. They are not in harmony.

Confucius warned that this type of behavior, which seeks gain at the expense of others, generates resentment and hatred from others. It also results in the fragmented person feeling chronically stressed. Confucius said, "Behaviors that are based on self-gain result in much resentment" (*Lun Yu*, IV-12).

Confucius said, "The fully integrated person [*jun zi*^{g}] is calm and at ease, the fragmented person is chronically stressed [sad, worried, anxious, sorrowful, distressed]." (*Lun Yu,* VII-37)

The phrase "chronically stressed" in the preceding quote is a translation/interpretation of *chang*^{l} *qi*^{m} *qi*^{m}. The character *chang*^{l} is a radical, which are the basic building blocks of the Chinese language, and represents/ is a picture of long hair held together by some implement; thus giving rise to extended interpretations such as long, lasting, growing, and ongoing. The character *qi*^{m}, which occurs twice, consists of the radical *wu*^{n}, which means "battle axe," and the component *shu*^{o}, which is an old form or way of writing "bean" or "beans." The repetition of the same character in a phrase gives emphasis or intensity to its meaning. The combination of the three characters then creates a picture or image of a battle axe continually and intensely dividing, separating, or chopping beans into small bits. It does not take much of an imagination to extend this image to the feelings associated with chronic stress.

According to Buss (2004), practitioners of evolutionary psychology are concerned with the psychological mechanisms that assist human beings in adapting to their environments. These psychological mechanisms are part of our nature, due to natural selection, because they were functional. They increased the probability of our distant ancestors surviving and reproducing. Insofar as these psychological mechanisms or variations increased the probability of surviving, reproducing, and maintaining the gene pool more so than other variations, they were passed on through natural selection to successive generations (see Nesse & Williams, 1994, pp. 13–25). Because these variations worked, all people today have the same physical and psychological mechanisms of our distant ancestors. They are the simple beginnings of behavior. Though he was not aware of the biology, this is what Confucius meant when he said, "By their nature people are close."

These psychological mechanisms alerted our distant ancestors to problems revolving around survival, reproduction, and maintaining their gene pool. These mechanisms contributed to behaviors that generated solutions to the problems and assisted the human being in adapting to the environment. Because of these various psychological mechanisms, the interactions between the human beings and various environmental contexts, the learning experiences, and the application of what was learned, the subsequent manifested behaviors may appear quite different and far apart. Though he was not aware of modern evolutionary theory and evolutionary psychology, this is what Confucius meant when he said, "Through their practice they are distant."

Case in point is the psychological and behavioral differences between the fully integrated person (*jun zi*^{g}) and the fragmented person (*xiao ren*^{h}). Although they both exist in the same geographical location and address common issues regarding functioning in their environment, they are, for

Confucius, quite different in their thinking, feeling, and behaving. The fully integrated person is calm, open minded, self-reflective, whole psychologically because cognitions and emotions are unified; understands existence as a continually changing process; and is focused through contextually appropriate behavior to be in a harmonious relationship with the environment and the people who populate it. The fragmented person is driven by habits, chronically stressed, resented by others, focused on self-gain, and disconnected from the environment and the people who populate it.

A Historical Example

The teachings of Confucius as presented in the *Lun Yu* were addressed to the ruling class, the literate. These teachings, which are fully addressed in Chapter 6, were an attempt to provide a solution to an adaptive problem. The adaptive problem was social and political instability. The various kingdoms were continually fighting with each other, did not trust each other, were unable to maintain relationships with each other, and were driven toward acquiring anything that would benefit them at the expense of the other kingdoms. Society was not in harmony.

This problem was approached by Confucius at the level of relationships between people. For society to be in harmony, the members of society, specifically the leaders, needed to be focused on their interrelationships and the overall well-being of the society. From the perspective of Confucius, these leaders were self-centered, fragmented, chronically stressed, and out for their own gain. They were the *xiao ren*[h]. In order for society to be in harmony, Confucius needed to guide the people such that they would reestablish positive relationships with each other. These positive relationships would lead to a harmonious society. His tool for guidance was education.

Confucius presented the fully integrated person (*jun zi*[g]) as a model for psychological and social health. The fully integrated person was concerned with the collective well-being of society, contextually appropriate behaviors (those that benefited society), and harmonious relationships. There was no concern for individual benefit or gain at the expense of others. Most important, for Confucius, the fully integrated person was constantly self-monitoring in order to develop and cultivate a psychologically healthy individual. It is clear from the *Lun Yu* that the fragmented person or *xiao ren*[h] was chronically stressed and was not psychologically healthy. Given the fact that the leaders were chronically stressed, it is easy to understand that the society as a whole would be socially and politically unstable or chronically stressed. The *Lun Yu* provides the theory and techniques of Confucius and his followers to address the chronic stress, guide the individual to a harmonious relationship with the environment, and reestablish a harmonious society.

The teachings of Confucius can be easily viewed through the perspective of evolutionary psychology. Confucius's teachings are an attempt to solve an adaptive problem occurring in an interrelated continually changing environment. The adaptive problem during the time of Confucius was that society itself was politically and socially unstable. It was not in harmony. The Confucian teachings can be seen as a way of reducing chronic stress (solving an environmental problem) that arises from utilizing contextually inappropriate behaviors (self-centered focus), for the purpose of assisting individuals in adapting to the environment. This would then lead, ideally, to a harmonious society.

This description can apply to the process of Western counseling. Western counseling is oriented toward helping individuals help themselves (solving an adaptive problem) so they can successfully function in (adapt to) their various environmental contexts. Thus, evolutionary psychology is an integral aspect of the integrative model being developed in this text.

In so far as evolutionary psychology is concerned with directing attention toward the function of behavior relative to addressing and solving basic environmentally generated problems, it is clearly grounded in the Daoist model of beginning points (behavior attempting to solve a problem generated by the interaction of the individual with the environment), commonalities (universal problems) and simplicity (adapting to the environment). At a level of beginning points, commonalities, and simplicity, Western counseling and Confucianism can be compared and explored.

Since we are attempting to integrate not only Confucianism into Western counseling, but also Daoism and Buddhism, it is necessary to explore these perspectives as well within the context of evolutionary psychology. We begin here with Daoism.

Daoism and Evolutionary Theory

According to tradition, Lao Zi (circa 6th century BCE), an older contemporary of Confucius, wrote the *Dao De Jing*. The *Dao De Jing,* like the *Lun Yu,* was written to address the same adaptive problem of social and political instability. It was addressed to the same literate population, the ruling class, and also focused on the problematic behavior of the individual. The *Dao De Jing,* however, provided a different solution than the *Lun Yu* and proposed that the Confucian solution was contributing to the ongoing problem of social and political unrest.

Like the Confucian perspective, Daoism looked at existence as an ongoing, interrelated process of change. This Daoist perspective is based on observation and direct experience. It is not based on speculation and logically reasoned argument. It is not based on faith.

Sincerely maintaining stillness, extreme emptiness is reached. All things simultaneously acting together, by which I nonjudgmentally [*guan*[p]] observe their cycles. Things are numerous. All cycles return to their root. Returning to the root is called stillness. This is said to be the cycle of destiny. The cycle of destiny is called the ordinary present.[5] (*Dao De Jing*, 16)

Guan[p], or what is translated in the preceding quote as "nonjudgmentally observe," is not merely looking or seeing. It is a nonjudgmental awareness of the "here and now" or ordinary present. To be nonjudgmental, the chattering mind/heart must be stilled and empty. The chattering mind/heart presents judgments, barriers, and filters that interfere with the direct experience of the process we call existence. Once the mind/heart is stilled and empty, such that judgments, barriers, and filters are suspended, existence is experienced. For the Daoist, the experience is that of interrelationships, continual change, and the process of all things cycling from and returning to their root. The root is the ordinary, unfiltered, empty present.

For the Daoist, when people interfere with themselves and others, they are not in touch with the ordinary present. They live in an artificial world of judgments, abstractions, *should*s and *ought*s, and absolute beliefs and values. This artificial world results in and is a result of a perspective that sees existence as fragmented, static, not interrelated, not changing, and as consisting of independent, distinct boundaries and categories. The consequence of this perspective is self-centeredness, contention, contrived desires, and stress. The self-centeredness, contention, contrived desires, and stress gives rise to social and political instability. The social and political instability, in turn, creates the potential for more stress. The solution, then, for this adaptive problem, of social and political instability, is to not interfere.

Not honoring the worthy allows the people not to contend. Not valuing goods difficult to obtain allows the people not to become robbers. Not looking at what may be desirable allows the people not to have a confused mind/heart. (*Dao De Jing*, 3)

As noted earlier in the chapter, the Confucian solution unfolds through the process of education. According to the Daoist perspective, this Confucian educational process teaches people what they should know about and how to behave in various environmental contexts. They are taught contextually appropriate knowledge and behavior that includes such areas as honoring, valuing, and desiring. The Daoists view the Confucian educational and learning process as contrived and artificial. They see it as interfering and giving rise to stress. Chapter 20 of the *Dao De Jing* shows the clear link among contrived, artificial knowledge, education, and learning and stress when it notes, "Discard learning, be without stress."

The character *you*[q], which is translated/interpreted here as "stress," gives considerable insight into the ancient Chinese understanding of stress. The character consists of three components. The component *shou*[r], the top section of the character, is a picture of a person's head without any hair. It is common to picture, when we think of a stressful situation, a person literally pulling his or her hair out of their head. The inference here, other than the common image, is that of problematic behavior. The second component, the middle section of the character, is the radical *xin*[s] or heart/mind. The inference here is that both cognitive and emotional functioning are compromised. The third component, the lower section of the character, is the radical *zhi*[t], which means to walk slowly. The inference here is that behavior is compromised or slowed down. If we look at the relationship among the three components, we can make inferences about negative effects on the body, thinking being slowed down, emotions being slowed down, and overall behavior being slowed down.

The character itself has many meanings, such as worry, anxiety, melancholy, sadness, sorrow, grief, or depression. The commonality among all of these meanings is that of stress. The placement/relationship of the three components, head on top, heart in the middle, and the feet on the bottom— in other words, a person—appears to indicate that the entire person is affected by stress.

For the *Dao De Jing,* the fact that you engage in interfering behavior means that you are stressed and are not in the here and now. You are fragmented or separated from the environmental context. You are not functionally adapted. The solution is to stop interfering.

> For learning/knowledge, there is daily accumulating. For *dao*[i], there is daily decreasing. Decreasing and again decreasing, arriving at noninterference [*wu wei*[u]]. Not interfering, there is nothing that is not accomplished. (*Dao De Jing,* 48)

By not interfering with yourself or others, the adaptive problem of social and political instability would be solved. Like the *Lun Yu,* the Daoist solution in the *Dao De Jing* is addressed at the level of the person. The *Dao De Jing* also has a model to guide one's behavior, and that model is called the *sheng ren*[v] or the naturally integrated person.

The character *sheng*[w] consists of three components. On the left-hand side on the top is the radical *er*[x], which is a picture of an ear. On the right-hand side on the top is the radical *kou*[y], which represents a mouth. Underneath these two radicals is the character *wang*[z], which is used to represent a king. The character *wang*[z] consists of three horizontal lines joined together in the middle of each line by a vertical line. The vertical line represents the ruler who joins the sky (top line), the people (middle line), and the earth (bottom line). When all three components are considered in relationship to each other, the character *sheng*[w] can be interpreted as an integrated (joining together), communicative process (ear and mouth) among all aspects (the sky, people, and earth) of existence. This communicative process, given the analysis of Daoism up to this point, must of course be seen as natural, not artificial. The character *ren*[aa] means a person. Thus, the *sheng ren*[v] is a person who is a part of the integrated, communicative process among the sky, the people, and the earth.

> Therefore the naturally integrated person/sage [*sheng ren*[v]] engages in affairs through noninterference [*wu wei*[u]], practices the teachings of no words, interacts with all things and does not try to control them. Produces yet does not possess. Acts yet does not make things rely on him. Achieves successful completion in his tasks, yet does not make any claims about them. By not making claims, there is no fragmentation. (*Dao De Jing,* 2)

By being integrated, there is no sense of a separate, distinct self. The person who is not integrated, which for the Daoist is most people, has a sense of a self that is separate and distinct from the various environmental contexts. It is this sense of separation or distinct self, generated by contrived, artificial knowledge and values, that causes people to interfere with others. This process eventually results in chronic stress.

> What is meant by excessive anxiety being associated with your distinct self? The reason I have excessive worry is that I have a distinct self. If I did not have a distinct self, why would I worry? If I considered my distinct self as instead being part of the world, it would seem to be possible to be integrated in the world. (*Dao De Jing,* 13)

The phrase *da huan*[ab] is here translated/interpreted as "excessive anxiety," which represents, once again, chronic stress. The radical *da*[ac] is a picture of a person with arms extended to the sides, thus the possible meanings of large, big, vast, or extended. The character *huan*[ad] consists of two components. The radical *xin*[b], which means heart/mind (thinking and feeling), and the character *chuan*[ae], which represents a sense of being strung, bunched, or clustered together. Given the two components of *huan*[ad], we can interpret this character as meaning the thinking and feeling of the individual is compromised or restricted, much as it is in anxiety and worry. By adding the character *da*[ac], we get a sense of extending outward, extended or vast. Placing this phrase *da huan*[ab] in the context of the *Dao De Jing,* it seems quite reasonable to refer to excessive anxiety or chronic stress.

The naturally integrated person is in harmony with the world. This person, to use the language of evolutionary theory/psychology, has adapted to the environment. For the *Dao De Jing,* most people are not really adapted to the environment. They are separate from natural ordinary present. The *sheng ren*[v], on the other hand, is in harmony with the natural ordinary present and realizes this to be the case.

> To realize harmony is called residing with the natural ordinary present. Residing with the natural ordinary present is called enlightenment. (*Dao De Jing,* 55)

In this quote, the character *ming*[af] is translated/interpreted as "enlightenment." The character *ming*[af] consist of the radical *ri*[ag], or sun, on the left and the radical *yue*[ah], or moon, on the right. Both give off light and allow the individual to see. The combination of the two radicals suggests being able to see very clearly and/or to truly understand. It is interesting to note that the sun is symbolic for *yang*[ai] and the moon is symbolic for *yin*[aj], suggesting a harmonious process of continual change. Given the depth of the character *ming*[af], enlightenment seems most appropriate to capture the Daoist sense of clearly seeing and participating as part of a harmonious process of continual change.

The *Dao De Jing* is consistent with the basics of evolutionary psychology. Like the *Lun Yu,* it views the environment as a continually changing, interrelated process. The problem of social and political unrest can be seen as an adaptive problem occurring in this continually changing, interrelated environment. It provides a solution to the problem in order to assist people in adapting to the environment. The teachings of the *Dao De Jing* can be understood as providing a solution for reducing chronic stress (environmental problem) that is due to a sense of a distinct, separate self that interferes with itself and others in order to assist individuals in adapting to their environment. This would lead, in theory, to an integrated, harmonious society.

As was noted in the Introduction, in this text we are utilizing the Daoist model of beginning points, commonality, and simplicity found in the *Dao De Jing.* It is clear that the *Dao De Jing* practices what it preaches, as it focuses on beginning points (behavior attempting to solve a problem generated by the interaction of the individual with the environment), commonalities (chronic stress), and simplicity (being integrated with the environment).

Buddhism and Evolutionary Theory

The foundation of Chinese Buddhism is Indian Buddhism. The Buddha (traditionally, 6th century BCE) views life as consisting of *dukkha* or, as it often translated/interpreted, suffering. Suffering is somewhat misleading, as the depth and breadth of *dukkha* is not expressed with the word *suffering*.[6] *Dukkha* does not just apply to the sick, the aged, or the dying. It applies to all people, no matter their status in life.

The Chinese character *ku*[ak], which has the meaning of "bitter" is used to translate/interpret the word *dukkha*. It consists of two components. The first component, on the top, is the radical *cao*[al], which is a picture of growing plants or grass. The second component, located on the bottom, is the character *gu*[am], which means "ancient" or "old." As the ancient Chinese used plants, herbs, and grasses for nutrition and medicinal purposes, it is not a stretch of the imagination to consider that old plants may have an unpleasant or bitter taste. The process of taste is directly linked to experience. It is this sense of experience, all experience, as being potentially bitter or dissatisfying that conveys the meaning of *dukkha*.

Thus, given the Chinese interpretation, a more encompassing term for *dukkha* is "dissatisfaction." No matter your position in life, according to the Buddha, if you do not experience and understand existence as it really is, impermanent and interdependent, you will be dissatisfied. You will be dissatisfied because you view existence as being permanent and consisting of tangible and nontangible independent components. You will behave as if you can actually obtain, accumulate, and possess, forever, these tangible and nontangible components.

Those with power, status, wealth, and material goods are dissatisfied as they want more and are afraid to lose what they do possess. Those who do not have power, status, wealth, and material goods are dissatisfied with what they have and are anxious about obtaining more and more. This dissatisfaction is ongoing and affects the individual at all levels: cognitive, emotional, behavioral, physical, and interpersonal. Thus, this universal dissatisfaction is, for Buddha, in the words of evolutionary psychology, the adaptive problem. Until this problem is solved, people will continually be dissatisfied. In other words, they will be, to varying degrees, chronically stressed.

The Four Noble Truths

Of the three non-Western approaches that are explored and integrated in this text, the teachings of Buddha are the closest and most obvious, on the surface, to the step-by-step process of modern-day counseling or psychotherapy. (See Table 1.2 for a comparison of approaches.) This step-by-step process, in which Buddha indicates the problem, the cause of the problem, the removal of the problem, and the path to the removal of the problem, is called the *Four Noble Truths*. He refers to his path to the removal of the problem of dissatisfaction as the *Middle Way*. The Middle Way is an approach to life that is in between the extremes of seeking constant pleasure on one side and total self-denial on the other side. Buddha lived both of these extremes, found them dissatisfying, and discovered, through his own experiences, the Middle Way. In his first teachings after his enlightenment, Buddha states:

> What is the Middle Way? It is that which is called the Eightfold Path. Correct Seeing. Correct Thoughts. Correct Speech. Correct Actions. Correct Livelihood. Correct Effort. Correct Mindfulness. Correct Concentration. This is the Middle Way. These are the Four Noble Truths: the Noble Truth of dissatisfaction, the Noble Truth of the cause of dissatisfaction, the Noble Truth of the cessation of dissatisfaction, and the Noble Truth of the path to the cessation of dissatisfaction.[7] (*Turning the Dharma Wheel*)

Table 1.2   Comparison of Approaches of Buddhism and Counseling or Psychotherapy

Buddhism	*Counseling/Psychotherapy*
First Noble Truth: Problem of *universal* suffering/dissatisfaction	**Diagnosis** of *specific* disorder/problem such as anxiety, depression, etc.
Second Noble Truth: Cause of *universal* suffering/dissatisfaction is twofold: 1. Ignorance of nature of existence 2. Craving and desire	**Cause** of *specific* disorder/problem is contingent upon the perspective of the counseling/psychotherapy theory. For example: 1. Medical model: Brain disease 2. Cognitive: Irrational thoughts/ inferences
Third Noble Truth: There is a release from *universal* suffering/ dissatisfaction: Nirvana	**Goal** of counseling/psychotherapy: Curing of *specific* disorder/problem

Fourth Noble Truth: Eightfold Path for the release from *universal* suffering/dissatisfaction	**Treatment plan** for the curing of *specific* disorder:
	1. Medical model: Drugs
	2. Cognitive:
	   a. Dispute irrational thoughts/ inferences
	   b. Replace irrational thoughts inferences with rational thoughts/inferences

The First Noble Truth

In the counseling context, a client comes in to see a therapist or counselor because she has a problem that is compromising her ability to be happy in her relationship with her various environmental contexts. The counselor or therapist, given the symptoms, makes some determination about the nature of the problem. Is it anxiety, depression, hostility, or some combination? Nonetheless, in both cases, an initial diagnosis occurs. For the Buddha it is a universal problem and applies to all people. For the counselor or therapist it is viewed, generally, as being based in the client. From the perspective of evolutionary psychology, whether it is universal or specific, it is still an adaptive problem relative to an environmental context. The problem is the First Noble Truth.

The Second Noble Truth

The second stage of this process, for Buddha, is explicating the cause of the dissatisfaction. For Buddha the cause is the same for everyone. People are ignorant of the nature of reality. Because of this ignorance, they crave and thirst for ongoing existence, sensual pleasure, and nonexistence. Nonexistence, for Buddha, refers to losing oneself in activities and thought such that your dissatisfaction, temporarily, does not, so you think, affect you. The cause is Buddha's Second Noble Truth.

Generally, a counselor or therapist approaches the client's problem from some therapeutic perspective. The therapeutic perspective determines the cause of the problem. For example, from the perspective of a cognitive therapist, the cause of, say, your anxiety is your absolute thoughts, beliefs, and inferences. How you are thinking has a direct impact on your feelings and behaviors. From a Rogerian perspective, the cause of your anxiety is due to the incongruency between your social self and your ideal self. From a behavioral perspective, the cause of your anxiety is due to reinforcement contingencies. In all cases, the problem is linked back to a theoretical perspective regarding the cause of the symptoms, feelings, and behavior.

At this point, it seems that Western psychotherapy and counseling is clearly following a Buddhist structure, more than 2,500 years old, when addressing psychological problems relative to adapting to the environment. For both Buddhism and Western therapy and counseling, there is the diagnosis of a problem and a determination of the cause of the problem. The process certainly seems to be the same up to this point.

The Third Noble Truth

The next step or stage for Buddha is the Third Noble Truth. This is the release from dissatisfaction. Not only does he say there is a universal problem of dissatisfaction, he also says that this problem can be eliminated. This step or stage is also referred to as *Nirvana*. Nirvana has over the course of time been associated with, unfortunately, in many instances, some rarified, otherworldly spiritual state or mystical experience. This is not what Buddha meant. In the context of his Four Noble Truths, Nirvana is the cessation of dissatisfaction. Nothing more!

This third step or stage certainly sounds like what the practitioners of modern-day counseling or therapy would call the goal of the counseling process. In the case of a diagnosis of anxiety and all that it entails, the goal of the therapy would be the elimination or at least significant reduction of the anxiety so the client can return to and functionally adapt to their various environmental contexts.

The final step or stage of the Buddha's grid for addressing the adaptive problem of dissatisfaction is called the Fourth Noble Truth. The Fourth Noble Truth is known as the Eightfold Path to the elimination of dissatisfaction. This Eightfold Path is Buddha's solution to the problem of universal dissatisfaction. This path simultaneously integrates the cognitive, emotional, affective, and physical components of the individual in its focus toward eliminating dissatisfaction.

This last step is, for the counselor or therapist, the treatment plan. The treatment plan, like the cause of the problem, is directly linked to the theoretical perspective of the counselor or therapist. In the case of cognitive therapy, the focus is on cognitive restructuring such that the client will become aware of his or her problematic thinking, thoughts, and beliefs; confront them; and then replace them with more appropriate beliefs, thoughts, and thinking. The behavior therapist will show the client how environmental contingencies, rewards, and punishments are maintaining the dysfunctional behavior and then work with the client relative to addressing and changing the contingencies in the environment and/or the environmental context itself.

Conditioned Arising

For Nisker (2000), the parallels between Buddhism and evolutionary theory are striking. He argues that Buddhism and evolutionary theory can inform and enhance each other. He see correct mindfulness, one of the steps on the Eightfold Path, as being particularly beneficial to psychotherapy (pp. 147–151). Watts (1995, pp. 22–23) contends that Buddha should be considered as the original "psychotherapist," as his Middle Way and Four Noble Truths are oriented toward healing "chronic frustration."

As noted throughout this chapter, evolutionary theory and evolutionary psychology view existence as a continually changing, integrated, interdependent process that is made up of and interacts with the temporary entities that populate it. This perspective is also incorporated in the teachings of Buddha. The very basis of dissatisfaction, for Buddha, is a result of people being ignorant of the fact that existence is a continually changing, integrated, interdependent, conditioning, and conditioned process.

For Buddha, this process is called "conditioned arising" (*yuan qi*[an]). In response to a question from his disciple Ananda, Buddha explains his experience of conditioned arising:

> When there is this, then there is that. When this arises, then that arises. When this is not, that is not. When this is extinguished, then that is extinguished. Thus, conditioned by ignorance there are the predispositions. Conditioned by predispositions there is consciousness. Conditioned by consciousness there is name and form. Conditioned by name and form there are the six senses. Conditioned by the six senses there is contact. Conditioned by contact there are sensations. Conditioned by sensations there are feelings. Conditioned by feelings there are cravings. Conditioned by cravings there is grasping-possessing. Conditioned by grasping there is becoming. Conditioned by becoming there is old age, death, anxiety, depression, dissatisfaction, anger and worry. Thus is the cause of all of this dissatisfaction.[8]
> (*Many Boundaries*)

It is important to note that, for Buddha, awareness of conditioned arising, like the Four Noble Truths and Eightfold Path, is based on direct experience. This is not a faith-based or logic-based perspective. The reason individuals are dissatisfied is contingent upon how they experience existence. If they want to remove dissatisfaction, they have to change how they experience existence. This focus on change is quite similar to expectations in counseling or therapy.

The teachings of Buddha are also consistent with the Daoist model of beginning points, commonalities, and simplicity. Fundamentally, all humans have the same common problem that compromises their existence. Everyone is dissatisfied. The cause of this dissatisfaction is quite simple. People are ignorant of the nature of existence and thus are subsequently controlled by their cravings. This is the beginning point of the problem.

Summary

The Daoist teachings described in the Introduction to this text set a foundation of exploration based on beginning points, commonalities, and simplicity to allow for a comparison and integration of Western counseling or psychotherapy with the Chinese teachings of Confucianism, Daoism, and Buddhism. Evolutionary psychology clearly fits into these teachings. It focuses on a behavioral process that is common to all people across all cultures, that of successfully adapting to the environment. It looks at behavior as selected, developing, and being maintained because it solved an adaptive problem in its beginning stages. It looks at this common, beginning stage, focused behavior as being, in a very real sense, quite simple: adaptation, survival, reproduction, and maintenance of the gene pool.

Evolutionary psychology operates from the perspective that existence is a continually changing, interdependent, integrated process. It is a process that affects and is affected by the temporary entities that make it up and populate it. Thus, the notion of behavior developing, being selected, maintained, and changing relative to solving adaptive problems in various environmental contexts.

The Confucian, Daoist, and Buddhist perspectives discussed up to this point are easily viewed, as has been demonstrated in this chapter, from the perspective of evolutionary psychology. As has also been demonstrated, all three perspectives focus on beginning points, commonalities, and simplicity.

The integration of evolutionary theory with the Daoist teachings of beginning points, commonalities, and simplicity can be easily applied to the counseling or therapeutic process. At its most basic, simple level, all counseling or therapy begins from the perspective of helping people help themselves develop solutions relative to adapting to an environmental context. All counseling or therapy is about change. Clients enter counseling or therapy because, for whatever reason, their current behavior is, in some sense, compromising their ability to functionally adapt to their environment.

The issue of chronic stress has been used as a basis for the psychological problems explored in the discussions of Confucianism, Daoism, and Buddhism. The stress response, through the process of natural selection, has been incorporated into the makeup of human beings and passed on through their genes to successive generations. It has been passed on because it assists human beings in becoming aware of problems in the environment, communicating about those problems, and solving the problems such that the humans can adapt to their environment. The stress response is a normal and valuable integrated tool for human beings. It is a fundamental aspect of evolution because it has and continues to work. Problems arise, however, when it is not allowed to turn off. At this point it becomes chronic stress. It is this chronic stress, albeit not by this name, that is addressed by Confucianism, Daoism, and Buddhism. Their adaptive solutions are, fundamentally, oriented toward its removal. In the same sense, counseling or therapy can be described as a process that is, fundamentally, attempting to assist the client in removing chronic stress. It is to this issue of the stress response and chronic stress that we turn to in the next chapter.

Important Terms

Adaptation

Adaptive problems

Continual process of change

Environment

Environmental contexts

Evolutionary psychology

Evolutionary theory

Functional behavior

Inclusive fitness

Natural selection

Physical mechanisms

Psychological mechanisms

Reproduction

Survival

Variation

Exercises

A. Think about your behavior (thinking, feeling, and acting) from a purely functional perspective. What problems in the environment (internal and/or external) does your behavior solve? How does your behavior allow you to adapt to the various environmental contexts wherein you interact? As you go thorough your normal day, try to look at your behavior from this perspective. Look at your life as a series of challenges and problems for which your behavior provides solutions and allows you to adapt.

B. Ask yourself why you interact with other people. What function does this behavior serve? What does interacting with other people do for you? What problems and challenges in your environment does this interactive behavior solve? How does interactive behavior allow you to adapt to various environmental contexts?

C. How would an understanding of adaptive/functional behavior relative to environmental demands help you as a counselor? How would teaching your client about adaptive/functional behavior relative to environmental demands help your client?

Chinese Characters

[a] 性	[u] 無為
[b] 忄 = 心	[v] 聖人
[c] 生	[w] 聖
[d] 習	[x] 耳
[e] 羽	[y] 口
[f] 白 = 自	[z] 王
[g] 君子	[aa] 人
[h] 小人	[ab] 大患
[i] 道	[ac] 大
[j] 和	[ad] 患
[k] 禮	[ae] 串
[l] 長	[af] 明
[m] 戚	[ag] 日
[n] 戊	[ah] 月
[o] 未	[ai] 陽
[p] 觀	[aj] 陰
[q] 憂	[ak] 苦
[r] 首	[al] 草 = 艹
[s] 心	[am] 古
[t] 夊	[an] 緣起

Notes

1. All translations/interpretations of the *Lun Yu* and the commentaries are my own. The format of XVII-2 refers to the Book (XVII) and Section (2) of the *Lun Yu*. The Chinese texts utilized for this translation can be found in Yang (1972b) and Hong (1973). Recommended English translations with introductions are *Confucius: The Analects (Lun Yu)* by Lau (1988) and *The Analects of Confucius: A Philosophical Translation* by Ames and Rosemont (1998).

2. The analysis and interpretation of the origins of Chinese characters, and the relationship between the components, if they consist of two or more components, is a fascinating and quite challenging endeavor. For assistance and guidance in this process I utilized Karlgren (1966, 1975), Mathews (1996), Peng (1998), Shi (1997), Wang (1997), Weiger (1965), Wenlin Institute (2004), and Wilder and Ingram (1974).

3. See Weiger (1965, p. 325), Kalgren (1975, p. 235), and Wenlin Institute (2004). I examined numerous texts, as noted in note 2, to unpack the Chinese characters. This current character and its references noted here is an example of the process. Given the extensiveness of the process, I do not repeat this reference procedure for additional characters in the text. All originality, creativity, and uniqueness of interpretations should be attributed to the references listed in note 2. I take responsibility for the mistakes.

4. The UNESCO statement on race can be found at http://unesdoc.unesco org/images/0012/001282/128291eo.pdf.

5. The translations/interpretations of the *Dao De Jing* are my own. The number after the text (*Dao De Jing*, 16) refers to the chapter number of the *Dao De Jing*. In this case the reference is to the Chapter 16. The primary text utilized for this translation is the standard transmitted text with the Wang Bi commentary. This Chinese text can be found in Yang (1972a). In addition, I also utilized Wang (1993). Recommended English translations with introductions are *Dao De Jing: A Philosophical Translation* by Ames and Hall (2003) and *Lao-Tzu's Tao Te Ching* by Pine (1996).

6. For a discussion of the term *dukkha*, see Rahula (1962), pp. 16–28.

7. The translations/interpretations, from the Chinese, of the Buddhist texts in this chapter and throughout the book are my own. Regarding specific Buddhist terms in Chinese, I relied on Soothill and Hodous (1962) for assistance. This particular text was taken from McRae (2003); the *Electronic Texts of the Chinese Buddhist Canon* Web site is located at http://www.indiana.edu/~asialink/canon.html. *Turning the Dharma Wheel (Zhuan Fa Lun Jing)*, in Chinese, can be extracted at this site from T22, 1421 [0104b08]. More commonly known as *Dhammakkappavattana*, it is translated from the Pali into English by Rhys Davids (1969).

8. The *Many Boundaries* (*Duo Jie Jing*), more commonly known as *Bahudhatukasutta*, is translated from the Pali into English by Horner (1967). It is #115 of the *Majjima Nikaya* or Middle Length Sayings. A copy from Fjland (2005) that I used for this translation/interpretation of this text, in Chinese, can be located at the Web site http://www.fjland.net/Article/ShowArticle.asp?ArticleID=202. This text is also found at http://www.indiana.edu/~asialink/canon.html, T01, 26 [0723a07].

References

Ames, R. T., & Hall, D. L. (Trans.). (2003). *Dao De Jing: A philosophical translation*. New York: Ballantine.

Ames, R. T., & Rosemont, H. (Trans.). (1998). *The analects of Confucius: A philosophical translation*. New York: Ballantine.

Buss, D. M. (2004). *Evolutionary psychology: The new science of the mind*. Boston: Pearson.

Darwin, C. (1979/1859). *The origin of species*. Random House: New York.

Darwin, C. (2004/1871). *The descent of man*. London: Penguin Group.

Fjland. (2005). *Duo jie jing*. Retrieved December 21, 2005, from http://www.fjland .net/Article/ShowArticle.asp?ArticleID=202

Hergenhahn, B. R. (1997). *An introduction to the history of psychology*. Pacific Grove, CA: Brooks/Cole.

Hall, D. L., & Ames, R. T. (1987). *Thinking through Confucius*. Albany: State University of New York Press.

Hong, C. H. (Xiao Zhe). (1973). *Si shu shou ji, zhu xi shou ji*. Taibei: Hua Lian Chu Ban.

Horner, I. B. (Trans.). (1967). *The collection of the Middle Length Sayings (Majjhima-Nikaya), Vol. III: The final fifty discourses (Uparipannasa)*. London: Luzac & Company.

Karlgren, B. (1966). *Grammata serica: Script and phonetics in Chinese and Sino-Japanese*. Taipei: Ch'eng-Wen.

Karlgren, B. (1975). *Analytic dictionary of Chinese and Sino-Japanese*. Taipei: Ch'eng-Wen.

Lau, D. C. (Trans.). (1988). *Confucius: The analects (Lun Yu)*. London: Penguin Group.

Mathews, R. H. (1996). *Mathews' Chinese-English dictionary*. Cambridge, MA: Harvard University Press.

McAdams, D. P., & Pals, J. L. (2006). Fundamental principles of an integrative science of personality. *American Psychologist, 61,* 204–217.

McRae, J. R. (2003). *Electronic texts of the Chinese Buddhist canon*. Retrieved December 21, 2005, from http://www.indiana.edu/~asialink/canon.html

Nesse, R. M., & Williams, G. C. (1994). *Why we get sick: The new science of Darwinian medicine*. New York: Random House.

Nisker, W. (2000). *Buddha's nature: A practical guide to discovering your place in the cosmos*. New York: Bantam Books.

Peng, T. H. (1998). *What's in a Chinese character*. Beijing: New World Press.

Pine, R. (Trans.). (1996). *Lao-tzu's Tao Te Ching*. San Francisco: Mercury House.

Rahula, W. (1962). *What the Buddha taught*. New York: Grove.

Rhys Davids, T. W. (Trans.). (1969). *Buddhist sutras*. New York: Dover.

Shi, Z. Y. (1997). *Picture within a picture: An illustrated guide to the origins of Chinese characters*. Beijing: New World Press.

Soothill, W. E., & Hodous, L. (1962). *A dictionary of Chinese Buddhist terms*. Kaohsiung: Buddhist Culture Service.

UNESCO. (1950). *UNESCO and its programme, III: The race question*. Retrieved December 14, 2005, from http://unesdoc.unesco.org/images/0012/001282/ 128291eo.pdf

Wang, H. Y. (1997). *The origins of Chinese characters*. Beijing: Sinolingua.

Wang, K. (Dian Xiao). (1993). *Lao zi dao de jing he shang gong zhang zhu*. Beijing: Zhong Hua Shu Ju.

Watts, A. (1995). *Buddhism: The religion of no-religion*. Boston: Tuttle.

Weiger, L. (1965). *Chinese characters: Their origins, etymology, history, classification and signification*. New York: Dover.

Wenlin Institute. (2004). *Wenlin software for learning Chinese*, version 3.2.2. Eureka, CA: Author. Available at http://www.wenlin.com

Wilder, G. D., & Ingram, J. H. (1974). *Analysis of Chinese characters*. New York: Dover.

Yang, J. L. (Zhu Bian). (1972a). *Lao zi ben yi, Lao zi xin kao shu lue*. Taibei: Shi Jie Shu Ju.

Yang, J. L. (Bian Ci). (1972b). *Lun yu zhu shu bu zheng*. Taibei: Shi Jie Shu Ju.

2

Stress and the Stress Response

The second component of the bamboo bridge is stress and the stress response. We first examine the classical Buddhist, Daoist, and Confucian experience regarding stress and the stress response. Having provided the reader with a concrete sense of the experience of stress within the context of classical Buddhism, Daoism, and Confucianism, the Western perspective is presented and explored.

Buddhism

What is meant by the Noble Truth of dissatisfaction/chronic stress [dukkha]? Birth is dissatisfying/stressful, old age is dissatisfying/ stressful, sickness is dissatisfying/stressful, death is dissatisfying/ stressful, anxiety, depression and anger are dissatisfying/stressful, resenting and hating is dissatisfying/stressful, being separate from pleasure is dissatisfying/stressful, not getting what you seek is dissatisfying/stressful. This simply means that the five heaps/ aggregates [the sense of self] are dissatisfying/stressful. This is the meaning of the Noble Truth of dissatisfaction/chronic stress.[1]

—Turning of Dharma Wheel

This description provided by Buddha (traditionally, 6th century BCE) is a picture, in actuality, of chronic stress. The very basis of his teachings, his focal point, is that life itself, the interaction of the individual with the environment, is stressful or *dukkha*. Physically, birth, old age, sickness, and death are stressful to the body and the mind. Psychologically, the emotions of anxiety, depression, anger, resentment, and hate are clear examples of feelings people express when they are stressed out and that affect both body and mind. Behaviorally, being separate from pleasurable objects and not obtaining what you desire also gives rise to dissatisfaction and stress.

The Components of Self

Buddha goes on to point out that the combination of the physical, psychological, and behavioral, the sense of self, the personality, the "I" itself, is dissatisfying or stressful. The five components (heaps or aggregates) that make up the sense of self are (1) form, (2) sensation, (3) perception, (4) mental disposition, and (5) consciousness.[2] (See Table 2.1.)

These five heaps or components that make up the self must not be seen as being distinct or separate from each other. Consistent with Buddha's conditioned arising, which was briefly discussed in Chapter 1, these five components are simultaneously interdependent, cause and effect, and conditioned and conditioning.

The Chinese character *se*[a], which is translated/interpreted as "form," has the meaning of color or expression. It refers to the physical features of the person. The tangible aspect, if you will. On initial observation it is the body. For Buddha, *form* includes the six senses (the five physical senses and the thinking component/mind) and their objects. It includes all that is observable.

Table 2.1　　The Five Heaps/Aggregates of the Buddhist Sense of Self

Heaps/Aggregates	Content
Form	Physical aspects/features of person
Sensation	Most basic level of experience across six senses (eye, ear, nose, mouth, body, and mind) and their objects; sensations are positive, negative, or neutral
Perception	Recognition of the objects of the six senses
Mental disposition	Conditioned and conditioning outlook we have of ourselves and the world around us
Consciousness	The result of contact between a sense and its object; thus there are six types of consciousness

Sensation, which is a translation/interpretation of the Chinese character *shou*[b], has the meaning of receiving or accepting. It refers to what is experienced at the most basic level when contact or interaction occurs between the six senses and their respective objects. For Buddha, what is experienced at this level is a positive, negative, or a neutral sensation. Thus, the sensation experienced as a result of the contact between the eye and its visual object would be would be positive, negative, or neutral. This process would follow for all of the remaining five senses. It must be noted that sensation is not something *in* the human being or the world. It is what *occurs* when contact is made between one of the senses and its respective object.

Perception is the recognition of the objects of the six senses. It is a translation/interpretation of the Chinese character *xiang*[c], which has the meaning of thinking, feeling, and considering. The character consists of two components. The top component, the character *xiang*[d], has meanings of looking at, mutual, and appearance. The bottom component is the radical *xin*[e], which means heart/mind and thus incorporates both cognitive and emotional aspects. The relationship between the two components represents an interaction among thinking, feeling, the senses, and their objects, resulting in perception.

The Chinese character *xing*[f], which has meanings of action, behavior, and performance is here translated/interpreted as "mental disposition." These *mental disposition* make up the conditioned and conditioning outlook we have of ourselves and the world around us. It is the repository of all that has influenced our formation of our sense of self and our environment. It is our perspectives about the nature of reality, people, and the relationship between them. It is our belief about how the world ought to behave and incorporates our values and judgments about right and wrong, good and evil, and beauty and ugliness. As it is what directs our behavior, it is called *karma*. The Chinese character *xing*[f] conveys the sense of acting upon or in various environmental contexts, and thus the mental disposition incorporate our will or volition regarding each of the senses and their respective objects. For Buddha, it is because of our mental disposition that we experience dissatisfaction and chronic stress. If we change our mental disposition, we can remove our chronic stress and dissatisfaction.

The final component of the human being is *consciousness*. Consciousness is a translation/interpretation of the Chinese character *shi*[g]. This character consists of three components. On the left-hand side is the radical *yan*[h], which means words, speech, and talk. The middle component is the character *yin*[i], which means sound. The final component, on the right-hand side, is the radical *ge*[j], which is a picture of an ancient Chinese weapon. The combination of the three gives the sense of being aware of or conscious of the sound of words or weapons, both of which are important for survival.

For Buddha, there are six types of consciousness: one for each of the six senses (five physical senses plus the mind) and their respective objects.

Consciousness occurs only when there is contact between a sense and its corresponding object.[3] For example, visual consciousness is the result of contact between the eyes and the forms of the environment. This process of contact is also the case for the five remaining senses. This Buddhist sense of consciousness is quite different from the Western concept of consciousness, in which consciousness is viewed as being the fundamental ground. In the West, consciousness is viewed as an arena, if you will, where all types of activities occur. This is simply not the case for Buddhism.

For Buddha, these five components or sense of self (form, sensation, perception, mental disposition, consciousness) are a source of dissatisfaction or chronic stress. While this statement points to the problem or cause of stress, it also provides the solution. The solution to the problem of ongoing dissatisfaction or chronic stress can be found within the individual himor herself. The solution is the realization, based on direct experience, of the nature of self and of reality.

> Buddha spoke to the monks. Form is impermanent. Being impermanent it is dissatisfying/*dukkha*. Being dissatisfying it is without a Soul/Self. Sensation is impermanent. Being impermanent it is dissatisfying/*dukkha*. Being dissatisfying it is without a Soul/Self. Perception is impermanent. Being impermanent it is dissatisfying/*dukkha*. Being dissatisfying it is without a Soul/Self. Mental dispositions are impermanent. Being impermanent they are dissatisfying/*dukkha*. Being dissatisfying they are without a Soul/Self. Consciousness is impermanent. Being impermanent it is dissatisfying. Being dissatisfying it is without a Soul/Self.[4] (*Sutra on Impermanence*)

This quote introduces the nature of the self. The self, the five aggregates or components, is impermanent, dissatisfying/chronically stressful, and nonsubstantial: without an absolute, underlying, distinct, separate, permanent self or soul. For Buddha, this is not only the nature of the self but also the nature of reality or all that conditions and is conditioned. For Buddha, there is no underlying, unchanging, absolute, separate, distinct substance, soul, self, or God.

> All that is conditioned and conditions are impermanent. All that is conditioned and conditions are dissatisfying [*dukkha*]. All dharma (things) are without a self.[5] (*Sutra of Statements on Dharma*, vv. 277–279)

The nature of reality and the self, for Buddha, is an ongoing process of change, interdependency, interrelatedness, nonseparateness, impermanence, and nonsubstantiality. People suffer, are dissatisfied and chronically stressed, because they act as if and believe they have a distinct, permanent, unchanging, substantial, and independent sense of a self or soul. This is not the case for Buddha. People also act as if and believe that reality, the world they live and function in, is permanent, distinct, unchanging, substantial, and independent. As such they suffer, are dissatisfied and chronically stressed. This is not the case for Buddha.

Buddha diagnosed the problem of living as chronic stress/dissatisfaction. Buddha sees this ongoing stress as the fundamental barrier to achieving real peace and tranquility. In the language of evolutionary theory/psychology, this ongoing stress is the adaptive problem. Buddha's Fourth Noble Truth, the Eightfold Path, is his solution to the problem of ongoing or chronic stress that will allow people to functionally adapt to their environment.

Daoism

The issue of chronic stress is also the primary focus of Zhuang Zi (circa 4th century BCE), the second major Daoist thinker after Lao Zi, the traditional author of the *Dao De Jing*. Unlike Lao Zi, who saw chronic stress as the fundamental cause of social and political instability and focused on establishing social and political harmony through its removal, Zhuang Zi was not focused on establishing social harmony. His major concern was helping people help themselves to become free from self-imposed and society-imposed absolute restrictions, judgments, and values. From the perspective of Zhuang Zi, these restrictions, judgments, and values resulted in physical and psychological distress.

The Daoist text *Zhuang Zi,* written in part by Zhuang Zi, clearly paints a landscape wherein chronic stress was quite prevalent more than 2,000 years ago. This theme of chronic stress, albeit by different names, and all it entails occurs throughout the text.

> When people are asleep their spirits are knotted up. When they are awake their form is scattered. Interacting in the world creates entanglements. Daily their mind/hearts battle: plodding, concealing, and tentative. Their small fears result in apprehensiveness. Their large fears result in being overwhelmed. In their judging of right and wrong their words shoot out as if an arrow was released from a bow. They hold onto their judgments as if they were sacred oaths. Guarding what they call their victory, they are executed like autumn moving into winter.[6] (*Zhuang Zi*, 3/2/10–12)

This passage from the *Zhuang Zi* unmistakably presents an environment permeated with fear, anxiety, doubt, restrictions, absolute values and judgments, impulsiveness, impatience, control issues, and insecurity. It is clear that the *Zhuang Zi* is discussing chronic stress by its reference to daily battles. It is these daily battles that result in entanglement—cognitively, emotionally, behaviorally, and physically—in the affairs of the world. An entanglement that is so stressful that it eventually leads to physical deterioration and death. The character $kong^k$, which is translated/interpreted in the preceding quote as "fears," strongly indicates the notion of stress. This character consists of two components. The top component, the character $gong^l$, has the meaning of binding. The bottom component, the radical xin^e, refers to mind/heart or both the cognitive and affective processes. The combination of these two components gives the picture of the heart/mind being bound or restricted in its activities and/or focus.

This is exactly what happens with the fear or the flight-or-fight response: the stress response! The body goes through a series of massive physiological changes as it prepares to fight or flee. The individual is hyper-vigilant or apprehensive—as part of the normal evolutionary process of self-protection—as he or she scans the environment for potential threats. The focus is quite restrictive or bound. Once the threat is gone, however, the stress response, normally, turns off. If the stress response does not turn off, then the individual will remain apprehensive. Thus, for the *Zhuang Zi*, the small fears and all that they entail. If the apprehensiveness is ongoing, the stress response not turning off, the fears increase and the individual becomes overwhelmed. This is chronic stress. This chronic stress compromises the very health of the body. Chronic stress interferes with the overall functioning—cognitively, emotionally, behaviorally, and physically—of the individual to such an extent that he or she can become sick, and in the worst-case scenarios, die. Thus, for the *Zhuang Zi*, the great fears and all that they entail.

> That which is respected in the world is wealth, status, longevity and approval. That which is enjoyed is a comfortable life, tasty food, beautiful clothes, pleasant sights and sweet sounds. That which is not respected is poverty, dishonor, dying young and disapproval. That which is dissatisfying/stressful is a life that is not comfortable, a mouth that does not have tasty food, a body that does not have beautiful clothes, eyes that do not have pleasant sights and ears that do not have sweet sounds. If these are not attained, there is chronic stress as well as fear. Those who treat the body in this way are indeed foolish. Now for those who are rich, the body is stressed and is made ill as they accumulate more wealth than they can possibly use. Those who treat the body in this manner are disconnected. Now those of status, day and night think about right and wrong. Those who treat their body in this manner are out of touch. People are born and all of life is a participation in anxiety/depression [chronic stress]. Those who seek a long life are of a confused mind. They are endlessly anxious/depressed [chronically stressed] about death. Why do they bother? To treat the body in this manner is to be far away from it. (*Zhuang Zi*, 46/18/2–6)

This sense of chronic stress and its physical and psychological impact is even more evident in the preceding passage of the *Zhuang Zi*. The *Zhuang Zi* presents life as a participation in continual worry about not having wealth, honor, longevity, and approval from others. This section of the *Zhuang Zi* examines four groups of individuals relative to the dissatisfaction/stress associated with living: the common people, the rich, those with status, and those seeking to live forever.

The common people are dissatisfied/stressed because they believe that in order to be happy they must have a comfortable life, tasty food, beautiful clothes, pleasant things to look at, and to be able to hear sweet sounds. If they do not obtain these, they become depressed and anxious. In other words, they are chronically stressed in their ongoing struggle to obtain, based on other people's values and judgments, these material goods. For the *Zhuang Zi*, to become depressed and anxious in an ongoing struggle over obtaining material goods is indeed foolish and harmful to the body! It is an absurd way to look at life.

Rich people, in their greed to obtain and keep on obtaining more wealth than they can possibly use, become chronically stressed and eventually physically ill. They are oblivious of the harm they do to their bodies. For the *Zhuang Zi*, this one-track mind results in a disconnection from the body. It is a superficial way to look at life.

People who have status, who are higher up the food chain if you will, are always thinking about what is right and what is wrong. Given their status, they are obsessed about how people ought to behave. Behave according to standards they set for right and wrong behavior. For the *Zhuang Zi*, the thinking of the people of status is out of touch with the people interacting in the world and out of touch with what their own bodies tell them about right and wrong.

The *Zhuang Zi*, like the Buddha, sees life as being chronically stressful. You are born and then life is an ongoing participation in anxiety and depression. The problem is that people are not aware of this chronic stress. Instead of trying to find a solution to the problem of the chronic stress associated with life, people focus their attention on worrying about dying, which results in more ongoing stress. People seeking a long life, living forever if possible, do not seem to understand that the human body is going to eventually die. They are confused in their understanding about life and death. They spend their time obsessing about not dying. They are obviously afraid of death. All their obsessing, however, is not going to change the fact that one day they will be dead. The *Zhuang Zi* finds these people to be quite distant, far apart from their own bodies and what will eventually happen to them.

The *Zhuang Zi* presents the facts of life and death to the reader in a straightforward, no-punches-pulled manner. Existence is all about change. Life is simply a change. Death is simply a change. In relationship to the universe, you are but an instant. One moment you are here. The next moment you are gone.

> The life of a human between the sky and the earth is like glimpsing through a crack and seeing a white colt passing by. A sudden moment and it is gone. Pouring forth and resonating, there is nothing that is not produced. Slipping and drifting there is nothing that does not return. A change and there is life. Another change and there is death. Living things grieve. Humans are saddened. The release of nature's bow. A dropping of nature's cover. One after another, all things give way. Consciousness leaves, followed by the body. Such is the great return. (*Zhuang Zi*, 59/22/39–41)

The problem is that people do not see reality. They do not see change. They do not believe that the process of change really applies to them. They fight against the inevitable. They become entangled in the affairs of the world as they seek to obtain and hold on to that which society tells them to value. In the process of this fight and struggle they become dissatisfied, chronically stressed, and ill. For the *Zhuang Zi*, people's very existence is compromised by self-imposed and society-imposed restrictions, values, and judgments. They do not take the opportunity to engage in life and the process of change. Instead, they attempt to deny and resist the very nature of existence.

> Once a person receives his complete form, it is not lost until it is used up. Interaction with things is that of destruction and waste. This goes on until exhaustion. Like a galloping horse unable to stop. Is this not sad? All one's life is that of labor and toil. Not seeing the completion of your work. So tired, exhausted, and weary! Not knowing where you will return. How can this not be tragic? People say they are not dead. Of what benefit is this? Your form changes and your mind/heart goes along with it. Is it possible not to call this tragic? (*Zhuang Zi*, 4/2/18–20)

For the *Zhuang Zi*, these are unhappy people. Like the Buddha, the *Zhuang Zi* diagnosed the problem as, essentially, chronic stress. This is the adaptive problem. People do not understand reality and their place in it. They resist accepting the facts of reality. Everything is an interrelated, interdependent ongoing process of continual change. Everyone and everything is going to die! People must remove the restrictions, values, and judgments that compromise engaging their environment. The *Zhuang Zi* offers a solution to the problem of chronic stress. Like Buddhism, people must change how they view themselves and their environment. The solution of the *Zhuang Zi* for changing one's viewpoint is to be empty.

> Don't be the corpse of fame. Don't be the residence of schemes. Don't be controlled by interaction in the world. Don't be ruled by knowledge. Live your life in the endless and roam in the boundless. Use up that which you received from nature, yet do not see any attainment. Be empty that is all! (*Zhuang Zi*, 21/7/31–32)

Confucianism

As noted in Chapter 1, Confucius made a distinction between the fully integrated person (*jun zi*[m]) and the fragmented person (*xiao ren*[n]). (See Table 2.2.) The fully integrated person was calm and relaxed, while the fragmented person—most of the population—was chronically stressed. This chronic stress occurs because people do not understand their role and function in society. Because fragmented people are self-centered and not society-centered, they compete with each other, at the expense of each other, for their own individual gain and benefit. They are not concerned with establishing a relationship with another person unless it is to their advantage.

Table 2.2   Confucius's Fully Integrated Person and Fragmented Person

Fully Integrated Person (*jun zi*[m])	Fragmented Person (*xiao ren*[n])
Cognitive, emotional, behavioral, and interpersonal components are all integrated and in harmony.	Cognitive, emotional, behavioral, and interpersonal components are all fragmented and disconnected.
Focused on establishing and maintaining a positive and harmonious relationship with people and their environment.	Looks at other people as threats to their own personal gain. Other people are seen as competition and cannot be trusted. Other people must be kept at a distance, for they will take advantage of you. Isolated from society and environment.
Focused on helping people help themselves for the overall benefit of society as a whole.	Self-centered, narcissistic, and self-entitled. Driven by greed, personal gain, and personal benefit.
Healthy, happy, and authentic.	Chronically fearful, stressed, and confused. Not healthy and inauthentic.

Fragmented people look at other people as threats to their own personal gain. Others are the competition and cannot be trusted. They must be kept at a distance or otherwise they will try to take advantage of you. The behavior of the fragmented person results in separation and isolation from the overall well-being of society as a whole. This separation, self-centeredness, greed, fear, and viewing other people as threats results in ongoing or chronic stress.

Confucius said, "Fragmented people! How is it possible to interact with your sovereign with such people? Having not yet attained anything, they are anxious about attaining something. Having attained something, they are anxious about losing it. If they are anxious about losing it, they will stop at nothing." (*Lun Yu*, XVII-15)[7]

It is clear from this quote that, for Confucius, fragmented people are anxious or stressed all the time. They are stressed as they seek for personal gain. They are stressed by the fear they may lose what they have gained. Given their fear about loss, their potential actions are compromised at the cognitive, emotional, and behavioral levels. Confucius certainly infers that this chronic stress associated with fear of not obtaining material goods and/or status or losing them will compromise their judgments and their actions. They will stop at nothing!

On the other hand, the fully integrated person (*jun zi*[m]) is not self-centered and is not driven by greed and personal gain. The fully integrated person is concerned with the well-being of society as a whole and is focused on maintaining positive interpersonal relationships. Other people are not the competition. As such, the fully integrated person is not chronically stressed.

> Si Ma Niu [a disciple of Confucius] asked about the *jun zi*[m]. The Master replied, "The *jun zi*[m] has neither sorrow nor fear [not chronically stressed]." Si Ma Niu said, "If he has neither sorrow nor fear, how can he be called a *jun zi*[m]?" The Master said, "Finding neither chronic illness nor sorrow within himself, why should he be worried or fearful?" (*Lun Yu*, XII-4)

This quote centers on its last line. Of special interest is the Chinese character *jiu*[o], which has the meaning of chronic illness and/or sorrow. This character consists of two components. The outside component is the radical *ni*[p], which has the meaning of "sick" or "ill." The inside component is the character *jiu*[q], which has the meaning of "long lasting" or "ongoing." The combination then has the meaning of chronic illness and/or sorrow.

Given the context of Confucius's teachings regarding the fully integrated person (*jun zi*[m]) and the fragmented person (*xiao ren*[n]), *jiu*[o] is best understood as an ongoing problem that gives rise to anxiety or fear; in other words, gives rise to chronic stress. The ongoing problem is that the fragmented person (*xiao ren*[n]) is threatened by not obtaining status and/or material goods, and if obtained, losing the status and/or material goods. This threat gives rise to anxiety and fear. As it is an ongoing threat, there is chronic stress.

This threat is because the fragment person (*xiao ren*[n]) views the world from the perspective of self-centeredness, greed, desire, and isolation from society. This being the case, the fragmented person is chronically stressed.

Fully integrated people (*jun zi*[m]), on the other hand, view the world from a perspective that is not self-centered, not isolated from the environment, not focused on controlling and manipulating others, not driven by greed, and is absent of any desire for obtaining and maintaining material goods and social status for their own personal benefit. Instead, integrated people are focused on establishing and maintaining a positive and harmonious relationship with people and their environment. Integrated people are focused on helping people help themselves for the overall benefit of society as a whole. Because of their perspective and the behaviors that occur as a result of their perspective, when they look within themselves they find no ongoing threats or chronic problems. This being the case, there is no anxiety, fear, or chronic stress.

> Confucius said, "The path [*dao*^{r}] of integrated people [*jun zi*^{m}] has three aspects. I am not able to accomplish them. In establishing relationships [*ren*^{s}] they are not stressed. Being wise, they are not confused. Being courageous they are not fearful." Zi Gong [a disciple of Confucius] said, "Master, this is your path!" (*Lun Yu*, XIV-28)

This quote provides a powerful picture of the degree of integration Confucius expects for the *jun zi*^{m}. Cognitive, emotional, behavioral, and interpersonal components are all integrated and in harmony for the *jun zi*^{m}. As such, the fully integrated person is not chronically stressed, confused, or fearful. The fully integrated person is someone whom we would today refer to as a healthy person. Given the humanistic aspect of the teachings of Confucius, the fully integrated person may well be considered an authentic person.

Like the Buddha and the *Zhuang Zi*, Confucius, diagnoses the problem as chronic stress. This is the adaptive problem. People do not understand reality and their place in it. Although society during the time of Confucius is socially and politically unstable, it is so because of chronic stress. People are chronically stressed because of their viewpoint and behavior relative to their fellow human beings and their social structure. This viewpoint sees other people as being disconnected from them, as threats, and as competition. By changing the problematic viewpoint and subsequent behavior derived from the problematic viewpoint, people will not be chronically stressed. The solution, for Confucius, to the problem of chronic stress is to develop proper, trusting relationships. It is to view the world from the perspective of the importance of positive interrelationships that set the foundation for social and political stability.

The Stress Response

Human beings are genetically wired, as a result of the evolutionary process, with physical and psychological mechanisms that assist them in adapting to challenges in their ever-changing environment. These physical and psychological mechanisms increase the probability of adapting, surviving, maintaining the gene pool (inclusive fitness), and reproducing. The challenges in the environment result in both physical and psychological adaptive changes in the body. These adaptive changes are normal and are part of the everyday process of providing solutions for living such that the human being is able to adapt to the various environmental contexts wherein he or she exists. These normal changes are what we call "stress."

Seyle (1978) defined *stress* as "the nonspecific response of the body to any demand" (p. 1). He further noted, "Complete absence of stress is incompatible with life since only a dead man makes no demand upon his body" (p. 422). Any demand in the environment, internal or external, results in general changes in the body as the body attempts to adapt and solve a contextual problem. Seyle referred to the "totality" of the nonspecific changes in the body, as a result of the demands (stressors) of the environment, which occurs on a consistent and integrated basis as the "general adaptation syndrome (G.A.S.)" or "stress syndrome" (p. 1).

The body is able to make these changes relative to the demands of the environment because the evolutionary process has provided it with the appropriate physical and psychological mechanisms. Through the process of natural selection, these mechanisms were incorporated into the makeup of the human being because they worked. They allowed the human being to adapt, survive, maintain the gene pool, and reproduce. As a result, these physical and psychological mechanisms have been and will continually be passed on to succeeding generations.

Although the concept of stress referred simply to these normal changes, the concept has, over the passage of time, come to be associated with chronic negative events, contexts, relationships, feelings, thoughts, and behaviors. In order to differentiate among the normal, positive stress response and the more chronic, negative stress response, Bruce McEwen (2002) uses the terms *allostasis* and *allostatic load*.

Allostasis

According to McEwen (2002), *allostasis* refers to the variable, normal changes in the human being (physical and psychological) that allow it to adapt to the ever-changing challenges in its various environmental contexts. He notes:

> Remember, the purpose of allostasis is to help the organism remain stable in the face of any change and to provide enough energy to cope with any challenge—not just life threatening ones. Take the simple act of getting up in the morning. Some people consider it to be the first major trauma of the day, but even for the birds, moving from sleep to wakefulness and from lying down to standing makes demands on the body. To ensure sufficient

energy to meet these demands, allostasis provides for a higher level of stress hormones in the morning. (McEwen, 2002, p. 7)

Consistent with Seyle, McEwen recognizes stress as being a normal response of the body to the demands of the environment. He calls this normal response allostasis to differentiate it from the more chronic, negative stress, which he calls *allostatic load* (McEwen, 2002, pp. 6–10). Sapolsky (1998) also utilizes the concept of allostasis to explain that the stress response is part of the natural makeup of the human being. He states:

> Allostasis refers to the notion that different circumstances demand different homeostatic set points (after all, the ideal blood pressure when you are sleeping is likely to be quite different than when you are bungee jumping), and that maintaining whatever an optimal set point might be demands far flung regulatory changes throughout the body instead of just local adjustments. . . . Within that framework, a stressor can be defined as anything that throws your body out of allostatic balance. . . . The stress response, in turn, is your body's attempt to restore balance. (Sapolsky, 1998, p. 7)

In describing the process of allostasis, McEwen (2002) states:

> Allostasis is produced by a swift and intricately organized system of communication. It links the brain, which perceives a novel or threatening situation; the endocrine system (chiefly the adrenal glands), which is primarily responsible for mobilizing the rest of the body; and the immune system for internal defense. Allostasis is often thought of as the fight-or-flight response because, when taken to the extreme, it prepares for just those two eventualities. The main idea is to get maximum energy to those parts of the body that need it most. . . . Fight-or-flight is allostasis with a sense of urgency. (pp. 6–7)

The fight-or-flight response is the wired response of the human organism to perceived, acute threats in the environment. The fight-or-flight response is one of the natural, evolutionary mechanisms passed down through the process of reproduction. Benson (1975) argued for this evolutionary aspect of the fight-or-flight response when he noted:

> Because we tend to think of man in Cartesian terms, as essentially a rational being, we have lost sight of his origins and of his Darwinian struggle for survival where the successful use of the fight-or-flight response was a matter of life or death. Man's ancestors with the most highly developed fight-or-flight reactions had an increased chance of surviving long enough to reproduce. Natural selection favored the continuation of the response. (p. 24)

The activation of the fight-or-flight response results in massive chemical, physical, and biological changes in the body in order to allow it to protect itself from perceived threats by fighting or fleeing.[8] These massive changes include, but are not limited to, those noted in Table 2.3.

Table 2.3

Body Focal Point	Body Changes
Respiratory system	Airways dilate. Breathing is rapid and shallow.
Endocrine system	1. Levels of adrenalin and noradrenalin (epinephrine and norepinephrine) increase. 2. Glucocorticoid (cortisol) levels increase, preventing inflammation, decreasing lymphocyte discharge, and contributing to increasing energy.
Vascular system	1. The heart rate increases. 2. Blood pressure rises. 3. Rate of clotting increases. 4. Blood flow is changed as (a) arteries to the heart, lungs, and active muscles dilate and (b) arteries to skin, abdominal organs, hands, feet, and some skeletal muscles constrict.
Elimination	Sweating increases. Urine production decreases. Digestion slows.
Attending to the environment	Hyperarousal. Pupils dilate. Muscles tense for fighting or fleeing. Anxiety increases. Hypervigilance occurs as the individual scans the environment for potential threats.
Energy production and utilization	Blood sugar levels rise. Metabolic rate increases.

These changes are normal and allowed our distant ancestors to deal with their threat, survive, adapt, reproduce, and maintain their gene pool. When the threat was gone, the fight-or-flight response was turned off by the parasympathetic nervous system and the body was allowed to return to normal (see Brehm, 1998; Lovallo, 2005; McEwen, 2002; Sapolsky, 1998; and Schafer, 1996). Sapolsky (1998) points out that the stress response is not restricted to perceived threats in the external environment. The stress response can be activated by thoughts, judgments, and even the anticipation that a threatening event may or may not occur. Thus, the very act of worrying about something is enough to activate the fight-or-flight response and all of its physiological changes. He states:

But unlike less cognitively sophisticated species, we can turn on the stress-response by thinking about potential stressors that may throw us out of allostatic balance far in the future. . . .

When we activate the stress response out of fear of something that turns out to be real, we congratulate ourselves that this cognitive skill allows us to mobilize our defenses early. And when we get into a physiological uproar for no reason at all, or over something we cannot do anything about, we call it things like "anxiety," "neurosis," "paranoia," or "needless hostility." Thus, the stress-response can be mobilized not only in response to physical or psychological insults, but also in expectation of them. (Sapolsky, 1998, pp. 7–8)

This perspective, that the mind can activate the stress response/ fight-or-flight response simply by thinking, is echoed by Stefano, Fricchione, Slingsby, and Benson (2001); Kabat-Zinn (2005); and Webster, Stuart, and Wells-Federman (1993). Stefano, Fricchione, Slingsby, and Benson argue:

Our physiological systems are not designed for long-term stress, such as prolonged immune compromise. We may also bring upon ourselves a long-term stress resulting from our perception of the stressor itself. Perhaps, with the appearance of cognitive appraisal capabilities human beings were, as a side effect, able to translate the short-term stress process into a long-term stress process simply by thinking about it and moreover dwelling on it (such as contemplating a boss firing you for several months). Cognitive abilities have allowed us to appreciate stressors that may not be immediately apparent to anyone else, but may be internally apprised as such. (Stefano, Fricchione, Slingsby, & Benson, 2001, p. 7)

Kabat-Zinn (2005) notes how thoughts and stress are linked together, pointing out how the mind can produce its own stress independent from any real threats in the environment. He argues that this self-generated stress can significantly compromise the functioning and health of an individual. He observed that

from the inside our mind not only changes in response to our perception of . . . outer forces; it also generates its own reactive energies, producing another whole set of pressures and demands on the organism. . . . Even our thoughts and feelings can act as major stressors if they tax or exceed our ability to respond effectively . . . even if the thought or feeling has no correspondence with "reality." . . . The mere thought that you have a fatal disease can be a cause of considerable stress and could become disabling, even though it may not be true. (Kabat-Zinn, 2005, p. 250)

Stuart, Webster, and Wells-Federman (1993) describe our everyday life as consisting of a number of potential stressors that are not really appropriate for the activation of the fight-or-flight response. Remember that the fight-or-flight response evolved as part of the human composition in order to assist us in addressing real threats. Massive physiological changes occur in the body to prepare us to fight or flee. Once the threat has been addressed through some physical action, which utilizes the changes in the body, the fight-or-flight response is turned off and the body returns to normal. Stuart et al et argue that if the fight-or-flight response is activated by potential stressors when a physical response of fighting or fleeing is not appropriate, there may be considerable difficulty in utilizing and dissipating the physiological changes that have occurred as a result of the activation of the fight-or-flight response.

> Our difficulty in the twentieth century is that many of the stresses we face (relationships, work, family, money, etc.) are not amenable to the physical reaction of fight-or-flight, yet the physiology elicited by the stress remains the same. In these situations, however, the physical response has no way to dissipate. Imagine driving behind a car which is traveling slowly. You begin to fume because you are "late" and "have important things to do." Your brain receives the urgent message—"going to be late"—and triggers the fight-or-flight response, even though it is not useful in this situation. Without the ability to dissipate the increased adrenalin circulating through your body, you probably remain angry and physically aroused for some time after the incident. Over time, chronic excessive exposure to stress can lead to physical symptoms and exacerbate many illnesses. Just as stress affects our body, so to it affects the ways we feel and think. Confronted by stress we may feel anxious, helpless, overwhelmed or angry. Our thinking style can be affected: it may be more difficult to concentrate, think clearly or make decisions. It is not uncommon to change our behavior (e.g. smoke more, eat more junk food, or drink more alcohol) when under stress. (Stuart, Webster, & Wells-Federman, 1993, pp. 180–181)

Thus not only do real physical threats activate the fight-or-flight response, but your very thinking about negative events has the potential of activating your fight-or-flight response. Seligman (2006) argues that the individual's explanatory style for negative or bad events may lead to illness and depression. Specifically, if the individual has a pessimistic explanatory style, he or she is much more likely to become depressed or ill. For Seligman, individuals with a pessimistic explanatory style blame themselves for the negative or bad events (personal), see the events as spilling over into other aspects of their lives (pervasive), and see these events as being ongoing (permanent).

Thus, in many cases, it is not so much the event itself that is problematic; it is how the individual perceives the event that leads or may lead to depression and illness. According to Seligman (2006), if the individual perceives the event as a threat, has a pessimistic explanatory style, and keeps thinking about it, he or she is likely to become depressed.

> Here's how the pessimism-rumination chain leads to depression: First, there is some threat against which you believe you are helpless. Second, you look for the threat's cause, and if you are a pessimist, the cause you arrive at is permanent, pervasive and personal. Consequently you expect to be helpless in the future and in many situations, a conscious expectation that is the last link in the chain, the one triggering depression. The expectation of helplessness may arise only rarely, or it may arise all the time. The more you are inclined to ruminate, the more it arises. Brooding, thinking about how bad things are, start the sequence. Ruminators get this chain going all the time. Any reminder of the original threat causes them to run off the whole pessimism-rumination chain, right through to the expectation of failure and depression. People who do not ruminate tend to avoid depression even if they are pessimists. For them, the sequence runs itself off infrequently. . . . We find, then, that pessimistic ruminators are most at risk for depression. (Seligman, 2006, p. 83)

It is important to note that in Seligman's description of the chain of events that may lead to depression, the chain is activated by a perceived threat. A perceived threat is what often activates the fight-or-flight or stress response. Kabat-Zinn notes:

> Much of our stress comes from threats, real or imagined, to our social status, not to our lives. But the fight-or-flight reaction kicks in even when there is no life-threatening situation for us to feel threatened. It is sufficient for us to just feel threatened. By causing us to react so quickly and so automatically, the fight-or-flight reaction often creates problems for us in the social domain rather than giving us additional energy for resolving our problems. Anything that threatens our sense of well-being can trigger it to some degree. (Kabat-Zinn, 2005, p. 254)

Allostatic Load

For McEwen (2003), *allostatic load* refers to the chronic activation of the fight-or-flight response. The individual is continually hyperaroused. In other words, the fight-or flight response is not allowed to operate in a normal manner. It is not serving a useful function. It is not assisting the individual in addressing and solving an adaptive problem in the environment.

As the individual continues to worry and/or ruminate about the self-generated threat, the fight-or-flight response continues to cause massive physiological changes in the body. As a result, excessive stress hormones continually circulate throughout the body.

In these types of cases, as Stuart et al. (1993) previously noted, there is no way to dissipate the excessive hormones in your body because there is no physical reaction you can make to the self-generated threat. There is no real physical threat in the present world confronting the individual to which fighting or fleeing would be an appropriate response. As long as the worry and/or rumination continue, the fight-or-flight response will remain activated. The human organism will be chronically stressed. The body will be continually flooded with physiological changes that over time may result in both psychological and physical dysfunctionality.

The psychological dysfunctionality may be manifested cognitively, affectively, and behaviorally.[9] This translates as chronic problems with attention, focusing, memory, decision making, logical thinking, and perceived sense of control. Chronic feelings such as low self-esteem, low motivation, tension, feeling overwhelmed, worry, anxiety, depression, helplessness, anger, fear, and hostility may be present. Maladaptive behaviors such as alcohol abuse, drug abuse, physical abuse, and sexual abuse may occur. The individual may miss a lot of work and/or be injury prone both at work and outside of work.[10]

The physical dysfunctionality may result in a chronically depressed immune system that may contribute to various diseases. This physical dysfuntionality may also contribute to various lifestyle disorders such as cancer, heart disease, strokes, hypertension, diabetes, digestive disorders, breathing disorders, skin disorders, digestive disorders, and chronic pain.[11]

The medical doctor Herbert Benson (1998, p. 3) noted in his testimony before the U.S. Senate Appropriations Subcommittee on Labor/HHS & Education that research indicates that between 60 and 90 percent of all office visits to medical doctors "are related to stress and other mind/body interactions." What this means is that although the symptoms are real, there are no identifiable physiological correlates. A physical cause for the disease cannot be identified. In other words, the symptoms are related to or generated by chronic stress.

Seventy-four percent of the complaints patients bring to medical clinics are of unknown origin and are probably caused by "psychosocial" factors, according to a study reported by Dr. Kurt Kroenke of the Uniformed Services University of Health Sciences in Bethesda, Maryland, and A. David Manglesdorff, Ph.D., MPH, of the Brooke Army Medical Center in Houston, Texas. Other studies indicate that between 60 and 90 percent of all our population's visit to doctors' offices are stress-related and probably cannot be detected, much less treated effectively, with the medications and procedures on which the medical profession relies almost exclusively. In other words, the vast majority of the time, patients bring medical concerns to the attention of a healing profession that cannot heal them with external tools or devices. (Benson, 1996, pp. 49–50)

Seyle (1978) linked a number of illnesses to an overtaxed general adaptation syndrome (G.A.S.). Because of continual demands or threats, the general adaptation syndrome, or as it is more commonly known, the fight-or-flight response, is not able to function in its normal capacity. Its normal adaptive role relative to assisting the human organism of becoming aware of, addressing, and solving a problem or threat is compromised. As it is chronically activated, the massive nonspecific changes in the body and the flooding of it with stress/adaptive hormones is ongoing. The body is not allowed to recover and rest. The stress/adaptive hormones flooding the body are not dissipated in a timely manner. The immune system is suppressed. (See also Ader, 2005; Cohen, 2005; Kemeny, 2005; McEwen, 2002; Overmier & Murison, 2005; and Sapolsky, 1998.) This is detrimental to the body. In other words, Seyle linked illness to chronic stress.

> The last concept which we have to define is that of the "disease of adaptation." These are the maladies in which imperfections of the G.A.S. play a major role. Many diseases are actually not so much the direct results of some external agent (an infection, intoxication) as they are of the body's inability to meet these agents by adequate adaptive reactions, that is, by a perfect G.A.S. (Seyle, 1978, p. 83)

Seyle clearly links the excessive flooding of the body with stress/adaptive hormones to illness. The excessive flooding is associated with adaptive problems relative to demands or threats in the environment.

> It is still largely a matter of debate which of the diseases of adaptation are due to an actual overproduction of, hypersensitivity to, adaptive hormones. But this is a point of secondary importance. The most significant practical outcome of our experiments was to demonstrate that hormones participate in the development of numerous nonendocrine diseases, that is, of maladies which are not primarily due to derangements originating in the endocrine glands themselves. (Seyles, 1978, p. 207)

> If a microbe is in or around us all the time and yet causes no disease until we are exposed to stress, what is the "cause" of our illness, the microbe or the stress? I think both are—and equally so. In most instances disease is due neither to the germ as such, nor to our adaptive reactions as such,

but to the inadequacy of our reactions against the germ. . . . If a company goes bankrupt and the owner develops a gastric ulcer, what is the cause of the disease, the bankruptcy or the owner's inability to adapt himself to his losses? (Seyle, 1978, p. 300)

The stress hormones are not only linked to so-called physical illnesses. There is also a clear connection between stress hormones and "psychological illnesses." Sapolsky (1998) links the stress hormones adrenalin and noradrenalin (epinephrine and norepinephrine), produced by the adrenal medulla, to anxiety. He links glucocorticoids (stress hormones), produce by the adrenal cortex, to depression. He notes that

about half of depressives have resting glucocorticoid levels that are dramatically higher than in other people, often sufficiently elevated to cause problems with metabolism and immunity. Or in some cases, depressives are unable to shut off glucocorticoid secretion, their brains less sensitive to a shut-off signal. A theme . . . on some troubled nonhuman primates is that there is a discrepancy between the sorts of stressors they are exposed to and the coping responses they come up with. Learned helplessness . . . an underpinning of depression, appears to be another example of such discrepancy. A challenge occurs, and what is the response of a depressive individual? "I can't, it's too much, why bother doing anything, it isn't going to work anyway, nothing I do ever works. . . ." The discrepancy here is that in the face of stressful challenges, depressives don't even attempt to mount a coping response. (Sapolsky, 1998, pp. 272–273)

Not surprisingly, anxiety disorders are associated with chronically overactive stress responses. Surprisingly, though, glucocorticoid excess is not the usual response. Instead, it is too much sympathetic activation, an overabundance of catecholamines (epinephrine and norepinephrine). . . . When it comes to human psychiatric disorders, it seems that increases in the catecholamines have something to do with still trying to cope and the effort that involves, where overabundance of glucocorticoids seems more of a signal of having given up coping with that stressor. (Sapolsky, 1998, pp. 274–275)

Sapolsky's linking of depression to "having given up" and "learned helplessness" is certainly connected to the work of Seligman. Seligman's (2006) work with depression, explanatory styles, and learned helplessness is linked to perception of personal control. Seligman argues that in contexts in which you do have some potential sense of personal control, your thinking about these contexts will have a direct influence on your actions.

Many things in life are beyond our control—our eye color, our race, the drought in the Midwest. But there is a vast, unclaimed territory of actions over which we can take control—or cede control to others or fate. These actions involve the way we lead our lives, how we deal with other people, how we earn a living—all the aspects of existence in which we normally have some degree of choice. The way we think about this realm of life can actually diminish or enlarge the control we have over it. Our thoughts are not merely reactions to events; they change what ensues. For example, if we think we are helpless to make a difference in what our children become, we will be paralyzed when dealing with this facet of our lives. The very thought "Nothing I do matters" prevents us from acting. And so we cede control to our children's peers and teachers, and to circumstances. When we overestimate our helplessness, other forces will take control and shape our children's future. (Seligman, 2006, p. 7)

According to Seligman, this type of thinking, in which individuals feel they do not really have any control over the events in the world they perceive as threatening, when they actually *do* have potential control, leads to learned helplessness. Learned helplessness leads to an overall pessimistic explanatory style that then reinforces the perception that the individual is helpless and has no personal control when addressing situations that are perceived as threatening. This pessimistic explanatory style, by which individuals continue to ruminate over threats or negative events, is likely to lead to depression, as noted earlier, and illness.

Optimism and pessimism affect health itself, almost as clearly as do physical factors. Most people assume that physical health is wholly a physical matter and that it is determined by constitution, health habits and how well you avoid germs. . . . This conventional view omits a major determinant of health—our own cognitions. Our physical health is something over which we can have far greater personal control than we probably suspect. For example:

- The way we think, especially about our health, changes our health.
- Optimists catch fewer infectious diseases than pessimists do.
- Our immune system may work better when we are optimistic.
- Evidence suggests that optimists live longer than pessimists. (Seligman, 2006, p. 14)

Seligman's (2006) work linking threats, pessimistic explanatory style, learned helplessness, and rumination to depression and illness clearly supports the hypothesis of an overactive fight-or-flight response. In other words, it is indicative of chronic stress or allostatic load. As noted previously in the work of Sapolsky (1998) and Seyle (1978), the circulating of excessive quantities of stress hormones, due to chronic stress, is linked with anxiety, depression, and physical illness. This link between chronic stress and psychological dysfunctionality and physical illness is further supported by the previously examined work of Stuart et al. (1993), Benson and Stuart (1993, 1996), Stefano, Fricchione, Slingsby, and Benson (2001), and Kabat-Zinn (2005).

Yalom (1980) links psychopathology with stress and the individual's inability to successfully defend against it. For Yalom, stress is everywhere. It part of the normal human being's existence. He notes:

> How then, one may ask, can a theory of psychopathology rests on factors that are experienced by every individual? The answer, of course, is that each person experiences the stress of the human condition in highly individualized fashion. . . . The overwhelming majority of patients suffer from stress that to differing degrees is part of every person's experience. In fact, only the universality of suffering can account for the common observation the patienthood is ubiquitous. The universality of stress is one of the major reasons that scholars encounter such difficulty when attempting to define and describe normality: the difference between normality and pathology is quantitative, not qualitative. . . . Thus, all human beings are in a quandary, but some are unable to cope with it: psychopathology depends not merely on the presence or absence of stress but on the interaction of the ubiquitous stress and the individual's mechanisms of defense. (Yalom, 1980, pp. 12–13)

For Yalom, stress is linked to four fundamental existential issues that provide the basis for potential threats to the individual: death, freedom, isolation, and meaninglessness. The awareness of these threatening ultimate concerns gives rise to anxiety (fight-or-flight response), which in turn give rise to various defense mechanisms or coping responses. The inability of the individual's defense mechanisms or coping responses to adequately transcend these threats gives rise to chronic stress, allostatic load, or, in Yalom's terminology, psychopathology.

> The existential position emphasizes . . . a conflict that flows from the individual's confrontation with the givens of existence. And I mean by "givens" of existence certain ultimate concerns, certain intrinsic properties that are a part, and an inescapable part, of the human being's existence in the world . . . such experiences as a confrontation with one's own death, some major irreversible decision or the collapse of some fundamental meaning-providing schema. . . . "Existential psychodynamics" refers, thus, to these four givens, these ultimate concerns, and to the conscious

and unconscious fears and motives spawned by each. . . . These four ultimate concerns—death, freedom, isolation and meaninglessness—constitute the corpus of existential psychodynamics. (Yalom, 1980, pp. 8–10)

The issue of death, one's own death, is quite likely the most threatening and fearful situation to any individual. From the perspective of evolutionary theory, the human organism is wired to protect itself from threats, with death being, far and away, the most threatening. The fight-or-flight response or stress response (*acute allostasis*) is an evolutionary mechanism that assists individuals in addressing immediate threats to their very existence. The fact, however, that individuals do not know (threat) what happens when they die gives rise, for most people, to considerable continuous stress. In other words, the fight-or-flight response is chronically activated. Continuous or chronic stress (allostatic load) is detrimental to physical and psychological health.

To suppress this threat and the subsequent stress, individuals develop or accept various coping mechanisms. In the case of the threat of individual death, one of the more salient coping mechanisms is that of religion. Religion offers a solution to the problem of the threat of individual death. Through religion, individuals will be saved. There will be no individual death. There is an afterlife where individuals live forever. By believing in religion and the various deities that populate it, the threat of individual death is suppressed. As long as this defense mechanism works and the threat of individual death is suppressed, the fight-or-flight response is turned off. There is no longer a fear of death. The threat is gone. Unless of course, something happens that raises doubt.

All individuals are confronted with death anxiety; most develop adaptive coping modes—modes that consist of denial-based strategies such as suppression, repression, displacement, belief in personal omnipotence, acceptance of socially sanctioned religious beliefs that "detoxify" death, or personal efforts to overcome death through a wide variety of strategies that aim at achieving symbolic immortality. Either because of extraordinary stress or because of an inadequacy of available defensive strategies, the individual who enters "patienthood" has found insufficient the universal modes of dealing with death fear and has been driven to extreme modes of defense. These defensive maneuvers, often clumsy modes of dealing with terror, constitute the presenting clinical picture. (Yalom, 1980, pp. 110–111)

Psychopathology, to a very great extent, is the result of failed death transcendence; that is, symptoms and maladaptive character structure have their origins in the individual terror of death. (May & Yalom, 2000, p. 284)

Thus, for Yalom, the very core of psychopathology is based on inadequate defense mechanisms relative to addressing, essentially, in one form or another, the perceived threat of an individual's death. As has been previously noted, threats activate the fight-or-flight response. If the defense mechanisms are not working adequately, the perceived threat is maintained. Consequently, acute stress moves into chronic stress, which is then manifested as various physical and/or psychological symptoms.

Chronic stress (allostatic load) is not restricted, however, to an overactive fight-or-flight response relative to addressing specific ongoing demands in various environmental (external and/or internal) contexts. Inadequate sleep, poor diet, and lack of exercise, which can also be a result of chronic stress, can, as well, contribute to chronic stress. These behaviors essentially result in the human organism being out of harmony or balance. As a result, they all may compromise an individual's ability to adapt to various environmental demands. In other words, our lifestyle contributes significantly to chronic stress.

> Allostatic load does not always denote a failure of the body's efforts to cope with change or emergency. We can create it for ourselves by living in a way that makes for internal imbalance. Sleep deprivation, for example, leads to elevations in blood glucose and cortisol; chronic elevation of this sort can lead to bone mineral loss and increase the amount of fat that accumulates in the abdominal area (considered the unhealthiest type of fat). Eating a rich diet or overeating produces a metabolic load on the body, thereby increasing fat deposition and hardening of the arteries, both risk factors for heart disease and other ailments. Lack of regular exercise is another major contributor to allostatic load: regular exercise increases energy expenditure and boosts muscles to burn glucose. Exercise works against the bad effects of a rich diet and increased body fat, enhances well-being, and improves sleep. Quite often, bad habits reflect our personal efforts to deal with stress. Eating the wrongs things, sleeping irregularly, and not exercising compound the effects of stress to make our lives miserable. (McEwen, 2003, p. 9)

Given the discussion to this point, it should be clear, given the pervasiveness of stressors and the stress response, that it is a mistake to try and consider physical and psychological problems as being distinct and not related to each other. There is a need for a truly integrative approach when addressing not only "physical problems" but also "psychological problems." With evidence suggesting that chronic stress (allostatic load) is intimately involved with both types of problems, it is of utmost importance to understand that both mind and body are intertwined in these problems.

> Western medicine still makes serious distinctions between mental, emo-
> tional and physical roots of illness despite the amassing of research that
> finds the mind and body are so interwoven that such distinctions are not
> only artificial, they're unscientific. (Benson, 1996, p. 50)

It is not enough, however, just to say that mind and body are intimately
intertwined relative to physical and/or psychological illness. If, as has been
demonstrated, chronic stress is a significant contributor to illness, then it
is necessary to link mind and body to the environment. That is, one must
assume, in many cases of illness, there is a perceived threat in the environment for which the stress response has been activated to assist the individual in solving the problem. In other words, the stress response was activated
to help the individual adapt to the environment. The difficulty is that the
perceived threat in the environment was not of the nature that the activation
of the fight-or-flight response was appropriate. This being the case, the
threat is maintained and the fight-or-flight response is chronically activated
(allostatic load).

In the case of psychological problems, it is necessary for counselors
and psychotherapists to see the problem as one of perceived threats giving
rise to difficulties in adapting to the environment, which, if the threat is not
resolved, leads to chronic stress. The linking of psychological problems, in
most cases, with perceived threats, which are in fact adaptive problems in
the environment and chronic stress, must serve as the foundation for understanding the client.

> Although . . . the conditions for which psychotherapy is sought or offered
> are protean, all can be viewed as temporary or persistent unsuccessful
> adaptations to stress. Everyone must deal with experiences that temporar-
> ily disturb equanimity and create tensions with others. The healthy person
> is able to handle most such experiences promptly and effectively. Others
> cannot. It is useful to think of all illnesses as "non-adaptive" states . . .
> characterized by disability and distress. Failures of adaptation imply an
> imbalance between the severity of an environmental stress and the
> person's susceptibility to it. . . . When attempts to overcome the distress
> caused by adversity are ineffective, the person or family may come to
> regard their disequilibrium as illness and seek expert help. By and large
> persons who attribute their distress and disability to bodily causes turn to
> physicians; those who perceive their illnesses as related primarily to dis-
> turbed relations with others or to internal psychological conflicts gravitate
> toward psychotherapists. . . . Such persons have much in common with
> other victims of interpersonal stress—for example the villager who con-
> sults a shaman about a curse, and the outcast on verge of religious con-
> version. Psychotherapy is commonly offered to those who seem basically

intact yet are unable to handle usual environmental demands. (Frank & Frank, 1993, pp. 22–23)

Given the analysis of allostatic load and its relationship to psychological dysfunctionality, and the perspectives of Frank and Frank (1993), Kabat-Zinn (2005), May and Yalom (2000), Seligman (2006), and Yalom (1980) regarding psychopathology, it is reasonable to infer that clients coming to counselors or psychotherapists for help are suffering from chronic stress (allostatic load). Clients are having difficulties solving various problems in a diverse set of environmental contexts. Essentially, they are having problems adapting to the demands of some aspect of their environments.

As these problems and demands are perceived, in some manner or other, as threats, the fight-or-flight responses of these individuals are activated. Because the activation of the fight-or-flight response is not appropriate for addressing these perceived threats, and the clients do not have appropriate, functional coping mechanisms to address the threats, the problem or demand is not resolved. Insofar as the problem or demand is not resolved, the stress is maintained. The maintenance of this stress results in allostatic load or chronic stress. Allostatic load or chronic stress significantly compromises the cognitive, emotional, behavioral, social, and physical functioning of the individual in relationship to various environmental contexts. As the clients were unable to resolve their adaptive problem and find the ongoing symptoms disabling and distressful, they sought the help of a counselor or psychotherapist. The interventions by the counselors and psychotherapists are, even though they may not acknowledge it or even be aware of it, for all intents and purposes addressing and attempting to alleviate chronic stress.

Summary

The focus of this chapter was to establish the second component of the foundation that will allow for building a bridge between Chinese thought, specifically Confucianism, Daoism, and Buddhism, and Western counseling and psychotherapy. This bridge will allow, we hope, for the insights of Confucianism, Daoism, and Buddhism to be utilized and incorporated, when appropriate, into Western counseling and psychotherapy.

This second component is that of stress and the stress response. The analysis has clearly demonstrated that the fundamental issue addressed by Confucianism, Daoism, and Buddhism is, in fact, that of chronic stress or allostatic load. Although the language is different, the descriptors are in complete agreement with the language used today in regard to stress, the stress response, and chronic stress.

Buddha's First Noble Truth of suffering or dissatisfaction (*dukkha*) is a statement about the universal condition of all people. It is, essentially, a statement about chronic stress (allostatic load). His analysis is clearly applicable today. It is consistent with Yalom's (1980) statements about the "universality of suffering" and the "universality of stress." Life is inherently stressful.

Whether the discussion is oriented toward a time frame 2,500 years ago or to the very present moment, the relationship among solving an adaptive problem in the environment, perceived threats in the environment, inadequate coping mechanisms, and chronic stress is the same. The evolutionary process has provided all human beings with a tool to assist them in becoming aware of threats in the environment and mobilizing their energy to address the threat. The tool is the fight-or-flight response.

The fight-or-flight response or stress response (allostasis) evolved to help provide solutions to acute physical threats in the environment. Our distant ancestors were challenged with the basic problem of adapting to their environments so that they could survive and pass on their gene pool. When they were threatened with real physical threats, the fight-or-flight response was activated, the problem was addressed and resolved with some type of physical response such as fighting or fleeing. In the process of solving the problem, the stress hormones were dissipated due to the physical response, and as the threat was removed, the fight-or-flight response was deactivated. Our ancestors returned to normal. The fight-or-flight response was selected for, maintained, and passed on through the reproductive process to succeeding generations because it worked. It allowed individuals to perceive problems, adapt, survive, and reproduce.

The difficulty associated with chronic stress is that, in general, the threats addressed by Confucius, Buddha, the Daoists, and the counselors and psychotherapists today are not really physical in nature. These threats are more of a result of how individuals or clients view, judge, and/or think about their various environmental contexts. As these threats are not physical in nature or really acute, the activation of the fight-or-flight response is not appropriate. The problem is that the brain does not make a distinction between a real physical threat and a self-generated, imagined one. The fight-or-flight response will still be activated.

Unfortunately the activation, by the mere thoughts of an individual or client, of the fight-or-flight response does not result in the removal the threat or solve the problem. Insofar as the threat or problem is not removed or solved, the fight-or-flight response is chronically activated. Threats generated by our thinking do not go away unless we stop thinking about them. If we do not stop thinking about them, our fight-or-flight response is chronically activated, resulting in ongoing significant physiological changes that are detrimental to our physical, social, cognitive, affective/emotional, and behavioral well-being.

It is this problem of chronic stress to which the thinking of Confucius, the Buddha, and the Daoists was addressed. It is this problem of chronic stress to which the interventions of counselors and psychotherapists is addressed. All are concerned with helping individuals adapt to their environment. All are concerned with teaching people how to live so they will be able to, essentially, work out their own destinies.

This component, stress and the stress response, easily fits into the Daoist model of simplicity, beginning points, and commonality that was set forth in the Introduction. Whether we are talking about individuals addressed by Buddha, Confucius, or the Daoists 2,500 years ago or those individuals addressed today by counselors and psychotherapists, they share, have in common, the fight-or-flight response. They have in common the fact that the primary source of their stress was/is not really physical threats but their perspective or worldview, which generated/generates perceived threats about their various environmental contexts. They have in common inadequate coping mechanisms/defense mechanisms that resulted/results in the chronic activation of the flight-or-fight response. They had/have in common the subsequent cognitive, emotional, behavioral, interpersonal, and physical dysfunctionalities associated with chronic stress as a consequence of the continual activation of the fight-or-flight response.

Self-generated perceived threats, worldview, the activation of the stress response, and inadequate coping mechanisms are the beginning points for the subsequent development of chronic stress. These beginning points are quite simple in nature when compared with the eventual complexity associated with the endpoint cognitive, emotional, behavioral, interpersonal, and physical problems generated by chronic activation of the fight- or-flight response.

Evolutionary theory and psychology, and stress and the stress response make up two-thirds of the bridge, allowing for the utilization of the perspectives of Confucius, Buddha, and the Daoists within the context of counseling and psychotherapy. The third component, that of stress management, is the final element of establishing a bridge, a bamboo bridge if you will, between Western counseling and psychotherapy and the teachings of Confucius, Buddha, and Daoism. It is to stress management that we turn in the next chapter.

Important Terms

Acute

Adaptation

Adaptive problems

Allostasis

Allostatic load

Coping mechanisms/responses

Chronic

Chronic stress

Disease

Distress

Dukkha

Environment

Existential position

Fear

Fight-or-flight response

General adaptation syndrome (G.A.S.)

Illness

Learned helplessness

Mind and body

Optimism

Perceived threat

Pessimism

Physical dysfunctionality

Psychological dysfunctionality

Rumination

Physical symptoms

Psychological symptoms

Stress hormones

Stressors

Stress response

Threats

Exercises

A. While stress is part of being human and is normal, some stress significantly compromises your ability to function and adapt to the challenges in your environment. Ask yourself, For you, what is problematic stress? What does being stressed mean to you? How do you know when you are stressed? How often do you feel stressed? How do you feel when you are stressed? How does stress affect you physically, psychologically, emotionally, and interpersonally? Do you have any particular triggers that set off your stress? Are they contextually bound? Do you have enough time in the day to do what you want to do? If not, how does this affect you? Ask yourself, on a scale of 1–10, with 1 being minimal and 10 being overloaded, how much stress, honestly, do you have daily?

B. How can an understanding of stress and the stress response (fight-or-flight response) be helpful to you as a counselor? How can teaching a client about the stress response (fight-or-flight response) be helpful to the client?

Chinese Characters

[a] 色	[h] 言	[o] 疒
[b] 受	[l] 音	[p] 广
[c] 想	[j] 戈	[q] 久
[d] 相	[k] 恐	[r] 道
[e] 心	[l] 巩	[s] 仁
[f] 行	[m] 君子	
[g] 識	[n] 小人	

Notes

1. All translations/interpretations, from the Chinese, of the Buddhist sutras are my own.

The original Chinese texts can be found at McRae (2003), the *Electronic Texts of the Chinese Buddhist Canon* Web site, located at http://www.indiana.edu/~asialink/canon.html. The reference for finding the *Turning the Dharma Wheel (Zhuan Fa Lun Jing)* at this site is T22, No. 1421 [0104b08].

2. See *Miscellaneous Sutras (Za A Han Jing)*. The Chinese text can be found at McRae (2003), T02, No. 99 [0126c20].

3. See *Miscellaneous Sutras (Za A Han Jing)*. The Chinese text can be found at McRae (2003), T02, No. 99 [0767a22].

4. *Sutra on Impermanence (Wu Chang Jing)*. The Chinese text can be found at McRae (2003), T01, No. 26 [0609c04].

5. The translations/interpretations from the Chinese are my own. The source for the original Chinese text of *Sutra of Statements on Dharma (Fa Ju Jing)* or more commonly known as the *Dharmapada* or *Dhammapada* can be found at Dhammapada (2004): http://myweb.ncku.edu.tw/~lausinan/Tipitaka/Sutta/Khuddaka/Dhammapada/Dhammapada.htm. The reference for finding verses 277–279 is MAGGAVAGGO (273–289).

6. All translations from the Chinese are my own. The format of 3/2/10–12 indicates the page/chapter/lines in the *Harvard–Yenching Institute Sinological Index Series Supplement 20, A Concordance to Chuang Tzu* (Cambridge, MA: Harvard University Press, 1956). The text *Zhuang Zi Bai Hua Ju Jie* (Hong Kong: Feng Hua Chu Ban Shi Ye Gong Se, 1989) was used as a supplement for the translation/interpretation. Focus of translation/interpretation is on inner chapters (1–7) and Chapters 17–22. For chapter authenticity, see Slingerland (2003), pp. 285–286. I consider Chapters 1–7 and Chapters 17–22 in the *Zhuang Zi* text to be representative of the teachings of the person Zhuang Zi.

7. All translations/interpretations of the *Lun Yu* and the commentaries are my own.

The format of XVII-15 refers to the Book (XVII) and Section (15) of the *Lun Yu*. The Chinese texts utilized for this translation can be found in Yang (1972) and Hong (1973).

8. For more in-depth analyses of the physiological and psychological changes occurring during the activation of the fight-or-flight response, see Benson (1975); Benson and Stuart (1993); Brehm (1998); Kabat-Zinn (2005); Lovallo (2005); McEwen (2002); Sapolsky (1998); Schafer (1996); and Seyle (1978).

9. For more in-depth analyses regarding the relationship between psychological dysfunctionality and chronic stress, see Jones and Bright (2001); Kabat-Zinn (2005); Lovallo (2005); Miller and Chen (2005); and Sapolsky (1998).

10. For concerns regarding the relationship between chronic stress and workplace performance both in China and the United States, see http://yourmedical

source.com/library/stress/STR_whatis.html; http://my.webmd.com/content/pages/ 19/103374.htm; http://www2.chinadaily.com.cn/english/doc/2005–05/20content_ 444337.htm; and http://english.runsky.com/homepage/english/news/soci/userobject 1ai544292.html.

11. For more in-depth analyses regarding the relationship among physical dysfunctionality, illness, and chronic stress see Benson (1975, 1998); Brehm (1998); Jones and Bright (2001); Kabat-Zinn (2005); Lovallo (2005); McEwen (2002); Miller and Chen (2005); Sapolsky (1998); Schafer (1996); and Seyle (1978).

References

Ader, R. (2005). Psychoneuroimmunology. In G. Miller & E. Chen (Eds.), *Readings from the American Psychological Society: Current directions in health psychology* (pp. 86–92). Upper Saddle River, NJ: Pearson Prentice Hall.

Benson, H. (1975). *The relaxation response.* New York: Avon Books.

Benson, H. (1996). *Timeless healing: The power and biology of belief.* New York: Scribner.

Benson, H. (1998). Testimony of Herbert Benson regarding mind/body interventions, healthcare and mind/body medical centers before the United States Senate Appropriations Subcommittee on Labor/HHS & Education, Senator Arlen Specter, chairman, September, 22, 1998.

Benson, H., & Stuart, E. M. (Eds.). (1993). *The wellness book: The comprehensive guide to maintaining health and treating stress-related illness.* New York: Simon & Schuster.

Brehm, B. A. (1998). *Stress management: Increasing your stress resistance.* New York: Longman.

Cohen, S. (2005). Psychological stress, immunity, and upper respiratory infections. In G. Miller & E. Chen (Eds.), *Readings from the American Psychological Society: Current directions in health psychology* (pp. 3–10). Upper Saddle River, NJ: Pearson Prentice Hall.

Dhammapada. (2004). Available at htttp://myweb.ncku.edu.tw/~lausinan/Tipitaka/ Sutta/Khuddaka/Dhammapada/Dhammapada.htm

Frank, J. D., & Frank, J. B. (1993). *Persuasion and healing: A comparative study of psychotherapy.* Baltimore: John Hopkins University Press.

Hong, C. H. (Xiao Zhe). (1973). *Si shu shou ji, zhu xi shou ji.* Taibei: Hua Lian Chu Ban.

Jones, F., & Bright, J. (Eds.). (2001). *Stress: Myth, theory and research.* New York: Prentice Hall.

Kabat-Zinn, J. (2005). *Full catastrophe living: Using the wisdom of your body and mind to face stress, pain, and illness.* New York: Random House.

Kemeny, M. E. (2005). The psychobiology of stress. In G. Miller & E. Chen (Eds.), *Readings from the American Psychological Society: Current directions in health psychology* (pp. 55–63). Upper Saddle River, NJ: Pearson Prentice Hall.

Lovallo, W. R. (2005). *Stress and health: Biological and psychological interactions.* Thousand Oaks, CA: Sage.

May, R., & Yalom, I. (2000). Existential psychotherapy. In R. J. Corsini & D. Wedding (Eds.), *Current psychotherapies* (pp. 273–302). Itasca, IL: F. E. Peacock.

McEwen, B. (2002). *The end of stress as we know it*. Washington, DC: Joseph Henry Press.

McRae, J. R. (2003). *Electronic texts of the Chinese Buddhist canon*. Retrieved December 21, 2005, from http://www.indiana.edu/~asialink/canon.html

Miller, G., & Chen, E. (Eds.). (2005). *Readings from the American Psychological Society: Current directions in health psychology*. Upper Saddle River, NJ: Pearson Prentice Hall.

Overmier, B. N., & Murison, R. (2005). Animal models reveal the "psyche" in the psychosomatics of peptic ulcers. In G. Miller & E. Chen (Eds.), *Readings from the American Psychological Society: Current directions in health psychology* (pp. 78–85). Upper Saddle River, NJ: Pearson Prentice Hall.

Sapolsky, R. M. (1998). *Why zebras don't get ulcers: An updated guide to stress, stress-related diseases, and coping*. New York: W. H. Freeman.

Schafer, W. (1996). *Stress management for wellness*. Fort Worth, TX: Harcourt Brace & Company.

Seligman, M. E. P. (2006). *Learned optimism: How to change your mind and your life*. New York: Random House.

Seyle, H. (1978). *The stress of life*. New York: McGraw-Hill.

Slingerland, E. (2003). *Effortless action: Wu wei as a conceptual metaphor and spiritual ideal in early China*. New York: Oxford University Press.

Stefano, G. B., Fricchione, G. L., Slingsby, B. T., & Benson, H. (2001). The placebo effect and relaxation response: Neural processes and their coupling to constitutive nitric oxide. *Brain Research Reviews, 35*, 1–19.

Stuart, E. M., Webster, A., & Wells-Federman, C. L. (1993). *Managing stress*. In H. Benson & E. M. Stuart (Eds.), *The wellness book: The comprehensive guide to maintaining health and treating stress-related illness* (pp. 177–188). New York: Simon & Schuster.

Yalom, I. D. (1980). *Existential psychotherapy*. New York: Basic Books.

Yang, J. L. (Bian Ci). (1972). *Lun yu zhu shu bu zheng*. Taibei: Shi Jie Shu Ju.

3

Stress Management

Chapters 1 and 2 established (1) that change is a fundamental aspect of existence for evolutionary theory and evolutionary psychology and for Buddhism, Confucianism, and Daoism; (2) that the challenge of functionally adapting to the ever-changing environment is common to all people, across cultures; and (3) the subsequent stress response (the fight-or-flight response), also common to all people across cultures and part of the evolutionary process, is activated when a threat is perceived in the environment (internal and/or external) and maintained when the threat is not successfully removed. It was argued that both the challenge of adapting to an ever-changing environment and the chronic activation of the stress response are common to problems encountered in counseling and psychotherapy on the one hand, and in Buddhism, Confucianism, and Daoism on the other.

This chapter presents the third component of the bamboo bridge: stress management. Given (1) the challenges of adapting to the various environmental contexts, (2) the chronic activation of the stress response associated with the process of adaptation, and (3) the physical, psychological, and interpersonal problems linked to the chronic activation of the stress response, it is necessary to stop the chronic activation of the stress response. Stopping the response and providing the individual with the tools for a healthy lifestyle change is the function of stress management programs. Buddhism, Daoism, and Confucianism all offer solutions for eliminating chronic stress—although it may be expressed in different terms—and provide guidelines for a healthier life. Each of these individual solutions is addressed in detail in Part II.

This chapter explores two contemporary holistic stress management programs: those of Herbert Benson and Jon Kabat-Zinn. Both approaches integrate non-Western components, the meditative practices of the relaxation response and mindfulness, respectively, as the focal point of their approach to stress management. Walsh and Shapiro (2006, p. 229) note that research studies "suggest that meditation can ameliorate a variety of psychological and psychosomatic disorders, especially those in which stress plays a causal or complicating role."

Herbert Benson

The cardiologist Herbert Benson is considered to be one of the pioneers in mind/body medicine. He is the founder of the Mind/Body Institute of Harvard Medical School and Deaconess Hospital. The centerpiece to his approach in addressing chronic stress is called the "relaxation response" (RR). The concept of the relaxation response evolved out of his study of high blood pressure (Benson, 1975, 1993; Harris, 1999). After noticing that the blood pressure of his patients increased when it was taken in the office, he considered stress as a possible cause. Initially he studied this phenomenon with monkeys and then moved on to human beings who practiced transcendental meditation.

Benson's (1975) experiments clearly indicated that blood pressure was linked to stress and that it could be lowered through the practice of transcendental meditation, a yogic practice developed in India. Reasoning that it was unlikely that the ability to lower blood pressure was restricted to the practice of transcendental meditation, he then examined the mechanics of this meditative practice and discovered two basic components. He stated in an interview with Gail Harris:

> It made no sense to me that transcendental meditation would be the only way to evoke these physiological changes, so I went back to the steps that they used in transcendental meditation. First there was the repetition of a word, a sound, a prayer, a phrase or even a repetitive muscular activity. The second step was when other thoughts would come to mind, they would passively let them go and come back to the repetition. Using that model, I went back to the religious and secular literatures of the world to see whether or not these two steps had been described before, and it was amazing. Every single culture of humankind that had a written history had these two steps within it, normally within a religious context. And ultimately, the state of deep calm and physical changes achieved by practicing the two-step process we started calling the "relaxation response." (Harris, 1999, p. 4)

Benson (1975) discovered that the relaxation response appeared to be the exact opposite of the fight-or-flight response (the stress response) and that its function was to bring the body back into harmony and balance. Its activation not only reduced blood pressure, it also reduced heart rate and breathing rate and returned to normal all other physiological changes that occurred as a result of the activation of the fight-or-flight response. He viewed both responses as innate and as mechanisms that were part of the evolutionary package of being human. This evolutionary package assisted individuals in solving continual challenges relative to adapting to their environment. He noted:

> If the continual need to adjust to new situations can bring on a detrimental flight-or-flight response, and if we live continuously with stressful events which trigger that response, it is natural to question whether we know how to check the dangerous results that invariably follow. Take this line of reasoning one step further. If the flight-or-fight response resides within animals and humans, is there an innate physiological response that is diametrically different. The answer is Yes. Each of us possesses a natural innate protective mechanism against "overstress," which allows us to turn off harmful bodily effects, to counter the effects of the flight-or-fight response. This response against "overstress" brings on bodily changes that decrease heart rate, lower metabolism, decrease the rate of breathing and bring the body back into what is a probably healthier balance. This is the Relaxation Response. (Benson, 1975, pp. 25–26)

The relaxation response is the center of Benson's holistic, integrated stress management program. The practice of the relaxation response should not be viewed as simply another stress management technique but as part of a lifestyle change that is fundamental to resolving the problem of chronic stress. Being nonjudgmental and changing/eliminating/letting go of problematic cognitive and emotional patterns are fundamental to this lifestyle change (Benson, 1975, 1996; Benson & Proctor, 2003; Benson & Stuart, 1993).

This stress management program (Benson, 1996; Benson & Stuart, 1993) is both psychoeducational and practical. His holistic stress management program discusses and explains such areas as

- His model of health and illness from the perspective of the relationship between the mind and body
- The physiology of stress, stressors, the stress response and their physical, psychological, behavioral, and interpersonal impact on individuals
- Lifestyle changes
- Exercise
- Nutrition
- Components of stress management
- Cognitive therapy
- Faith and belief
- Interpersonal communication
- Sleep
- Yoga

- The relaxation response, and
- His three-legged stool approach to health and well-being, consisting of
  1. Surgery and procedures
  2. Pharmaceuticals, and
  3. Self-care, stress management, which has been essentially neglected because of a bias of Western medicine toward surgery and drugs.

As previously noted, the foundation of Benson's program is a perspective based in the Darwinian evolutionary theory of natural selection relative to adapting to the environment. The fight-or-flight response and relaxation response are both mechanisms that were naturally selected for, as they enhanced the probability of individuals surviving in their various environmental contexts. Esch, Stefano, Fricchione, and Benson (2002a) note:

> The interest of various medical fields and disciplines in the area of stress-related diseases and research is rapidly growing: The idea that challenging stimuli (stressors) elicit a stress response, which eventually leads to physiological, behavioral and psychological adjustments in order to enhance the organism's chances to cope (and—ultimately—survive) is now widely accepted.... All life forms have developed mechanisms to overcome immediate perturbations, i.e., protective perturbation response. It can also be said that the ability to overcome perturbations is essential to survival and longevity, as it ensures the "molecular messenger" is passed on. Thus, keeping a dynamic physiological balance throughout ongoing (environmental) perturbations is a crucial step to maintain survival, biological integrity, and health. (p. 94)

The difficulty arises when the naturally selected fight-or-flight response is not allowed to turn off (allostatic load) because there are continual challenges in the environment and/or the chronic activation of the fight-or-flight response does not resolve or is not appropriate for the specific challenges being faced. Citing considerable research, Esch, Stefano, Fricchione, and Benson (2002b) indicate that the chronic activation of the fight-or-flight response contributes to and/or results in physical diseases such as immunological diseases, cardiovascular diseases, neurodegenerative diseases, and mental disorders. Regarding mental disorders, they state, "Stress in general has been demonstrated to be part of mechanisms related to anxiety, and chronic stress, involving chronic sympathetic activation, has specifically been linked to the onset of anxiety and depression" (Esch et al., 2002b, p. 112).

Benson (1975) has argued that the relaxation response is a natural innate mechanism that was selected through the process of evolution to turn off or to counter the physiological changes of the fight-or-flight response once it served its purpose. The activation of the relaxation response can be used to address current stress associated with mental and physical disorders and provide protection against future stress. In both cases the relaxation response leads to a physically and psychologically healthier existence. Benson (1996) citing numerous studies regarding the elicitation of the relaxation response, notes:

> For all patients the relaxation response is not only a short-term boon but a long-term balm. My colleagues and I at the Mind/Body Medical Institute have amassed evidence of the tremendous diversity of medical conditions that the elicitation, together with other self-care strategies such as nutrition, exercise, and self management can heal or cure. . . . Patients with hypertension experienced significant decrease in blood pressure and needed fewer medications. . . . Patients with chronic pain experienced less severity of pain, more activity, less anxiety, less depression, less anger. . . . Seventy-five percent of patients with sleep-onset insomnia (meaning they couldn't fall asleep easily) were cured and became normal sleepers. Sleeping also improved for the other 25 percent. . . . Patients with complaints described by the admitting personnel as psychosomatic and who were frequent users of a health maintenance organization reduced their number of visits by 50 percent. . . . Patients with cancer and AIDS experienced decreased symptoms and better control of nausea and vomiting associated with chemotherapy. . . . Patients with cardiac arrhythmias experienced fewer of them. . . . Patients who suffered from anxiety or mild or moderate depression were less anxious, depressed, angry and hostile. . . . Migraine and cluster headache suffers found they had fewer and less severe headaches. . . . Working people experienced reduced symptoms of depression, anxiety and hostility. . . . Working people had fewer medical symptoms, fewer illness days, improved performance and lower blood pressure. (pp. 146–148)

Benson and his colleagues continue to gather evidence supporting both the short-term and long-term benefits, both physically and psychologically, of practicing the relaxation response on a regular and consistent basis. Research (Dusek et al., 2006; Stefano, Esch, Cadet, Zhu, Mantione, & Benson, 2003) indicates that there are numerous ways to elicit the relaxation response, that it is clearly antagonistic to the stress response, that it produces significant physiological changes, and that it is effective when dealing with both physical and psychological conditions.

> Numerous mind/body approaches can elicit the RR including: meditation, repetitive prayer, yoga, tai chi, autogenic training, deep breathing exercises, progressive muscle relaxation, biofeedback, guided imagery and Qi gong. The RR can be elicited as individuals repeat a word, sound, phrase, prayer, or focus on their breathing and disregard intrusive everyday

thoughts. The RR is described as a coordinated physiological response that is characterized by decreased arousal, diminished heart rate, respiratory rate, and blood pressure, in association with a state of well being. The physiological responses of the RR occur in the opposite direction from those of the stress response, described as the "fight or flight" response and the "general adaptation response" to stress by Cannon and Seyle respectively. . . . The elicitation of the RR is characterized by measurable, predictable, and reproducible physiological decreases in volumetric oxygen consumption (VO_2). In addition to decreased VO_2, other consistent physiological changes include decreased carbon dioxide elimination, reduced heart rate and respiration rates, lower arterial blood lactate, reduced systolic and diastolic blood pressure, decreased responsivity to norepinephrine, decreased theta and beta waves and increased alpha frontal activity on EEG, prominent low frequency heart rate oscillations and alterations in cortical and sub-cortical brain regions. Clinically, the RR has been shown to counteract the negative effects of long-term stress. The RR is often utilized as an adjunct to medical treatment, in conditions that are caused or exacerbated by stress. (Dusek et al., 2006, p. 2)

Benson and his colleagues have been searching for the underlying biological mechanism associated with the clinical effects of the relaxation response. Research (Benson & Proctor 2003; Esch et al., 2002b; Stefano, Fricchione, Slingsby, & Benson, 2001; Stefano et al., 2003) has focused on nitric oxide (NO) as that mechanism. Recent research (Dusek et al., 2006) has provided some initial evidence establishing the link between nitric oxide (NO) and the relaxation response utilizing volumetric oxygen (VO_2) and fractional exhaled nitric oxide (F_ENO) as variables.

Our current data demonstrate that depth of RR elicitation (as defined by the VO_2 slope) is associated with increased percentage changes of F_ENO. This observation suggests that NO may serve as a biological mechanism underlying the RR and provides the first empirical support for the hypothesis that NO is a mediator of the RR. Our study provides evidence of a possible mechanism underlying the widely reported clinical effects of RR. Future, larger scale studies are needed to confirm our study findings. (Dusek et al., 2006, p. 8)

There is substantial evidence supporting the efficacy of Benson's holistic stress management program relative to resolving the physical and psychological problems associated with stress. His approach is clearly grounded in evolutionary theory with such concepts as survival, natural selection, the fight-or-flight response, physiological changes, adaptation to the environment, biological integrity, survival, and the relaxation response itself being fundamental. His stress management program provides a solution for addressing and resolving allostatic load (chronic activation of the stress response) and the subsequent physical and psychological dysfunctionality associated with it. It is an approach grounded in a cost-effective, non-Western approach to health and well-being known as the relaxation response.

Jon Kabat-Zinn

Jon Kabat-Zinn, a molecular biologist, is the founder and past director of the Stress Reduction Clinic and the Center for Mindfulness in Medicine, Health Care and Society at the University of Massachusetts Medical School. The central focus of his stress management approach is based on the Buddhist meditative practice of *mindfulness*. His approach to stress management is called mindfulness-based stress reduction (MBSR).

Kabat-Zinn's (2005b) own study of Zen Buddhism, which is based in mindfulness, eventually led him to integrate the practice of mindfulness into the Western world of medicine and healing. He found the hospital environment to be a center of suffering and stress (*dukkha*), the very focus of the teachings of Buddha. He notes:

> Whether you want to call it stress or dis-ease or *dukkha,* it is pretty obvious that hospitals function as major *dukkha* magnets. Their force fields pull in those among us who are suffering the most at any given time either from disease or dis-ease or both; from stress, pain, trauma, and illness of all kinds. People go or are taken to the hospital when there is literally nowhere else to go, when they have run out of other options and resources. Given the level of suffering hospitals attract, one might think, "What better place to offer training in mindfulness said by no less an authority than the Buddha himself to be the direct path for the surmounting of sorrow and lamentation and the disappearance of pain and grief, in a word, the relief of suffering? Might not some exposure to mindfulness, if it is indeed as powerful and as fundamental and as universal as the Buddha was claiming, be of significant benefit to many of the people who walk or are carried through its doors?" . . . And what better place to offer such training, not only for the patients but for the staff as well, who in many instances are just as stressed as the patients? This is how mindfulness-based stress reduction (MBSR) came to be born. At first, it was offered primarily for those medical patients who could be said to be falling through the cracks of the health care system, people who were not being completely helped by the medical treatment available to them. That turned out to be a lot of people. It also included a great many people who had not improved with traditional medical

treatments or were suffering from intractable conditions for which medicine has few options and no cures. . . . From its inception, the Stress Reduction Clinic gave physicians across a wide range of disciplines and specialties a new option for their patients. It was a place within the hospital where medical patients could, on an outpatient basis, learn to do something for themselves as a compliment to all that was being done for them, something potentially extremely powerful and also hard to come by, precious. (Kabat-Zinn, 2005b, pp. 130–131)

While the focus of Kabat-Zinn's (1993, 2005a, 2005b) MBSR program is on mindfulness, it also incorporates explorations and discussion of such areas as stress, stress response, health and illness, yoga, physical and emotional pain, mind/body integration, fear, panic and anxiety, diet, sleep, and interpersonal relationships. The MBSR program is clearly a holistic, integrated approach for addressing chronic stress and the need for significant lifestyle changes relative to optimal health and well-being.

Kabat-Zinn (2005a) also sees evolution as being fundamental for understanding chronic stress and the solution to it. Evolutionary theory postulates that existence is a continually changing, interrelated, and interdependent process. Organisms that are able to solve the challenges presented by this ever-changing environment, in other words adapt or survive. Chronic stress is linked to problems associated with adapting to the process of change.

The concept of stress suggests that . . . we are continually faced with the necessity of adapting to all of the various pressures we feel in life. Basically this means adapting to change. If we can learn to see change as an integral part of life and not as a threat to our well-being, we will be in a much better position to cope effectively with stress. The meditation practice itself brings us face-to-face with the undeniable experience of continual change within our own minds and bodies as we watch our constantly changing thoughts, feelings, sensations, perceptions and impulses. . . . We may find it comforting to know that our bodies have very robust and resilient built-in mechanisms, developed over millions of years of evolution, for maintaining stability and vitality in the face of change. This biological resilience and stability is a major ally when it comes to facing stress and change in our lives. . . . The ultimate effect on our health of the total psychological stress we experience depends in a large measure on how we come to perceive change itself, in all of its various forms, and how skillful we are in adapting to continual change while maintaining our own inner balance and sense of coherence. It is here . . . that mindfulness most needs to be applied. (Kabat-Zinn, 2005a, pp. 242, 245, 247)

The definition of mindfulness on one level is quite straightforward. Mindfulness is a flexibly focused, nonjudgmental engagement with the here and now. It is about being in the present without judging, fully experiencing, without any barriers, all aspects of one's existence.

On another level, regarding empirical studies, Bishop et al. (2004), Brown and Ryan (2004), and Dimidjian and Linehan (2003) argue for the need of a concise operational definition of mindfulness so that it can be consistently measured. Kabat-Zinn (2003, p. 145) offered the operational definition of "an awareness that emerges through paying attention on purpose, in the present moment, and non-judgmentally to the unfolding of experience moment by moment." In describing mindfulness, he stated:

> Mindfulness can be thought of as a moment-to-moment, non-judgmental awareness, cultivated by paying attention in a specific way, that is, in the present moment, and as non-reactively, as non-judgmentally, and as openheartedly as possible. When it is cultivated intentionally, it is sometimes referred to as deliberate mindfulness. When it spontaneously arises, as it tends to do more and more the more it is cultivated intentionally, it is sometimes referred to as effortless mindfulness. Ultimately, however arrived at, mindfulness is mindfulness. (Kabat-Zinn, 2005b, pp 108–109)

Kabat-Zinn (1994, 2003, 2005a) makes it clear that the practice of mindfulness is not to be viewed as a technique among many other techniques utilized for healing or relaxation. It is a way of life or of being. Mindfulness is simply about being, nonjudgmentally, in the present. There are no expectations about what will happen. The practice of mindfulness is about getting out of your own way and experiencing the present. When you are able to do this, as paradoxical as it may sound, the natural healing and relaxing aspects of the body/mind will begin to wash away the suffering and chronic stress. In regard to the development of MBSR, Kabat-Zinn notes:

> The primary intention was to see if it were possible to create a vehicle for the effective training of medical patients in relatively intensive mindfulness meditation (including mindful hatha yoga) and its immediate application to the stress, pain, and illness people were grappling with in their lives. . . . The objective was not to teach Buddhism or even "to make great meditators" out of people, but to offer an environment within which to experiment with a range of novel and potentially effective methods for facing, exploring, and relieving suffering at the levels of both mind and body, and understanding the potential power inherent in the mind/body connection itself in doing so. (Kabat-Zinn, 2003, pp. 148–149)

Baer's (2003) review of the empirical literature on mindfulness-based approaches suggests there is support for the effectiveness of mindfulness as an intervention for chronic pain, generalized anxiety disorders, panic disorders, depressive relapse, fibromyalgia, psoriasis, depression, and stress-related problems. She noted, however, that the studies were few in number and that there were methodological and design issues, such as no control groups in many studies.

Kabat-Zinn (2003), in his response to Baer's article, acknowledges concerns with design and methodological issues. He cites more recent rigorous studies, one on psoriasis and one on the immune system and brain activity, from the Center for Mindfulness that demonstrate the effectiveness of MBSR.

In the immune system and brain activity study, the authors (Davidson et al., 2003) argue that their study is the first to provide empirical evidence that MBSR positively affects brain activity and the immune system. They note:

> The findings from this study are the first to suggest that meditation can produce increases in relative left-sided anterior activation that are associated with reductions in anxiety and negative affect and increase in positive affect. . . . To our knowledge, this is the first demonstration of a reliable effect of meditation on an in vivo measure of immune function. The findings may reflect a relatively more rapid peak rise in antibody titers among the mediators compared with controls. The observation that the magnitude of change in immune function was greater for those subjects showing the larger shift toward left-sided activation supports earlier associations between these indices. (p. 569)

Grossman, Niemann, Schmidt, and Walach's (2004) meta-analysis of empirical studies support Baer's finding regarding the effectiveness of MBSR as an intervention for both physical and mental health issues. Across both nonclinical and clinical populations and examining such areas as stress, anxiety, depression, cancer, chronic pain, and heart disease, MBSR was found to be beneficial in assisting individuals manage their health issues. Like the Baer article, they raised concern with the small number of studies, methodological issues, and design problems.

The practice of mindfulness has been found to integrate quite well with the practice of Western counseling and psychotherapy (Germer, Siegel, & Fulton, 2005; Shapiro & Walsh, 2006). The integration of mindfulness and Western counseling and psychotherapy (Brantley, 2003; Epstein, 1995; Germer, Siegel, & Fulton, 2005; Hayes, Follette, & Linehan, 2004; Segal, Williams, & Teasdale, 2002) has been used to address a variety of psychological concerns, such as anxiety, depression, relationships, fear, panic, alcohol abuse, substance abuse, and chronic pain.

There is considerable evidence supporting the effectiveness of Kabat-Zinn's MBSR program in addressing and resolving both physical and psychological problems associated with stress. His approach is consistent with evolutionary theory, as he acknowledges change as a fundamental aspect of human existence, the importance of being able to adapt to the ever-changing environment, how stress is a fundamental component of this adaptive process, how chronic stress is related to both physical and psychological problems, and how humans have innate mechanisms that give rise to and allow us to address stress relative to adapting to change.

Kabat-Zinn's stress management program, like Benson's, provides a solution for addressing and resolving allostatic load and the subsequent physical and psychological dysfunctionality associated with it. It is an approach grounded essentially in a cost-effective, non-Western approach to health and well-being known as mindfulness.

Summary

The focus in this chapter was in establishing the third component, stress management, of the bamboo bridge that will allow for the integration of Chinese thought, specifically Buddhism, Daoism, and Confucianism into Western counseling and psychotherapy. The bamboo bridge is now complete.

Using the Daoist model of simplicity, beginning points, and commonalities that was set out in the Introduction, Western counseling and psychotherapy and Chinese Buddhism, Daoism, and Confucianism can be viewed as operating in the same arena: evolutionary theory and psychology, stress and the stress response, and stress management. It is in this arena the bridge for intercultural communication and exchange is built.

At the most basic and simple level, life is about adapting to change. This is a simple beginning point that is common to all human beings. Common to all human beings are innate, evolutionary derived mechanisms that assist them in adapting and surviving. One of the most fundamental of these mechanisms is that of the stress response (the fight-or-flight response).

When the stress response, however, is chronically activated and its activation is unable to resolve the adaptive challenges in the environment (internal and/or external), significant physical, psychological, and interpersonal problems arise. This is a simple beginning point for the origin of physical, psychological, and interpersonal problems common to all human beings.

Stress management deals at the level of simplicity. Given the problem of chronic stress, common to all human beings, the least complex or simplest solution is to manage, holistically, the stress and the challenges in the environment (internal and/or external). Thus, the problem is addressed at its beginning points: the human being, the environment, and their interaction.

Common to all human beings are innate, powerful tools and mechanisms that allow for and assist in the process of self-cultivation, healing on all levels, and a positive, full-engaged interaction with the environment and all that populates it. When chronic stress is present, learning how to activate these tools and mechanisms is essential to adapting to and surviving in the environment. Whether it is called counseling and psychotherapy or the teachings of Chinese Buddhism, Daoism, and Confucianism, they are all approaches for activating these tools and mechanisms in order to manage, eliminate, and prevent chronic stress. Thus, the commonality between their approaches is quite apparent.

The three chapters in Part II, which represent the core of this text, present the perspectives of Chinese Buddhism, Daoism, and Confucianism relative to addressing and offering a solution for (albeit under different terminology) chronic stress. Each of these chapters contains a significant number of translations from the original texts to provide the reader with a more in-depth understanding of the contextual perspectives and solutions of Chinese thought.

Important Terms

Holistic

Meditation

Mindfulness

Nonjudgmental

Relaxation response

Stress management

Exercises

A. For this exercise, I want you to try to not think. Isolate yourself away from external distractions. For 10 minutes, simply see if you can shut off any thoughts. Having spent 10 minutes on this exercise, what did you notice? Did you notice, almost immediately, even though you were trying not to think about anything, thoughts arose? If you were in control of your thoughts, how could they arise? Did you start to notice a lot of activity going on in your mind? Even though you were trying to not think, thoughts still arose. What kind of thoughts did you have? Were you in control of them? Did they arise on their own? Did you start thinking about the thoughts and thus create additional thoughts? Thinking about thoughts and/or making judgments about thoughts, which are in themselves thoughts, maintains thoughts in awareness.

Did you notice any feelings connected with certain thoughts? Anxiety? Anger? Frustration? Did you get anxious about when the time limit of 10 minutes was up? Did you get frustrated and/or angry and simply stop before the passing of 10 minutes? Did you tell yourself the exercise was stupid and a waste of your time? Did you come up with another excuse to discontinue the exercise?

B. Imagine a burning fire. As you add wood to the fire, the fire continues to burn. Some types of wood burn more than others. As you continue to add wood to the fire, the fire continues to burn. At times the fuel that you add results in the fire getting out of control and overwhelming the surrounding area.

Look at your thought-filled mind as the burning fire and your adding of thoughts (judging) as pieces of wood that feed the fire. As you continue to feed your mind (the fire) with your thoughts and judgments (wood), your mind gets more and more agitated. Negative judgments (a type of wood that burns faster and quicker) tend to cause your mind to get more and disturbed/restless (fire out of control) and affect your feelings, your body, and often others around you (a spreading out-of-control fire).

C. A second analogy has to do with water. Imagine a clear pond of still water. You can see the bottom. Now stir the pond up with a stick. All the particles, debris, dust, and muck will cloud up the pond. The water is quite agitated and not still. As long as you continue to stir up the pond with the stick, the pond will not be still, the pond will not be clear, and you will not be able to see to the bottom. The continuing stirring of the pond negatively compromises the overall environment of the pond.

Look at the still, clear pond as your mind. Look at the swirling stick as your thoughts and judgments. As long as your thoughts and judgments run rampant, your mind will be cloudy and agitated. This cloudy and agitated mind will negatively affect its own environment (feelings and body functioning) and the environment around it.

How is this agitated mind related to chronic stress? How can teaching a client about this agitated mind be helpful to the client? How is the practice of meditation related to calming the mind, removing the agitation, and eliminating chronic stress?

References

Baer, R. A. (2003). Mindfulness training as a clinical intervention: A conceptual and empirical review. *Clinical Psychology: Science and Practice, 10,* 125–143.

Benson, H. (1975). *The relaxation response.* New York: Avon Books.

Benson, H. (1993). The relaxation response. In D. Goleman & J. Gurin (Eds.), *Mind body medicine: How to use your mind for better health* (pp. 233–257). Yonkers, NY: Consumer Reports Books.

Benson, H. (1996). *Timeless healing: The power and biology of belief.* New York: Scribner.

Benson, H., & Proctor, W. (2003). *The break-out principle.* New York: Scribner.

Benson, H., & Stuart, E. M. (Eds.). (1993). *The wellness book: The comprehensive guide to maintaining health and treating stress-related illness.* New York: Simon & Schuster.

Bishop, S. R., Lau, M., Shapiro, S., Carlson, L., Anderson, N. D., Carmody, J., Segal, Z. V., Abbey, S., Specca, M., Velting, D., & Devins, G. (2004). Mindfulness: A proposed operational definition. *Clinical Psychology: Science and Practice, 11,* 230–241.

Brantley, J. (2003). *Calming your anxious mind: How mindfulness and compassion can free you from anxiety, fear, and panic.* New York: New Harbinger.

Brown, K. W., & Ryan, R. M. (2004). Perils and promises in defining and measuring mindfulness: Observations from experience. *Clinical Psychology: Science and Practice, 11,* 242–248.

Davidson, R. J., Kabat-Zinn, J., Schumacher, J., Rosenkranz, M., Muller, D., Santorelli, S. F., Urbanowski, F., Harrington, A., Bonus, K., & Sheridan, J. F. (2003). Alterations in brain function produced by mindfulness meditation. *Psychosomatic Medicine, 65,* 564–570.

Dimidjian, S., & Linehan, M. M. (2003). Defining an agenda for future research on the clinical application of mindfulness practice. *Clinical Psychology: Science and Practice, 10,* 166–171.

Dusek, J. A., Chang, B. H., Zaki, J., Lazar, S. W., Deykin, A., Stefano, G. B., Wohlhueter, A. L., Hibberd, P. L., & Benson, H. (2006). Association between oxygen consumption and nitric oxide protection during the relaxation response. *Medical Science Monitor, 12*(1), 1–10.

Epstein, M. (1995). *Thoughts without a thinker: Psychotherapy from a Buddhist perspective.* New York: Basic Books.

Esch, T., Stefano, G. B., Fricchione, G. L., & Benson, H. (2002a). Stress in cardiovascular diseases. *Medical Science Monitor, 8*(5), 93–101.

Esch, T., Stefano, G. B., Fricchione, G. L., & Benson, H. (2002b). Stress-related diseases—A potential role for nitric oxide. *Medical Science Monitor, 8*(6), 103–118.

Germer, C. K., Siegal, R. D., & Fulton, P. R. (2005). *Mindfulness and psychotherapy.* New York: Guilford.

Grossman, P., Niemann, L., Schmidt, S., & Walach, H. (2004). Mindfulness-based stress reduction and health benefits: A meta-analysis. *Journal of Psychosomatic Research, 57,* 25–43.

Harris, G. (1999). *Body and soul: Your guide to health, happiness, and total well-being.* Watertown, MA: Beacon Productions.

Hayes, S. C., Follette, V. M., & Linehan, M. M. (2004). *Mindfulness and acceptance.* New York: Guilford.

Kabat-Zinn, J. (1993). Mindfulness meditation: Health benefits of an ancient Buddhist practice. In D. Goleman & J. Gurin (Eds.), *Mind body medicine: How to use your mind for better health* (pp. 258–275). Yonkers, NY: Consumer Reports Books.

Kabat-Zinn, J. (1994). *Wherever you go, there you are: Mindfulness meditation in everyday life.* New York: Hyperion.

Kabat-Zinn, J. (2003). Mindfulness-based interventions in context: Past, present and future. *Clinical Psychology: Science and Practice, 10,* 144–156.

Kabat-Zinn, J. (2005a). *Full catastrophe living: Using the wisdom of your body and mind to face stress, pain, and illness.* New York: Random House.

Kabat-Zinn, J. (2005b). *Coming to our senses: Healing ourselves and the world through mindfulness.* New York: Hyperion.

Segal, Z. V., Williams, J. M. G., & Teasdale, J. D. (2002). *Mindfulness-based cognitive therapy for depression: A new approach to preventing relapse.* New York: Guilford.

Stefano, G. B., Esch, T., Cadet, P., Zhu, W., Mantione, K., & Benson, H. (2003). Endocannabinoids as autoregulatory signaling molecules: Coupling to nitric oxide and a possible association with the relaxation response. *Medical Science Monitor, 9*(4), 83–95.

Stefano, G. B., Fricchione, G. L., Slingsby, B. T., & Benson, H. (2001). The placebo effect and relaxation response: Neural processes and their coupling to constitutive nitric oxide. *Brain Research Reviews, 35,* 1–19.

Walsh, R., & Shapiro, S. L. (2006). The meeting of meditative disciplines and Western psychology. *American Psychologist, 61,* 227–239.

PART II

Culturally Diverse Approaches to Managing Stress

Part II examines the solutions offered by Buddhism, Daoism, and Confucianism for managing stress and assisting individuals in functionally adapting to their environmental contexts. It is hoped that the solutions offered by these three forms of Chinese thought will inform, expand, and enhance the theoretical and application base of treatment modalities in Western counseling and psychotherapy. The goal is to lay a foundation for a truly integrative, culturally diverse approach to counseling and psychotherapy that is guided by the Daoist model of simplicity, beginning points, and commonality.

The chapters in Part II consist of extensive translations, or should I say interpretations, from Buddhist, Daoist, and Confucian texts. To attain a more in-depth understanding of these culturally diverse perspectives, both in theory and application, it is necessary to examine the original sources. These translations/interpretations provide an exploration into cultural perspectives relative to an adaptive problem, the stress response associated with the adaptive problem, and the solutions that are, essentially, holistic methods of managing stress. It is hoped that this examination and exploration will be of assistance in creating an environment in Western counseling and psychotherapy that is conducive to investigating, assessing, and integrating the solutions offered by Buddhist, Confucian, and Daoist teachings.

4

Buddhism and Stress Management

Buddha (tradition says he lived in India during 6th century BCE) was born into a noble class. His family was quite wealthy, and for all intents and purposes, all of his material needs were met. He was married and had a child. Nonetheless, he was not satisfied (Rahula, 1962).

Tradition says that one day Buddha was outside of his secluded compound and for the first time saw sickness, old age, and death. He saw *dukkha* (suffering/dissatisfaction). This experience and his compassion for his fellow human beings compelled him to give up his social status, his wealth, and his family, including his wife and child, and to seek out a solution to end this continuous suffering and dissatisfaction; to put an end to what we today call chronic stress.

Buddha went on a six-year journey, becoming a wandering ascetic. He sought out various religious and spiritual teachers and practiced many different techniques in his quest to end *dukkha*. Nothing worked. He was still dissatisfied (Jordan, 1998).

One day, probably tired and frustrated with his lack of success, he wandered off on his own and eventually sat down under a tree, a *bodhi* tree. He sat there vowing not to leave until he found a solution to the end of suffering and dissatisfaction. Tradition says he had his awakening experience under this tree and discovered his solution for the end of suffering and dissatisfaction (Jordan, 1998).

Buddha never wrote anything. He taught for many years and then died. About 100 years after his death, Buddhism had split into many schools, with two schools being prominent: the Theravada and the Sarvastivada (Conze, 1970). Sometime between 1st century BCE and 2nd century CE, the Mahayana tradition developed. As time passed, the Theravada and the Mahayana schools became the dominant schools. One of the primary differences between these two schools is that the Theravada school focused on individual liberation while the Mahayana school focused on salvation for all.

Buddhism, in its various traditions, forms, and schools, entered China somewhere between 1st century BCE and 1st century CE. It took approximately 500 years before it was fully integrated into the Chinese culture. During this time period Buddhism was translated and interpreted by and through the Chinese perspective. Buddhism clearly had a monumental impact on Chinese civilization, and Chinese civilization in turn affected and shaped Buddhism, giving birth to a distinctive Chinese form of Buddhism. The integration of Buddhism into the Chinese civilization constitutes one of the major cross-cultural events in the history of China (Ch'en, 1972).

Given that the focus of this book is on the Chinese tradition and its relevance to counseling and psychotherapy, the Chinese translations of the early teachings of Buddhism, from the Pali Canon of the Theravada school and its subsequent translation into Sanskrit by the Sarvastivada school, will serve as the basis for the English translations in this chapter.

As noted in the Introduction, there are a considerable number of translations/interpretations of Buddhist texts in this chapter. It is important for the reader to get a culturally sensitive, albeit in an English translation/interpretation, feel for and an understanding of Buddhism in the manner in which it is transmitted and applied.

The Four Noble Truths

> Friends. Now what is the Noble Truth of the path to the cessation of dissatisfaction/chronic stress [*dukkha*]? This is the Eightfold Noble Path: Correct Seeing, Correct Thinking, Correct Speaking, Correct Action, Correct Life, Correct Effort, Correct Mindfulness, and Correct Concentration.[1] (*Analysis of the Noble Truths*)

The First Noble Truth

For Buddha, existence itself—the very aspect of attempting to adapt to the environment on a daily basis, living in general—is the source for suffering, dissatisfaction, and chronic stress. It is this insight into the nature of existence that is represented in his First Noble Truth of *dukkha*. From the moment an individual is born through the moment the individual dies, all of it, according to Buddha, is intimately intertwined with suffering, dissatisfaction, and chronic stress.

> What is the Noble Truth of chronic stress [*dukkha*]? Birth is chronic stress, old age is chronic stress, death is chronic stress, worry is chronic

stress, grieving/depression is chronic stress, suffering is chronic stress, hostility is chronic stress, anxiety is chronic stress, and not getting what one is seeking/desires is chronic stress. All of these are chronic stress. In brief, the five grasping containers (the five components of the individual) are suffering-dissatisfaction. (*Analysis of the Noble Truths*)

With his reference to the five components of the individual[2] (form, sensation, perception, dispositions, and consciousness), Buddha is essentially saying that the very fact of being human is *dukkha*. It is interesting to note that the description of *dukkha* is oriented toward a psychological perspective. In her discussion of her translation of *dukkha* in the Buddhist sutras in *The Middle Length Sayings,* Horner (1967) notes:

I have translated this on the whole as "anguish" and have always done so in the various formulae such as the Four Truths. . . . "Anguish," I am aware, may be considered too strong. But where it has been used the stress appears to be wanted more on the mental than on the physical disease. (p. xxii)

The Second Noble Truth

Given the clear indication of the problem of *dukkha* and Buddha having, essentially, made a diagnosis regarding the disease or illness of the human race, the next step for him was to provide an explanation regarding the cause or origin of the problem of *dukkha* or chronic stress. This is his Second Noble Truth. This is the same process used by a physician, counselor, or a psychotherapist when addressing the disease or illness of the client. The physician, given the presenting problem of a chronic cough, may focus on a bacteria or a virus as the cause of the cough in the patient, while the counselor or psychotherapist will view the client's problem—say anxiety—through a specific theoretical perspective (cognitive, Freudian, or existential) and may view the cause of the anxiety as irrational thoughts, fixation of libidinal energy, or limited choices.

Friends, now what is the Noble Truth of the origin of chronic stress-dissatisfaction? Namely it is called craving for sense pleasure, craving for existence and craving for nonexistence. Friends this is the meaning of the noble truth of the origin of chronic stress-dissatisfaction. (*Analysis of the Noble Truths*)

The Second Noble Truth consists of two components, neither of which can be considered as a first cause. Everything, according to Buddha's concept of conditioned arising, is interdependent and relative. There is no first cause of anything. Everything simultaneously is both conditioned and conditions. Everything is both cause and effect.

The Component of Craving

The first component is that of *craving* or *desire*. The Buddha indicates three types of craving. The first craving is that of craving for sense pleasure. Sense pleasure for Buddha includes the fives senses plus the sixth sense of the mind. This one is quite obvious. It is whatever gives one pleasure. Certainly there is a connection to Freud's pleasure principle. Pleasure is, for all intents and purposes, a driving force in one's waking life. Buddha is not so much concerned with pleasure per se, recognizing that pleasure is part of being a human being. His concern is focused on the extent to which the individual is controlled by the resulting pleasure. The person becoming attached to the experience of pleasure is the problem. There is an ongoing need to continually obtain, possess, and maintain the pleasure. It is the desire to have all of one's needs continually met. Thus, the craving!

The second craving is the craving for *existence* or *life itself*. The desire to stay alive, protect oneself, to avoid sickness, old age, and death. It is a desire or craving to live forever. This craving serves as the basis for many religions and philosophies that offer the vanquishing of death, immortal souls, and eternality in a heaven far beyond the suffering of mere mortal life. Psychologically it is the basis of narcissism, self-centeredness, egotism, the demand for attention, and an individual's feelings of self-entitlement. The link to evolutionary theory, the stress response, and the instinct for survival should be quite apparent.

The third craving is the craving for *nonexistence*. Psychologically, it is the drive to avoid the threats, demands, expectations, and/or unpleasantness of various aspects of one's existence. It is the losing of one's self in some task, activity, or experience that allows the individual to escape self-awareness. At its more mundane end, this can be losing oneself in forms of entertainment such as watching TV, going to a movie, attending a sporting event or concert, reading a book, or participating in various activities where the sense of self disappears. It can also be argued that the religious or spiritual search or craving for a mystical experience with or absorption into a godhead or absolute state of existence is an attempt to lose one's self. Thus, it would be consistent with a craving for nonexistence. At its more problematic end, it is a way to avoid responsibility and escape from the self through behaviors that result in such psychological dysfunctionality as eating disorders, alcohol abuse, substance abuse, physical violence, hostility, anxiety, and depression.

The Component of Ignorance

The second component, that of ignorance, is the origin of craving through the process of conditioned arising. Cravings are due to feelings, which in turn are due to sensations. Sensations are due to contact, which in turn is due to the six senses. The six senses are due to name and form (mental and physical phenomena), which are in turn due to consciousness. Consciousness is due to the predispositions, which in turn are due to ignorance. Ignorance is the result of being born, and so the cycle continues endlessly.

For Buddha, ignorance is twofold. It is ignorance of the Four Noble Truths. Not knowing about or understanding the Four Noble Truths is the first aspect of ignorance. Imbedded in the Four Noble Truths is the path to the realization that existence is impermanent, interdependent, and nonsubstantial. The second aspect of ignorance is not knowing and understanding that existence is impermanent, interdependent, and nonsubstantial. It is the experiential realization of impermanence, nonsubstantiality, and interdependence that results in the end of dissatisfaction or chronic stress. It is this ignorance of the nature of existence that results in craving and thus *dukkha*.

Ignorance of the nature of existence results in people falsely believing they can satisfy their craving for pleasure. Because individuals view themselves and the components that make up their world as being permanent, substantial, and independent, they falsely believe they can satisfy their demand for sense pleasures. They believe they can obtain, possess, and maintain whatever is desired or craved. The problem is that existence does not behave according to the false beliefs of individuals. The craving will not stop as long as the belief in permanence, substantiality, and independence is maintained. People will never be satisfied, because everything is interdependent, nonsubstantial, and impermanent. They are unable to obtain, possess, or maintain anything. They are unable to get what they want or desire.

If they are unable to obtain and control the pleasures they crave or desire, then their very existence is threatened. Their self-esteem drops. Their self-worth is vulnerable. They generate doubt about themselves. They view themselves as unable to control the world around them. These are all threats to their sense of self. The threats activate the fight-or-flight response. As long as they continue to believe existence entails permanence, substantiality, and interdependence and are thus ignorant of the nature of existence, the activation of the fight-or-flight response will be ongoing. The ongoing activation of the fight-or-flight response is *dukkha* or chronic stress.

The craving for existence is intimately intertwined with the uncertainty and terror surrounding the death of the individual. It is an ignorance of existence as being impermanent, nonsubstantial, and interdependent. It is a denial of death. Nobody really knows what happens after the one dies. The fear is that death is the end of individual existence. If this is the case, it appears to make the life of an individual meaningless. This uncertainty is terrifying. This lack of control is frightening. This uncertainty is a clear threat to the individual. As a threat, it activates the fight-or-flight response and the individual becomes stressed. As people continue to worry about this possibility the stress becomes chronic or *dukkha*.

In an attempt to resolve the unpleasant feelings of chronic stress associated with the uncertainty surrounding death, people crave existence. This craving and belief in an eternal (permanent), unchanging (substantial) individual existence (independent) after death in some heaven or absolute state of existence temporarily relieves the stress. But only temporarily!

Every day presents the individual with occurrences that appear to contradict his or her view of permanence, substantiality, and independence. People get old, get sick, and die. The uncertainty is still present. There is doubt. The fears and threats are just beneath the surface. *Dukkha* is still present. The only way to eliminate *dukkha* is to realize and accept the fact that everything is impermanent, nonsubstantial, and interdependent. People's viewpoint of existence needs to be consistent with the way that existence actually behaves. As long as people remain ignorant of the nature of existence, and crave eternality, they will be chronically stressed.

Because people are not satisfied (are chronically stressed) in their constant battles to obtain, possess, and maintain their objects of pleasure, are continually presented with occurrences that threaten their worldview (chronic stress), and are ignorant of the nature of existence (chronic stress), they attempt to escape from existence. They seek activities that allow them to forget about their selves, their troubles, and their stressors. They crave nonexistence. They seek relief from their *dukkha*.

The problem is, as everything is impermanent, nonsubstantial, and interdependent, people cannot escape from existence. Their escape, as everything else about existence, is only temporary. People simply do not realize this state of affairs. Their ignorance of this fact gives rise to their craving for nonexistence. This craving results in *dukkha*.

Because of ignorance, there is craving for sense pleasures, existence, and nonexistence. This false view (ignorance) about existence that gives rise to craving results in *dukkha* or chronic stress. If people understood existence, there would be no craving, because there is nothing that is permanent, substantial, and independent.

The Third Noble Truth

Friends now what is the Noble Truth of the cessation of chronic stress-dissatisfaction? All that craving is gone, separated from attachment to it, extinguished, abandoned, abandoned and detached, free, not holding on to it. Friends this is the meaning of the Noble Truth of the cessation of chronic stress-dissatisfaction. (*Analysis of the Noble Truths*)

The Third Noble Truth is, from the perspective of counseling or psychotherapy, the goal of the treatment. It is the removal or reduction of the anxiety, depression, or hostility. From the perspective of the Buddha, it is the complete removal of and elimination of craving. Insofar as the craving ceases, the individual is free from chronic stress or *dukkha*. The Third Noble Truth is also known as Nirvana. Given that everything is impermanent, nonsubstantial, and interdependent, Nirvana is not some mystical experience with a god or absolute state of existence. Nirvana is not absorption into an unchanging, permanent oneness. Nirvana cannot be understood cognitively through logic, rationality, theories, books, discussions, or arguments. Nirvana cannot be taught. Nirvana is not a result of faith. Nirvana is not due to the grace of some deity. Nirvana is the complete and total stopping, cutting off, and cessation of craving. This must be experienced, realized, and validated by each individual.

The Fourth Noble Truth

Friends. Now what is the Noble Truth of the path to the cessation of dissatisfaction/chronic stress [*dukkha*]? This is the Eightfold Noble Path: Correct Seeing, Correct Thinking, Correct Speaking, Correct Action, Correct Life, Correct Effort, Correct Mindfulness, and Correct Concentration. (*Analysis of the Noble Truths*)

The Fourth Noble Truth of the path to the cessation of *dukkha* or the Eightfold Path (see Table 4.1) is essentially the treatment plan of the counselor or psychotherapist. It is the treatment of the problem. The treatment of a problem, say depression, for a cognitive therapist, such as Ellis, would focus on disputing irrational beliefs (which are viewed as the cause of the depression) of the client, assisting the client in replacing the irrational beliefs with rational beliefs and pointing out the new feelings, not being depressed, that occur as a result of the new rational thoughts.

The Eightfold Path

The Eightfold Path is Buddha's treatment plan for the removal of *dukkha*. It is a holistic approach addressing the individual on cognitive, emotional, behavioral, and interpersonal levels. All eight folds of this path are interdependent and linked together. Each fold conditions and is conditioned by the other folds. They should not be considered as independent from each other. The path is based in the practice of mindfulness, which is the core component for the cessation of *dukkha* or chronic stress.

Correct Seeing

Friends, now what is Correct Seeing? It is knowledge of chronic stress [*dukkha*], knowledge of the origin of chronic stress, knowledge of the cessation of chronic stress, and knowledge of the path to the cessation of chronic stress. Friends, this is the meaning of Correct Seeing. (*Analysis of the Noble Truths*)

Table 4.1   The Fourth Noble Truth: The Eightfold Path

Fold	Behavior
Correct Seeing	Seeing, understanding, and applying the Four Noble Truths Seeing and acting with the understanding that the nature of existence is impermanent, interdependent, and nonsubstantial
Correct Thinking	Thinking of the cessation of suffering/dissatisfaction (chronic stress) Thinking of not being hateful and angry Thinking of doing no harm
Correct Speech	Not speaking in a manner that is harmful Removal of negative speech
Correct Action	Not engaging in behavior that is harmful
Correct Livelihood	Not engaging in occupations that are harmful
Correct Effort	Willingness, commitment, discipline, determination, motivation, enthusiasm, and effort for removing suffering/dissatisfaction (chronic stress) Results in Correct Seeing, Thinking, Speech, Action, and Livelihood Guides Correct Mindfulness and Concentration
Correct Mindfulness	A flexibly focused, nonjudgmental engagement with all aspects of the present Central practice for elimination of suffering/dissatisfaction; applied to all of the folds Primary practice for experiencing all of existence as being subject to impermanence, interdependence, and nonsubstantiality
Correct Concentration	A single, nonjudgmental focused attention resulting in inner absorption; ultimately leads to stopping of all sensation and perception

Correct Seeing is being aware of and understanding the Four Noble Truths. Being aware of and understanding the Four Noble Truths is the understanding of and penetration into the nature of existence. It is seeing that the nature of existence is impermanent, nonsubstantial, and interdependent. This Correct Seeing is based on direct experience and self-validation. Correct Seeing is the goal of the Eightfold Path.

Correct Thinking

Friends, now what is Correct Thinking? It is thinking of the cessation of suffering, thinking of not being hateful and angry, thinking of not doing harm. Friends this is the meaning of Correct Thinking. (*Analysis of the Noble Truths*)

Cognitively, the individual should be focused on becoming detached from chronic stress or *dukkha*. The individual should be focused on being compassionate and not doing any harm. By focusing on the goal of the cessation of suffering and changing how one thinks about existence, how one feels and how one interacts with the people who populate existence, the individual will move closer to Correct Thinking. In a very real sense, this component indicates the importance of cognitive restructuring relative to the removal of chronic stress or *dukkha*.

Correct Speech

Friends, now what is Correct Speech? It is not speaking falsehoods, not speaking in a manner that causes dissension, not speaking in a slanderous manner, not speaking in an obscene manner. Friend this is the meaning of Correct Speech. (*Analysis of the Noble Truths*)

Correct Speech is about behavioral change relative to one's self and interacting with other people. It is about changing one's negative feelings. By removing negative speech, the individual will remove a source of chronic stress, as all the negative aspects of speech noted in the previous quotation are based in perceived threats to the individual. The removal of negative speech results in the removal of negative emotions. By removing negative speech, the individual will be honest and speak in a truthful manner that is conducive to positive relationships with other people. Correct Speech is an interrelated component of the treatment plan leading to Correct Seeing and the removal of chronic stress or *dukkha*.

Correct Action

Friends, now what is Correct Action? Not killing, not stealing, and not behaving wrongly in circumstances associated with the sense pleasures. Friends, this is the meaning of Correct Action. (*Analysis of the Noble Truths*)

Correct Action focuses on behavior that is conducive to not causing harm to others or to oneself. Killing and stealing harms others, is stress producing, and is not consistent with the teachings that are focused on the removal of *dukkha* or chronic stress. The teachings of Buddha are not pleasure denying. Obtaining pleasure is part of being human. However, when individuals behave in a manner that is guided by ignorance of the nature of existence, then pleasure will lead to *dukkha* or chronic stress.

Behaving wrongly is being controlled by pleasure, attached to pleasure, seeking to obtain, possess, and maintain whatever one desires, fearful of not getting what one desires, fearful of losing what one thinks one has obtained, and demanding that one's needs are continually met. This is craving driven by ignorance of the nature of existence. Not behaving wrongly regarding pleasure is recognizing that all pleasure, as is existence, is temporary.

Correct Livelihood

Friends, now what is a Correct Livelihood? Friends, disciples of the sages abandon unhealthy livelihoods and select Correct Livelihoods for their lives. This is the meaning of Correct Livelihood. (*Analysis of the Noble Truths*)

Unhealthy livelihoods are those occupations that harm others both physically and psychologically. They are occupations that give rise to and support craving for pleasure, existence, and nonexistence. Correct Livelihoods are those occupations that do not harm others and are conducive to the elimination of craving.

Correct Effort

Friends, now what is Correct Effort? Friends, monks are determined, are energetic, are devoted and industrious, are enthusiastic, and are motivated for not allowing the arising of evil unskilled methods that have not arisen and for abandoning evil unskilled methods that have already arisen. They are determined, are energetic, are devoted and industrious, are enthusiastic, and are motivated for the arising of all the skilled methods that have not arisen. They are determined, are energetic, are devoted and industrious, are enthusiastic, and are motivated for continuing, not confusing, increasing, expanding and cultivating all the skilled methods that have already arisen. Friends this is the meaning of Correct Effort. (*Analysis of the Noble Truths*)

Correct Effort is the willingness and motivation to stay on the path toward the cessation of *dukkha* or chronic stress. It is the drive and determination to see existence as it really is, to abandon behaviors that give rise to craving, to not allow behaviors to arise that give rise to craving, to maintain, cultivate, and increase behaviors that are conducive to the elimination of craving, and to create and develop new behaviors that are conducive to the elimination of craving. Correct Effort results in Correct Seeing, Correct Thinking, Correct Speaking, Correct Action, and Correct Livelihood. Correct Effort guides Correct Mindfulness and Correct Concentration.

Correct Mindfulness

Friends, now what is Correct Mindfulness? Friends, a monk follows along nonjudgmentally observing the body as the body. Enthusiastic, there is correct knowing and mindfulness. Controlling and subduing the greed and anxiety in the world. Then moving on to sensations, feelings, and then arriving at mental objects. The monk follows along nonjudgmentally observing mental objects as mental objects. Enthusiastic, there is correct knowing and mindfulness. Controlling and subduing the greed and anxiety in the world. Friends this is Correct Mindfulness. (*Analysis of the Noble Truths*)

Mindfulness is the central method for the elimination of *dukkha* or chronic stress. While the other seven folds of the Eightfold Path are important, they cannot be understood outside of mindfulness. Mindfulness is applied with each of the folds. As noted in the preceding quote, mindfulness is applied to the body, the sensations, the feelings, and mental objects. In other words, mindfulness is applied to the individual and the world around the individual.

Through the practice of mindfulness, the individual nonjudgmentally observes or experiences that all of existence is impermanent, nonsubstantial, and interdependent. The individual nonjudgmentally observes or experiences conditioned arising. It is the nonjudgmental observation or experience of conditioned arising that frees the individual from *dukkha*. The release from *dukkha* is not possible through reason, logic, science, faith, belief in a higher power, an absolute state of existence or a god/gods, being told by others, reading books, or engaging in intellectual discussions with other individuals. Buddha is quite clear: Release from *dukkha* or chronic stress is based on the individual's direct experience of the nature of existence. The experience can only be validated by the individual. This experience can only occur through the practice of mindfulness.

Correct Mindfulness

Then the Buddha said, "Monks. To purify all sentient beings, to overcome anxiety and depression, to eliminate bitterness and worry, to arrive at the correct path, to realize Nirvana, there is this one dharma [truth]: the four dwellings of mindfulness." (*The Dwellings of Mindfulness*)[3]

The conditions of anxiety, depression, bitterness, and worry are certainly indicative of chronic stress. There is a strong focus on the psychological aspects of problems relative to successfully adapting to the environment. These psychological issues, for Buddha, can only be addressed through the practice of mindfulness. The practice of mindfulness allows the individual to see existence as it really is: impermanent, nonsubstantial, and interdependent. In other words, the individual sees or experiences conditioned arising.

> All people! The Buddha also thus said, "If you see conditioned arising then you see the dharma [truth]. If you see the dharma then you see conditioned arising." (*The Metaphor of the Elephant's Footprint, Greater*)[4]

The concept of *dharma* has many meanings in Buddhism. Ultimately, though, it refers to the truth of Buddha's overall teachings. The truth is that only through the practice of mindfulness will the individual be able to observe that existence is impermanent, nonsubstantial, and interdependent. In other words, the individual will see conditioned arising.

The Chinese character for mindfulness is *nian*[a]. This character consists of two components. The first component, located on the top, is the character *jin*[b], which means the present, the here and now. The second component, located on the bottom, is the radical *xin*[c], which means the heart/mind. The combination gives the notion of the heart/mind in the present. In other words, the focus of thinking, feeling, and acting is in the present.

In one sense, mindfulness serves as a cue to the practitioner to remember the present, the here and now. Do not be obsessing about the past or worrying about the future. Do not let the attention become attached to the past or the future. Bring the attention to now.

Given that mindfulness is the key to understanding Buddhism, it is important to further analyze this practice so that its applicability to counseling and psychotherapy can be ascertained. Mindfulness is a flexibly focused, nonjudgmental engagement with the present. There are three key points to this definition: (1) to be flexibly focused, (2) to be in the present, and (3) to be nonjudgmentally engaged.

To be flexibly focused means to be attentive to the environment, both internal and external. It does not mean to be absorbed into a single object, thought, or sound. It is not a meditative device where everything disappears as the practitioner disengages from the environment. It is not a loss of awareness of the environment. In fact, it is an enhanced awareness of the environment.

This enhanced awareness is focused on the present. To practice mindfulness, the individual needs to be in the here and now. To fully engage the present, the individual cannot be holding on to the past or obsessing about the future.

The third key is that of nonjudgmental engagement. To be nonjudgmentally engaged is to observe the environment, internal and external, in a nonjudgmental manner. Observing in a nonjudgmental manner will allow the individual to experience existence as it really is: impermanent, nonsubstantial, and interdependent. This direct experience will change how one views and thinks about existence. This being the case, *dukkha* or chronic stress is eliminated.

The Four Dwellings of Mindfulness

The practice of mindfulness consists of four *dwellings* or focal points (see Table 4.2). It starts with the breath and the body. It then moves on to the sensations (pleasant, unpleasant, and neutral), the feelings or emotions, and then to mental objects or thoughts. The commonality at each of these four dwellings is that the practitioner observes that the content of each dwelling is impermanent, nonsubstantial, and interdependent.

Everything, at each level, is in a continual process of change. Everything is interdependent. Everything is simultaneously cause and effect. Everything conditions and is conditioned. There is no separate existence. Insofar as

Table 4.2   The Four Dwellings of Mindfulness

Dwelling	Content
Mindfulness and the Body	Mindfulness is directed toward all aspects and behaviors of the body. It begins with mindfulness of breathing.
	All aspects and behaviors of the body are experienced as being impermanent, interdependent, and nonsubstantial.
Mindfulness and Sensations	Mindfulness is directed toward all sensations. All sensations are pleasant, unpleasant, or neutral and are experienced as being impermanent, interdependent, and nonsubstantial.
Mindfulness and Feelings	Mindfulness is directed toward feelings. All feelings are experienced as being impermanent, interdependent, and nonsubstantial.
Mindfulness and Mental Objects	Mindfulness is directed toward thoughts and beliefs (mental objects). Thoughts and beliefs are observed as thoughts and beliefs. All thoughts and beliefs are experienced as being impermanent, interdependent, and nonsubstantial.

everything changes, is interdependent, is simultaneously cause and effect, and is not separate, then it makes no sense to talk about an unchanging, independent substance such as matter, soul, or self.

For Buddha, the fact that the individual is ignorant of the nature of existence results in the individual craving. This craving results in chronic stress that is manifested as psychological and physical misery. Thus it is one's false view of existence, how one thinks about and acts in the various environmental contexts, that ultimately results in *dukkha*. It is the continual perception of threats in the environment (internal and/or external) due to the individual's false view of existence (permanent, substantial, and independent) that results in chronic stress. The only way alleviate this is through the practice of the four dwellings of mindfulness.

What are these four? The Buddha said, "Monks, it is to follow along nonjudgmentally observing the body as the body, enthusiastic and attentive, maintaining mindfulness very deeply to eliminate the world of greed and anxiety. It is following along nonjudgmentally observing sensations as sensations, enthusiastic and very attentive, maintaining mindfulness to eliminate the world of greed and anxiety. It is following along nonjudgmentally observing feelings/emotions as feelings/emotions, enthusiastic and very attentive, maintaining mindfulness to eliminate the world of greed and anxiety. It is following along nonjudgmentally observing mental objects as mental objects, enthusiastic and very attentive, maintaining mindfulness to eliminate the world of greed and anxiety." (*The Dwellings of Mindfulness*)

While this gives a description of the four dwellings of body, sensations, feelings/emotions, and mental objects (thoughts), it does not really explain the practice. The practice begins with a process that fits easily into the Daoist teachings of simplicity, beginning points, and commonalities, that of simply focusing on breathing. The act of breathing is quite simple. The breath, which is impermanent, nonsubstantial, and interdependent, is the very basis of life. At birth, life begins with the first breath. At death, life ends with the last breath. Breathing is common to all human beings. It is with the breath that mindfulness begins.

Mindful Breathing

Monks! How does a monk follow along nonjudgmentally observing the body as the body? Monks! By this! A monk walked into a forest, he walked to the base of a tree, he walked to an empty place, folded his legs, sat cross-legged, and straightened his body, in the present, mindfully. At that point, mindful he exhales, mindful he inhales. Perhaps it is a long exhalation. Being aware he says, "I am breathing out a long breath." Perhaps it is a long inhalation. Being aware he says, "I am breathing in a long breath." Perhaps it is a short exhalation. Being aware he says, "I am breathing out a short breath." Perhaps it is a short inhalation. Being aware he says, "I am breathing in a short breath." Perhaps he cultivates himself nonjudgmentally observing, "I am aware of my entire body when I exhale." Perhaps he cultivates himself nonjudgmentally observing, "I am aware of my entire body when I inhale." Again cultivating himself he non-judgmentally observes, "I am making the actions of my body tranquil and still when I exhale." Cultivating himself he nonjudgmentally observes, "I am making the actions of my body tranquil and still when I inhale. . . . In this way he follows along nonjudgmentally observing the body in the body internally, the body in the body externally, the body in the body internally and externally. *(The Dwellings of Mindfulness)*

The description of the practice of mindfulness indicates that initially the practitioner is simply and only aware of his or her breathing (long or short) while inhaling and exhaling. The practitioner follows the breath. The attention is flexibly focused. It is not locked onto a single point. There is no thinking or judging. The practitioner is in the present totally aware of the process of inhalation and exhalation. As the individual practices, trains, and cultivates the process, the individual's awareness will expand becoming aware of the entire body and then the accompanying feelings with each inhalation and exhalation. The individual then applies this same process to nonjudgmentally observing other bodies in the environment. In this manner the practitioner moves on to nonjudgmentally observing the behavior of the body.

Mindfulness and the Body

In this way he follows along nonjudgmentally observing things originating in the body, in this way he follows along observing things ceasing in the body, in this way he follows along observing things origination and ceasing in the body. In the present, mindfully, he says, "The body is this." Thus is the establishment of his wisdom and his remembrance. In the world, he is without dependency or attachments. This, monks, is following along nonjudgmentally observing the body in the body. *(The Dwellings of Mindfulness)*

As the practitioner deepens into the practice of mindfulness, the body is seen as being impermanent. Things originate and then cease. Nothing in the body is permanent! With the body being seen as impermanent, its non-substantiality and interdependence is seen. Conditioned arising! With this nonjudgmental awareness of the nature of his body, he becomes detached and free from restrictions. This practice is then extended even further into the actions of the body in the various environmental contexts.

Monks, again! Perhaps a monk is walking, knowing this he says, "I am walking." Perhaps he is standing, knowing this he says, "I am standing." Perhaps he is sitting, knowing this he says, "I am sitting." Perhaps he is lying down, knowing this he says, "I am lying down." Whatever aspect of the body is indicated, he knows it is such. In this way, he follows along non-judgmentally observing the body . . . without dependency or attachments. This, monks, is nonjudgmentally observing the body as the body. Monks, again! A monk is going off, returning, truly aware, nonjudgmentally observing the front and the back, truly aware, desiring to bend or stretch, truly aware, desiring to hold his topcoat, robe or alms bowl, he is truly aware. Eating, drinking, chewing, tasting, he is truly aware. At the time of defecating or urinating, he is truly aware. (*The Dwellings of Mindfulness*)

This practice of mindfulness is directed to all aspects of the practitioner's physical form and the physical form of others, including dead bodies. The practitioner, having established mindfulness of the body, then moves on to nonjudgmentally observing sensations.

Mindfulness and Sensations

Monks! How does a monk following along nonjudgmentally observing sensations as sensations? Now, a monk, being aware of sensing a pleasant sensation says, "I am sensing a pleasant sensation." Being aware of sensing an unpleasant feeling says, "I am sensing an unpleasant sensation." Being aware of sensing a neutral sensation says, "I am sensing a neutral sensation." Being aware of sensing a pleasant sensation in regard to material objects says, "I am sensing a pleasant sensation in regard to material objects." Being aware of sensing a pleasant sensation in regard to nonmaterial objects says, "I am sensing a pleasant sensation in regard to nonmaterial objects." Being aware of sensing an unpleasant sensation in regard to material objects says, "I am sensing an unpleasant sensation in regard to material objects." Being aware of sensing an unpleasant sensation in regard to nonmaterial objects says, "I am sensing an unpleasant sensation in regard to non material objects." Being aware of sensing a neutral sensation in regard to material objects says, "I am sensing a neutral sensation in regard to material objects." Being aware of sensing a neutral sensation in regard to nonmaterial objects says, "I am sensing a neutral sensation in regard to nonmaterial objects." (*The Dwellings of Mindfulness*)

The same application of mindfulness thus occurs with the sensations as the practitioner nonjudgmentally observes the sensations of pleasant, unpleasant, or neutral. Mindfulness is directed to both material and nonmaterial objects. It should be noted that *material* and *nonmaterial* do not refer to spirit and matter or substance and soul. For Buddha, material is essentially that with form and nonmaterial (thoughts) is that without form, neither of which can be considered as permanent, substantial, or independent.

> Thus, following along nonjudgmentally observing sensations as internal sensations, following along nonjudgmentally observing sensations as external sensations, following along nonjudgmentally observing sensations as internal and external sensations, following along nonjudgmentally observing the sensation of things originating, following along nonjudgmentally observing the sensation of things ceasing, following along nonjudgmentally observing the sensation of things originating and ceasing. In the present, mindfully, he says, "The sensations are this." Thus is the establishment of his wisdom and his remembrance. In the world, he is without dependency or attachments. This, monks, is following along nonjudgmentally observing sensations as sensations. (*The Dwellings of Mindfulness*)

As with the body, under the eye of mindfulness, sensations, internal and external, are also experienced as impermanent, nonsubstantial. and interdependent. Through nonjudgmental observation, the practitioner is no longer controlled by the six senses. There is no attachment or dependency on people, things, or thoughts, as there is no sense of permanence, substantiality, or independence. There is nothing permanent to be attached to or dependent upon. Sensations associated with material and nonmaterial objects, including people, are experienced as impermanent, nonsubstantial, and interdependent. There is nothing to grasp, crave, or hold on to, as everything is impermanent, nonsubstantial, and interdependent. Therapeutically, for the Buddha, experiencing all aspects of existence as impermanent, nonsubstantial, and interdependent changes how the individual views the world and thus releases the individual from *dukkha* or chronic stress.

Mindfulness and Feelings

The next level at which mindfulness is applied, in order to change the individual's experience, view, and understanding of the world, is that of feelings or emotions. Buddha once again explains the process of applying mindfulness to the feelings. As with the body and the sensations, the focus, for the practitioner, is on being in the present, nonjudgmentally aware, simply observing feelings as feelings. Nothing else!

> Monks! How does a monk follow along nonjudgmentally observing feelings as feelings? Now, a monk aware of having the feeling of greed says, "I have the feeling of greed." Aware of not having the feeling of greed says, "I do not have the feeling of greed." Aware of having the feeling of hate says, "I have the feeling of hate." Aware of not having the

feeling of hate says, "I do not have the feeling of hate." Aware of having the feeling of confusion says, "I have the feeling of confusion." Aware of not having the feeling of confusion says, "I do not have the feeling of confusion." Aware of the feeling of absorption says, "I have the feeling of absorption." Aware of the feeling of distraction says, "I have the feeling of distraction." Aware of the feeling of expansion says, "I have the feeling of expansion." Aware of the feeling of nonexpansion says, "I have the feeling of nonexpansion." Aware of the feeling of being superior says, "I have the feeling of being superior." Aware of the feeling of not being superior says, "I have the feeling of not being superior." Aware of the feeling of concentrating says, "I have the feeling of concentrating." Aware of the feeling of not concentrating says, "I have the feeling of not concentrating." Aware of the feeling of being free says, "I have the feeling of being free." Aware of the feeling of not being free says, "I have the feeling of not being free." (*The Dwellings of Mindfulness*)

As with the breath, the body, and the sensations, mindfulness is applied to the feelings. The feelings are experienced, without any judgments, simply as feelings. The practitioner does not feed, think about, or ruminate on the feelings. The feelings are simply experienced.

While all of the feelings are subject to being experienced mindfully, the feeling of confusion is of special interest. The two Chinese characters that are combined and translated/interpreted as confusion are yu^d and chi^e. The first Chinese character yu^d consists of two components. The bottom component of this character is the radical xin^c, which means mind/heart. The top component of this character is the character yu^f, which means the spider monkey. The spider monkey is suggestive of an animal that appears easily frightened, hyperactive, distractible, and impulsive. Thus, the combination of the two components of mind/heart (xin^c) and spider monkey (yu^f) implies a mind/heart that is easily frightened, hyperactive, distractible, and impulsive.

The second character chi^e also consists of two components. The outside character is the radical ni^g, which means sick. The inside character is the character zhi^h, which means to know, to realize, to understand. The combination suggests the knowing process is sick or compromised.

The combination of yu^d and chi^e gives the sense of a compromised feeling and knowing process that is unable to focus (distractible), not in control (impulsive), unsettled (hyperactive), and, in a general sense, sick and dysfunctional. Given these descriptors, confusion is an apt translation/ interpretation for the cognitive and affective process of the individual. For all intents and purposes, this is what Buddha is saying about the general state of the human being who lives in the world of ignorance and thus craving.

The world honored one [Buddha] thus spoke, "Monks. When fears rise up, they all rise because the person is confused, not because the person is wise. When difficulties rise up, they all rise because the person is confused, not because the person is wise. When anxieties rise up, they all rise because the person is confused, not because the person is wise."
(*Many Boundaries*)[5]

The character that is translated as "confused" in the preceding quote is the Chinese character yu^d, which consists of the two components of mind/heart and spider monkey. It is not difficult to link fear, difficulties, and anxiety to a fragmented thinking and feeling process that is significantly compromised by the inability to (cognitively, affectively, and behaviorally) focus, be in control, and remain stable or grounded. This is a description of stress! It is, in fact, a general description for the symptoms of most, if not all, individuals who enter therapy or counseling. Their stress is simply ongoing or chronic. Buddha is just taking this one step further ins far as this is a description, from his perspective, of, unfortunately, the normal state for human beings: *dukkha.*

As with the body and the sensations, the application of mindfulness to the feelings results in the experience of the feelings being impermanent. If the practitioner remains nonjudgmental, the feelings simply arise and pass away. If, on the other hand, individuals do not practice mindfulness, are judgmental and confused about the nature of existence, their feelings will appear to be maintained and the individuals will experience fear, anxiety, and have difficulties in adapting to their various environmental challenges.

This being the case, it is imperative that mindfulness is practiced. Through the practice of mindfulness, individuals will experience their feelings as impermanent. This experience will be of benefit in reducing their chronic stress.

Thus, following along nonjudgmentally observing feelings as internal feelings, feelings as external feelings, feelings as internal and external feelings, following along nonjudgmentally observing the feelings of things originating, following along nonjudgmentally observing the feelings of things ceasing, following along nonjudgmentally observing the feelings of things originating and ceasing. In the present, mindfully, he says, "The feelings are this." Thus is the establishment of his wisdom and his remembrance. Wherever he goes in the world there is no dependence or attachment. This is a monk nonjudgmentally observing feelings as feelings. (*The Dwellings of Mindfulness*)

Mindfulness and Mental Objects

The final dwelling for the application of mindfulness is that of mental objects or thoughts. Even though one can experience the body, sensations, and feelings and observe their impermanence, there are still words and concepts for the body, sensations, and feelings that must also be nonjudgmentally observed. In fact, it is the words, the concepts, the theories, and the viewpoints that are generated as mental objects that present the individual with the greatest threat. For most people, their words, concepts, theories and viewpoints are viewed by them as being absolute. They are taken to be true without question. It is believed by people that the world is in direct correspondence with their viewpoint of it. Their viewpoint is that the world and all that it entails is permanent, substantial, and independent. This viewpoint or manner of thinking is, according to Buddha, the source of their *dukkha* or chronic stress.

It is only through the practice of mindfulness that the practitioner will be able to see and experience mental objects as mental objects, nothing more or less. Seeing and experiencing them simply as mental objects that are subject to arising and passing away. Like everything else, mental objects are impermanent.

Thus, mindfulness is applied not only to the actual body, sensations, and feelings but also to the words or concepts that label them. This allows for demonstrating or experiencing that thoughts or mental objects like the breath, the body/form, the sensations, and the feelings are all impermanent. From this it follows that theories and viewpoints are also subject to impermanence, including the very teachings of Buddha.

The Mental Objects

The process of applying mindfulness to mental objects begins with the five hindrances and follows along nonjudgmentally observing the five components of the individual, the six internal and external dwellings (six senses and their objects), and the Four Noble Truths themselves (see Table 4.3). This process is not simply replacing one viewpoint with another viewpoint. It is not about merely changing how one looks at the world. It is not a cognitive restructuring based on replacing irrational thoughts or inferences with rational thoughts or inferences. A cognitive restructuring occurs but as a result of the direct experience of all aspects of existence as impermanent, nonsubstantial, and interdependent.

Through this process the individual experiences and sees the impermanence, nonsubstantiality, and interdependence of everything. It is the direct experience of the body or form, sensations, feelings, and thoughts or mental objects as impermanent, nonsubstantial, and interdependent that

Table 4.3   Mindfulness and Mental Objects

Mental Object	Content
Five Hindrances	1. Internal craving for sense pleasure 2. Hatred 3. Laziness 4. Discontent and regret 5. Doubt
Five Grasping Containers. Also known as the five heaps or the five aggregates. Essentially Buddhist sense of self or person.	1. Form 2. Sensation 3. Perception 4. Mental disposition 5. Consciousness
Six Internal and External Dwellings	1. Eye and form 2. Ear and sound 3. Nose and smell 4. Tongue and taste 5. Body and touch 6. Mind and thoughts/beliefs
Seven Branches of Awakening	1. Awakening 2. Discrimination 3. Effort 4. Happiness 5. Peace 6. Concentration 7. Equanimity
Four Noble Truths	1. Suffering/dissatisfaction 2. Cause of suffering/dissatisfaction 3. Cessation of suffering/dissatisfaction 4. Path leading to the cessation of suffering/dissatisfaction

is the basis of the teachings of Buddha. This experience is freedom from *dukkha* or chronic stress.

The Five Hindrances

Monks! How does a monk follow along nonjudgmentally observing mental objects [thoughts] as mental objects [thoughts]? By this! A monk follows along nonjudgmentally observing the mental object of the five hindrances as a mental object. How does a monk follow along nonjudgmentally observing the mental object of the five hindrances as a mental object? Monks! Now, a monk, aware that he is having an internal craving for sense pleasure says, "I am having an internal craving for sense pleasure." If he is aware that he does not have an internal craving for sense pleasure he says, "I am not having an internal craving for sense pleasure." He is aware of a craving for sense pleasure that has not risen before, he is aware of getting rid of a craving for sense pleasure that has risen before, he is aware of no further arising of a craving for sense pleasure he has gotten rid of. In addition, being internally aware of having hatred, he says, "I internally have hatred." Being internally aware of not having hatred he says, "I internally do not have hatred." He is aware of the arising of hatred that has not risen before, he is aware of abandoning hatred that has already risen before, he is aware of abandoning hatred that has not yet arisen in the future. So it is with laziness, discontent and regret, as well as doubt which are moreover like this. (*The Dwellings of Mindfulness*)

For Buddha, the five hindrances (internal craving for sense pleasure, hatred, laziness, discontent, and regret, doubt) are mental obstacles that compromise experiencing the release from *dukkha* or chronic stress itself. The practitioner of mindfulness, through practice, becomes nonjudgmentally aware of each of the hindrances. By not feeding into or making judgments about the hindrances, in other words by not thinking about these mental objects (thoughts) and what they generate, the individual will not become attached to them or what they generate. These mental objects are simply experienced for what they are: impermanent, nonsubstantial, and interdependent mental objects or thoughts. This being the case, the individual will not be subject to being influenced or controlled by the mental object of the five hindrances.

Thus, following along nonjudgmentally observing mental objects internally as mental objects, following along nonjudgmentally observing mental objects externally as mental objects, following along nonjudgmentally observing mental objects internally and externally as mental objects, following along nonjudgmentally observing mental objects originating as mental objects, following along nonjudgmentally observing mental objects ceasing as mental objects, following along nonjudgmentally observing mental objects originating and ceasing as mental objects. In the present, mindfully, he says, "The mental objects are this." Thus is the establishment of his wisdom and his remembrance. Wherever he goes in the world there is no dependence or attachment. This is a monk following along nonjudgmentally observing the mental object of the five hindrances as a mental object. (*The Dwellings of Mindfulness*)

Through the practice of mindfulness, the practitioner will see the reality of the five hindrances. They are nothing more than mental objects (thoughts) subject to rising and passing away. Like the breath, the body, the sensations, and the feelings, the mental object of the five hindrances is impermanent and has no inherent control or influence on the individual.

The Five Grasping Containers

Next, monks! A monk follows along nonjudgmentally observing the mental object of the five grasping containers [the five aggregates or sense of self] as a mental object. Monks! How does a monk follow along nonjudgmentally observing the mental object of the five grasping containers as a mental object? From this! A monk says, "Thus is form, the origin of form, the disappearance of form. Thus is sensation, the origin of sensation, the disappearance of sensation. Thus is perception, the origin of perception, the disappearance of perception. Thus are mental disposition, the origin of mental disposition, and the disappearance of mental disposition. Thus is consciousness, the origin of consciousness, and the disappearance of consciousness." In this manner, following along, nonjudgmentally he says, "I am observing mental objects internally as mental objects." In the present, mindfully, he says, "The mental objects are this." Thus is the establishment of his wisdom and his remembrance. Wherever he goes in the world there is no dependence or attachment. This is a monk following along nonjudgmentally observing the mental object of the five grasping containers as a mental object. (*The Dwellings of Mindfulness*)

When mindfulness is applied to the mental object of the five grasping containers or the five aspects of the sense of self (form, sensation, perception, mental disposition, consciousness), the practitioner experiences the impermanence of this mental object. For the Buddha, the self or I or ego is nothing more than the interrelationship and interdependence between these five grasping containers or components that make up the individual person. There is nothing else. It makes no sense for the Buddha to talk about an unchanging, permanent, substantial, and independent soul. He is clear that it is foolish to even consider absolute existence or absolute nonexistence after death or even in life itself. There is nothing independent that can either exist or not exist. To try to make existence or aspects of it into what you would like it or wish it to be—permanent, substantial, and independent—results in suffering, dissatisfaction, and chronic stress. This is not how existence behaves. This is Buddha's core point!

All aspects of existence, including all the happiness and pleasure that is desired, are subject to change. To try to make something, including the Self or I, that is impermanent, nonsubstantial, and interdependent into something that is permanent, substantial, and independent is an exercise in wishful thinking. It will not happen! Unfortunately, people continue to try, and this is why they are ill and chronically stressed. When the individual is able to get beyond this wishful thinking, the individual will be at peace.

Next! In this way it is said, where one is at peace, all thinking about pleasure and happiness do not continue on. When all thinking about pleasure and happiness do not continue on, the Buddha is still and tranquil. So, what does this mean? Monk! To say "I have an I," this is wishful thinking. To say "I am that," this is wishful thinking. To say "I will exist," this is wishful thinking. To say that "I will not exist," this is wishful thinking. To say "I will be and have form," this is wishful thinking. To say that "I will be and not have form," this is wishful thinking. "I will be and think," this is wishful thinking. "I will not be and not think," this is wishful thinking. "I will be not thinking and not not thinking," this is wishful thinking. Monk, wishful thinking is an illness. Wishful thinking is an abscess. Wishful thinking is foreign body embedded in you. Monks! Thus, getting past and beyond all the wishful thinking, the Buddha is still and tranquil. (*Analysis of the Elements*)[6]

Through the practice of mindfulness, the practitioner will nonjudgmentally observe that impermanence is applicable to all thoughts or mental objects. All thoughts are impermanent. All thoughts arise and pass away. The very nature of the individual, the Self or the I as something or someone that is permanent, substantial, and independent, is experienced and seen as a fiction. This experience or awakening to the nature of all aspects of existence is liberating, and the practitioner becomes free from dependence and attachment as he or she wanders throughout the world.

The Six Internal and External Dwellings

Next, monks! A monk follows along nonjudgmentally observing the mental object of the six internal and external dwellings [six senses and their objects] as a mental object. Monks! How does a monk following along nonjudgmentally observing the mental object of the six internal and external dwellings [six senses and their objects] as a mental object? From this! A monk is aware of the eye, aware of the visual form, aware of the conditionality of these two which gives rise to restrictions. Is aware of the arising of the restrictions not risen before, is aware of getting rid of the restrictions already arisen before, is aware of the nonarising in the future of the restrictions that have been abandoned. Is aware of the ear, sound, aware of the conditionality of these two which gives rise to restrictions, and so it is with awareness of the nose, smells, and the conditionality of these two which gives rise to restrictions. Is aware of the tongue, taste, aware of the conditionality of these two which gives rise to restrictions, and so it is with awareness of the nose, smells, and the conditionality of these two which gives rise to restrictions. Is aware of the body, touch, and aware of the conditionality of these two which gives rise to restrictions. Is aware of thinking, mental objects, and is aware of the conditionality of these two which gives rise to restrictions. Is aware of the arising of restrictions having not arisen, is aware of getting rid of the restrictions already arisen before, and is aware of the nonarising in the future of the restrictions that have been abandoned. Thus, is following along nonjudgmentally observing mental objects internally as mental objects. . . . Thus is the establishment of his wisdom and his remembrance. Where ever he goes in the world, he is without dependency and attachment. This is a monk following along nonjudgmentally observing the mental object of the six internal and external dwellings [six senses and their objects] as a mental object. (*The Dwellings of Mindfulness*)

With the application of mindfulness to the mental objects of the six senses (the five physical senses and the mind) and their objects, the notion of conditionality or interdependence and the restrictions or entanglements associated with conditionality are clearly presented in regard to mental objects or thoughts. The application of mindfulness to the thinking process allows the practitioner to experience the mind as a process wherein thoughts arise and pass away. Mindfulness allows the practitioner to see or experience nonjudgmentally how thoughts or mental objects are subject to conditionality and the subsequent restrictions or entanglements that lead, ultimately, to *dukkha* or chronic stress. This occurs when individuals attempt to make thoughts permanent by not examining them, holding on to them, feeding them, worrying over them, or ruminating about them. This process then hardens, if you will, into a viewpoint that sees the mental object of the six senses and their objects as permanent, substantial, and independent. The six senses and their objects are viewed as independent things.

The ignorance of the nature of reality results in craving for sensual pleasure, existence, and nonexistence. This craving results in trying to make existence itself, which is impermanent, nonsubstantial, and interdependent, into something that is permanent, substantial, and independent. This attempt is made through the individual's thoughts, concepts, theories, perspectives, and viewpoints about the nature of existence. The map—mental objects—is mistaken for the territory, existence itself. The map, mental objects, and all that they entail are not questioned or examined. Because of this, individuals suffer or are chronically stressed because existence does behave according to the map. This chronic stress may be manifested in such forms as anxiety, depression, hostility, or as a general sense of dissatisfaction. The bottom line is that, according to Buddha, people suffer physically and psychologically because of their mistaken viewpoint about the nature of reality.

It is only through nonjudgmentally observing the mental objects as mental objects, in this case the six sense and their objects, through the practice of mindfulness that this entanglement and suffering can be overcome. The practitioner must experience mental objects as being impermanent, nonsubstantial, and interdependent in order to be free from the conditionality and entanglements associated with the map. Simply replacing one set of thoughts with another set of thoughts will not work, as the individual will still be entangled in the map.

The Seven Branches of Awakening

The next aspect of mental objects that is examined by mindfulness is that of the mental object of the seven branches (also called "levels") of awakening. Practitioners must experience the mental object of the seven branches of awakening in order to observe its impermanence, nonsubstantiality, and interdependence. Even though the feelings associated with the seven branches of awakening may be conducive to interpretations of permanence, substantiality, and independence, the practitioner must not crave or attempt to hold onto the seven branches of awakening. To do so results in suffering and chronic stress, because the seven branches of awakening, like everything else, are subject to impermanence, nonsubstantiality, and interdependence.

Next, monks! A monk follows along nonjudgmentally observing the mental object of the seven levels of awakening as a mental object. Monks, how does a monk follow along nonjudgmentally observing the mental object of the seven levels of awakening as a mental object? Monks! A monk aware that he is internally at the mindfulness level of awakening says, "I am internally at the mindfulness level of awakening." A monk aware that he is internally not at the mindfulness level of awakening says, "I am internally not at the mindfulness level of awakening." He is aware of the arising of the mindfulness level of awakening that had not risen before. He is aware of successfully cultivating the mindfulness level of awakening that has already risen. Being aware that he is internally at the level of awakening of the mental object of discrimination he says, "I am internally at the level of awakening of the mental object of discrimination." Being aware that he is internally not at the level of awakening of the mental object of discrimination he says, "I am internally not at the level of awakening of the mental object of discrimination." He is aware of the arising of the level of awakening of the mental object of discrimination that has not risen before. He is aware of successfully cultivating the mental object of discrimination level of awakening that has already arisen. And so it is with awareness of the levels of awakening of effort, happiness, peace, concentration, and equanimity. Thus he follows along nonjudgmentally observing mental objects internally as mental objects. . . . Wherever he goes in the world, he is without dependency and attachment. This is a monk following along nonjudgmentally observing the mental object of the seven levels of awakening as a mental object. (*The Dwellings of Mindfulness*)

As with the body, the sensations, the feelings, and the previous mental objects, the seven branches of awakening (awakening, discrimination, effort, happiness, peace, concentration, equanimity) are also subject to the same process. Everything is subject to impermanence, nonsubstantiality, and interdependence. Everything arises and then passes away. Even the seven branches of awakening are seen as mental objects that are subject to conditioned arising.

The monk practitioner must not become attached to these various branches of awakening. The monk practitioner must not become dependent upon these seven branches of awakening. To do so would be indicative of viewing aspects of existence as permanent, substantial, and independent. This viewpoint results in *dukkha* or chronic suffering.

Even the so-called positive and apparently quite beneficial aspects of existence must be seen as impermanent and subject to change. To discard the negative aspects of existence yet hold on, grasp, and become attached to the positive aspects will still result in *dukkha* or chronic stress. Thus it is with the final dwelling of mindfulness, that of the Four Noble Truths themselves. Buddha points out that the Four Noble Truths must also be seen as subject to impermanence, nonsubstantiality, and interdependence. The monk practitioner must not become dependent upon or attached to the Four Noble Truths.

The Four Noble Truths

Next, monks! A monk follows along nonjudgmentally observing the mental object of the Four Noble Truths as a mental object. Monks! How does a monk follow along nonjudgmentally observing the mental object of the Four Noble Truths as a mental object? Monks! A monk who is truly aware says, "This is *dukkha*, I am truly aware of this. This is the origin of *dukkha*, I am truly aware of this. This is the cessation of *dukkha*, I am truly aware of this. This is the meticulous path to the cessation of *dukkha*, I am truly aware of this." Thus is following along nonjudgmentally observing internally mental objects as mental objects. Thus is following along nonjudgmentally observing externally mental objects as mental objects. So it is with following along nonjudgmentally observing internally and externally mental objects as mental objects. So it is with following along nonjudgmentally observing the origination of mental objects as mental objects, the cessation of mental objects as mental objects, and the origination and cessation of mental objects as mental objects. In the present, mindfully, he says, "The mental objects are this." Thus is the establishment of his wisdom and remembrance. Where ever he goes in the world, he is without dependency and attachment. This is a monk following along nonjudgmentally observing the mental object of the Four Noble Truths as a mental object. (*The Dwellings of Mindfulness*)

Buddha does not want the monk practitioner to become attached to or dependent upon the Four Noble Truths. Like everything else, the Four Noble Truths (suffering/dissatisfaction, the cause of suffering/dissatisfaction, the cessation of suffering/dissatisfaction, and the path leading to the cessation of suffering/dissatisfaction) are mental objects subject to impermanence, nonsubstantiality, and interdependence. Release from *dukkha* or chronic stress is experiencing conditioned arising. It is the realization that if no-thing is permanent, substantial, or independent, then there is no-thing, ultimately, to which an individual can be dependent upon or attached to. This includes the Four Noble Truths. If an individual is attached to and dependent upon the Four Noble Truths, that individual will experience *dukkha* or chronic stress.

According to Buddha, people, unfortunately, do not view the world from the perspective of conditioned arising. Because people view existence from the perspective of permanence, substantiality, and independence, they are dependent upon and attached to a wide range of things both with form (such as people, property, and the environment) and without form (such as thoughts, beliefs, theories, truths, and concepts). When an adaptive problem in the environment presents itself, people try to solve the problem from a perspective that is based on dependency, attachment, and a false view of the nature of existence. This results in *dukkha* or chronic stress. *Dukkha* is contingent upon individuals trying to make that (form and nonform) which is impermanent, nonsubstantial, and interdependent into something that is permanent, substantial, and independent. This cannot happen! The adaptive problem is, thus, not really solved.

The frustration, dissatisfaction, anger, hostility, anxiety, depression, and other various manifestations of chronic stress arises because existence does not behave according to the individual's perspective or viewpoint about existence. When it does not behave according to their expectations, individuals feel threatened and the fight-or-flight response is automatically activated. Because their viewpoint (believing existence is permanent, substantial, and independent) about their various environmental contexts is the basis of the threat, their behavior or actions in their diverse environmental contexts are unable to, ultimately, eliminate the threat. Their thinking maintains the threat in one manner or another. This being the case, the fight-or-flight response is continually activated and the individual is chronically stressed. Such is *dukkha*!

As much as the Four Noble Truths provide assistance for the practitioner in being released from *dukkha*, they must be seen for what they are: mental objects subject to impermanence, nonsubstantiality, and interdependence. To see them otherwise will result in chronic stress. In the "Parable of the Raft" found in the sutra *The Parable of the Snake,* Buddha makes it crystal clear that even the Four Noble Truths must be let go of when they have served their purpose of assisting the individual in becoming released from *dukkha.* To become attached to and dependent upon the Four Noble Truths indicates that the individual still sees aspects of existence as permanent, substantial, and independent. This being the case, the individual is still subject to *dukkha.*

> Monks! I will speak to you the dharma of the parable of the raft for crossing over to the other shore and not retaining. Listen attentively. Be thoughtful and mindful. I will speak. The monks said, "We are willing to, are happy to, and want to listen. This we agree to world honored one." Thus the world-honored one said, "Monks! The parable has a man traveling on a mountain path and he sees a great river. The shore on this side is dangerous and furthermore frightening. The shore on the other side is peaceful and not frightening. In addition to go from this shore to the other shore there is neither boat to cross over with nor a bridge. That man thinks, "This is a very large river and moreover this shore is dangerous and frightening, while the other shore is peaceful and not frightening. In addition to go from this shore to that shore I do not have a boat to cross over with or a bridge. So! I will gather grass, wood, branches and leafs to make a raft. Depending on this raft and the effort of my hands and feet, I will cross over to that peaceful and secure shore." Monks! Thereupon that man gathered grass, wood, branches and leafs and made a raft. Depending on the raft and the effort of his hands and feet, he crossed over to that peaceful and secure shore. Crossing over he reached the other shore. Having reached the other shore he might give rise to the thought, "This raft was very beneficial to me. Depending on this raft and the effort of my hands and feet, I reached this peaceful and secure shore. This being so, I should place the raft on my head or perhaps carry it on my shoulders. Like this I would want to move onward." Monks! What about his thought? Should he act with the raft in this way? The monks said, "Not so, world-honored one." Monks! Suppose that man who crossed the river and arrived at the other shore had another thought and said, "This raft was very beneficial to me. I depended upon this raft and the effort of my hands and feet to reach this peaceful and secure shore. So, I will take this raft and perhaps place it on the river bank or submerge it in the back water. Like this I would want to move onward." Monks! That man acting in this way toward that raft is acting how he should act. Monks! In this way I speak the dharma of the parable of the raft which is for crossing over to the other shore and not for retaining. Monks! If you truly understand the raft parable then you should abandon the true mental objects. How much more the false mental objects? (*The Parable of the Snake*)[7]

Mental objects or thoughts are simply mental objects. Even if they are extremely beneficial to the individual in overcoming *dukkha* or chronic stress, they are still mental objects or thoughts. They must be seen as being impermanent, nonsubstantial, and interdependent. If even true, good and beneficial mental objects should not be craved for and must be abandoned or let go of, then certainly false, bad, and detrimental mental objects should not be craved for and must be abandoned or let go of.

The basis for nonjudgmentally observing mental objects or thoughts as being impermanent, nonsubstantial, and interdependent is the practice of mindfulness. Release from *dukkha* or chronic stress cannot occur as a result of faith, belief in the Buddha, books, logical arguments, scientific inquiry, or through the process of reasoning. Release is based on the direct experience of the individual during the practice of mindfulness. The truth about the nature of existence can only be validated by the individual through the direct experience of nonjudgmentally observing the four dwellings of mindfulness.

Correct Concentration

Friends, now what is Correct Concentration? Now monks, it is being separate from all sensory desire, apart from all evil and unskilled methods, it has discovery and analysis, it is born due to detachment, and it is happy and joyful. This is the place of the initial meditation [*dhyana*]. Causing discovery and analysis to stop, entering where the mind is peaceful, still, focused on one point, without discovery and analysis, it is born due to concentration, happy and joyful. It is the second meditation. And so it is with the place of the third and fourth meditations. Friends, this is Correct Concentration. (*Analysis of the Noble Truths*)

Correct Concentration is a meditative process in which the practitioner is trained to develop a one-pointed internal focus. The practitioner gradually becomes more focused and internally absorbed as he or she moves through the four levels of meditation. It is training of the mind that results in freedom from distraction and total oneness. The initial meditation is one of joy and happiness; the individual is detached and free from sensory desire, yet still engaged in discovery and analysis. As the practitioner becomes more internally focused and absorbed, he or she becomes less distracted and moves into the second level of meditation, where discovery and analysis stop. At this point the practitioner's mind is still and the experience of peacefulness, happiness, and joy is present.

This passage quoted, on the eighth component of the Eightfold Path—Correct Concentration—does not provide a description of the third and fourth meditations. It appears the written tradition followed the original oral tradition, Buddha did not write anything down, and assumed the disciple had familiarity with what was entailed by the third and fourth meditations. A description, with varying degrees of detail, of the third and fourth meditations can be found in other sutras.

The third meditation, essentially, eliminates happiness and retains joy. The fourth meditation eliminates joy, in fact all sensation is eliminated (neither suffering nor joy), and focuses on the place of abandonment or renunciation, mindfulness, and purity. The process of Correct Concentration leads the practitioner through varying degrees of absorption until all sensation and perception is stopped. The practitioner's mind/heart is free.

Table 4.4   The Four Meditations of Correct Concentration

Meditation	Content
First	1. Separate from all sensory desire 2. Apart from evil and unskilled methods 3. Discovery and analysis 4. Born due to detachment 5. Happy and joyful
Second	1. Discovery and analysis stop 2. Mind peaceful and still 3. Focus on one point 4. Born due to concentration 5. Happy and joyful
Third	1. Happiness eliminated 2. Joyful
Fourth	1. Joy eliminated 2. Sensation and perception stop

It is clear, however, that mindfulness guides the entire process of Correct Concentration including coming out of the final absorption where sensation and perception is stopped. In one sense, Correct Concentration appears to demonstrate that even levels of altered consciousness, often referred to as mystical states or union with a deity, are subject to impermanence, nonsubstantiality, and interdependence. For Buddha, nothing escapes impermanence, nonsubstantiality, and interdependence. Nothing!

Stress Management and Buddha

Buddha clearly indicates that the fundamental problem of human existence is that human beings suffer, are dissatisfied, and for all intents and purposes, are chronically stressed (allostatic load). He called this *dukkha*. This is the fundamental condition of human beings. Chronic stress prevents people from fully adapting to their environment.

Buddha indicated that the cause of chronic stress or *dukkha* is twofold: craving and ignorance. Ignorance refers to the fact that people believe, view, and act toward existence as if it is permanent, substantial, and independent. Psychologically, this gives people a sense of certainty and thus, security. With this sense of certainty and security, fears and threats seem to be reduced or eliminated. Because this viewpoint appears, on the surface, to work, it is functional, it is maintained.

Because people believe, view, and act toward existence as if it is permanent, substantial, and independent, they crave or desire things (material and/or immaterial) under the impression that they can actually possess and maintain these things. People become chronically stressed trying to possess and maintain things (they are threatened if they don't have it), and once they believe that they have actually possessed and are maintaining something, they become chronically stressed because they are fearful (threatened) of losing it.

Craving is also linked to avoidance or aversion. People do not want to have unpleasant experiences or feelings. Thus they crave for a life devoid of unpleasantness or of aversive conditions. As people view unpleasant feelings and experiences as if they were somehow permanent, substantial, and independent, as if somehow they should not be expected to have to feel uncomfortable, they attempt to avoid them or situations that may give rise to them. When the unpleasantness occurs anyhow, people become stressed because existence is not behaving how they expect it to behave. In their attempt to cope with the stress of being uncomfortable, craving the nonexistence of unpleasantness, people often engage in such dysfunctional behaviors as eating disorders, alcohol abuse, substance abuse, physical violence, hostility, anxiety, and depression.

For Buddha, the problem is that people are trying to make that which is impermanent, nonsubstantial, and interdependent, existence itself, into something that is permanent, substantial, and independent. This cannot occur! It never has! It never will! This is why people are chronically stressed. This is why there is *dukkha*. Existence, any aspect of it, does not behave the way people, who view it from the perspective of permanence, substantiality, and independence, want it to behave. It will not sit still. It continues to change. This being the case, it is not possible to actually possess and maintain anything. There is no thing that is permanent, substantial, and independent. Unfortunately, people believe, view, and act otherwise. Thus when existence does not behave according to their viewpoint and beliefs, they feel threatened (could they be wrong?) and become chronically stressed.

Buddha, without a single doubt, indicated that there is a release from *dukkha* or chronic stress. People can be free and happy in an environment that is impermanent, nonsubstantial, and interdependent. Thus there is a clear goal for his teachings: freedom from chronic stress.

Buddha's goal can be attained by following his *dukkha* management/ stress management program: the Eightfold Path. This stress management plan is a holistic approach to eliminating chronic stress. It addresses the individual at the cognitive, affective, behavioral, and interpersonal levels. Fundamentally, Buddha's approach is about changing the individual's view of existence and their behavior within their various environmental contexts. His focus is on assisting individuals in changing how they think, feel, and interact relative to overcoming or eliminating chronic stress.

At the cognitive level, the individual needs to become aware of, examine, and analyze the Four Noble Truths. It is about understanding and being aware of existence as being impermanent, nonsubstantial, and interdependent. It is becoming aware of the fact that one's worldview gives rise to chronic stress or *dukkha*. It is thinking about not doing harm, about not being hateful and angry, and about ending chronic stress. It is about eliminating negative thoughts. It is about removing perceived threats that are maintained due to negative thinking. It is about developing concentration. It is about developing one's attending skills, becoming focused, and being nonjudgmental in all interactions. It is learning how to be flexibly focused without getting distracted. It is about being aware of, attending to, and participating in the here and now. It is about having one's mind centered and stable. It is learning about being proactive and in control. It is learning how to be cognitively disciplined.

At the affective or emotional level, the focus is about individuals being aware of feelings or emotions when they are having them. It is about the individuals being aware of not having a feeling or emotion when they are not having it. At this level, the goal is to eliminate hurtful and harmful emotions relative to oneself and to other people. It is the removal of such emotions as hate, anger, hostility, anxiety, fear, depression, and worry. It is about being at peace with oneself and the environment wherein one exists.

At the interpersonal level it is about doing no harm. It is about not killing another person, not stealing, and not being physically/psychologically violent or abusive. It is about speaking in a truthful manner, not lying, not being insulting, not being malicious, not whining, not criticizing, not complaining, and not being demeaning. It is oriented toward removing negative speech that results in chronic stress both for the individual and for other people. The focus is on learning how to speak in a manner that creates an environment that is conducive to growth and well-being. The interpersonal level is about engaging in a livelihood that is not harmful, physically and/or psychologically, to oneself or others. The interpersonal level is about behaviors that are conducive to development, growth, and the removal of *dukkha* or chronic stress.

The behaviors at the cognitive, affective/emotional, and interpersonal levels are driven by Correct Effort and guided by the practice of Correct Mindfulness. Correct Effort is the enthusiasm, commitment, and motivation to eliminate chronic stress/*dukkha* and change how one views and behaves in the world. Correct Mindfulness is the practice of nonjudgmentally observing oneself (internally and externally) during all behaviors and the world wherein one behaves and interacts with others. Mindfulness is the essential practice of the teachings of Buddha. Actually, it is not so much a practice or technique as it is a way to encounter all aspects of existence. Mindfulness is a way of living life.

The Eightfold Path is a treatment plan, guided by mindfulness, that prepares the individual for release from *dukkha* or chronic stress. It is about removing chronic negativity from all aspects of the individual's life. It is oriented toward creating a positive and growth-producing environment. Ultimately, the Eightfold Path is about teaching an individual how to engage and embrace life while letting life engage and embrace the individual.

Summary

The teachings of Buddha clearly fit the three component structure of the bamboo bridge relative to (1) evolutionary theory and evolutionary psychology; (2) the stress response, which is activated when threats, relative to adapting, are perceived in the environment, and maintained (chronic stress) when the threats are not removed; and (3) the development of a treatment plan, a stress management program, to eliminate the source of the threats and the chronic stress. Both evolutionary theory and psychology and the teachings of Buddha view the continual process of change as a fundamental aspect of existence. Both see human beings involved in solving challenges relative to successfully adapting to the environment. For Buddha, chronic stress or *dukkha* is the fundamental problem for all human beings. Because of the prevalence of chronic stress or *dukkha,* people cannot successfully adapt to their various environmental contexts.

The source or cause of the perceived threats is ignorance and craving. It is ignorance and craving that give rise to the perceived threats and results in chronic stress. The presence of chronic stress prevents individuals from successfully adapting to their environment.

The Eightfold Path is the treatment plan or stress management program leading to the removal of ignorance and craving which then results in the elimination of *dukkha* or chronic stress. This being the case, individuals will be able to successfully adapt to their various environmental contexts.

The treatment plan or stress management program is centered on the practice of mindfulness. Mindfulness allows the individual to directly experience, at four levels or dwellings, the impermanence, nonsubstantiality, and interdependence of all aspects of experience. It is this direct experience that removes ignorance and craving, and thus *dukkha* or chronic stress.

For Buddha, the removal of ignorance and craving, and thus *dukkha,* cannot occur as a result of faith or belief in the Buddha, faith or belief some deity, listening to, reading or chanting Buddha's teachings as found in sutras or books, other sutras or books, lectures, discussions with others, or by rational or logical arguments. It can only occur through the direct experience of practicing mindfulness.

Buddha points out that even his teachings are subject to impermanence, nonsubstantiality, and interdependence. The practitioner must not crave for Buddha's teachings or attempt to make them permanent, substantial, or independent. In the "Parable of the Raft," he indicates that once the raft has served its purpose and carried the person to the other shore, the raft should be left behind. It would make no sense to carry the raft on one's head as the individual moved forward on the land of the other shore. The raft was symbolic for Buddha's own teachings. Once they have served their purpose, do not hold on to them. As is everything else, they are subject to impermanence, nonsubstantiality, and interdependence. To hold on to them would indicate that the individual was still entangled in *dukkha* or chronic stress.

The teachings of Buddha also fit the Daoist teachings guiding this ext of beginning points, simplicity, and commonality. The beginning points are *dukkha,* ignorance, and craving. The Four Noble Truths are quite simple: there is an adaptive problem, there is a cause, the problem can be solved, and there is a way of solving the problem. The commonality is quite obvious as everyone, no matter what culture they are from, have, essentially, the same physical and psychological mechanisms as result of the evolutionary process. This being the case, all humans have the fight-or-flight response and are subject to chronic stress. All human beings, no matter what culture, are attempting to solve adaptive problems in their various environmental contexts.

Finally, it is quite apparent, as noted in Chapter 1, that the Four Noble Truths are the forerunner to the diagnostic process used in psychotherapy and counseling: (1) diagnosis of the problem (say, depression); (2) theory-based cause of the problem (for example, cognitive therapy such as Rational Emotive Behavior Therapy (REBT) would view irrational thoughts as the cause of the depression); (3) the goal of the treatment (removal of the depression), and (4) the theory-based treatment. REBT would dispute the irrational thoughts, replace the irrational thoughts with rational thoughts, and then link the rational thoughts with the new, more positive feelings that are expected to occur as a result of the rational thoughts.

Important Terms

Correct Action

Correct Concentration

Correct Effort

Correct Life

Correct Mindfulness

Correct Seeing

Correct Speaking

Correct Thinking

Craving

Dukkha

Eightfold Path

Four Noble Truths

Ignorance

Impermanence

Interdependence

Nonsubstantiality

Exercises

A. Correct Speech and Correct Effort are important components of the Eightfold Path. Select a 24-hour period, say a Saturday, and practice Correct Effort and Correct Speech in all of your interpersonal encounters. Commit yourself (Correct Effort) to practice Correct Speech. Only speak in a positive and supportive manner (Correct Speech) both to yourself and to others. No whining, complaining, criticizing, moaning, nitpicking, sarcasm, or judging. Say nothing that can be construed as being harmful. Remember, to practice Correct Effort and Correct Speech, you must practice Correct Mindfulness. Be fully engaged and attentive (flexibly focused) in the here and now without being judgmental.

B. What do you observe in yourself and others when you engage in Correct Speech? When others speak in a negative or harmful manner, what do you observe and feel? How can Correct Effort and Correct Speech be helpful to you as a counselor? How can teaching a client Correct Effort and Correct speech be helpful to a client?

Chinese Characters

ª 念	ᵉ 痴
ᵇ 今	ᶠ 禺
ᶜ 心	ᵍ 广
ᵈ 愚	ʰ 知

Notes

1. The translations/interpretations, from the Chinese, of the Buddhist texts in this chapter are my own. The Chinese text for *Analysis of the Noble Truths* can be found at Jie Zhuang Buddhist Educational Web Site at http://www.jcedu.org/fxzd/ah/zb/16.htm. The Chinese *Agama* version of this text can be found in the *Madhyamagama*, number 31 [0467b01]. The *Madhyamagama* can be found at McRae (2003), the *Electronic Texts of the Chinese Buddhist Canon* Web site, T1, No. 26, located at http://www.indiana.edu/~asialink/canon.html. An English version, translated from the original Pali, can be found in Horner (1967), *The Collection of the Middle Length Sayings* (*Majhima-Nikaya*), Vol. III, No. 141, "Discourse on the Analysis of the Truths."

2. See Chapter 2 for a discussion of the five components of the self.

3. The Chinese text for *The Dwellings of Mindfulness* can be found at the Web site http://www.jcedu.org/fxzd/ah/zb/2.htm#10. The Chinese *Agama* version of this text can be found in the *Madhyamagama*, number 98 [0582b08]. The *Madhyamagama* can be found at McRae (2003), the *Electronic Texts of the Chinese Buddhist Canon* Web site, T1, No. 26, located at http://www.indiana.edu/~asialink/canon.html. An English version, translated from the original Pali, can be found in Horner (1967), *The Collection of the Middle Length Sayings* (*Majhima-Nikaya*), Vol. I, No. 10, "Discourse on the Application of Mindfulness."

4. The Chinese text for *The Metaphor of the Elephant's Footprint, Greater* can be found at the Web site http://www.jcedu.org/fxzd/ah/zb/4.htm#28. The Chinese *Agama* version of this text can be found in the *Madhyamagama*, number 30 [0464b19]. The *Madhyamagama* can be found at McRae (2003), the *Electronic Texts of the Chinese Buddhist Canon* Web site, T1, No. 26, located at http://www .indiana.edu/~asialink/canon.html. An English version, translated from the original Pali, can be found in Horner (1967), *The Collection of the Middle Length Sayings (Majhima-Nikaya),* Vol. I, No. 28, "The Simile of the Elephant's Footprint (Greater)."

5. The Chinese text for *Many Boundaries* can be found at the Web site http://www.jcedu.org/fxzd/ah/zb/13.htm#115. The Chinese *Agama* version of this text can be found in the *Madhyamagama*, number 81 [0723a10]. The *Madhyamagama* can be found at McRae (2003), the *Electronic Texts of the Chinese Buddhist Canon* Web site, T1, No. 26, located at http://www.indiana.edu/~asialink/ canon.html. An English version, translated from the original Pali, can be found in Horner (1967), *The Collection of the Middle Length Sayings (Majhima-Nikaya),* Vol. III, No. 115, "Discourse on the Manifold Elements."

6. The Chinese text for *Analysis of Elements* can be found at the Web site http://www.jcedu.org/fxzd/ah/zb/15.htm#140. The Chinese *Agama* version of this text can be found in the *Madhyamagama*, number 162 [0690a20]. The *Madhyamagama* can be found at McRae (2003), the *Electronic Texts of the Chinese Buddhist Canon* Web site, T1, No. 26, located at http://www.indiana.edu/ ~asialink/canon.html. An English version, translated from the original Pali, can be found in Horner (1967), *The Collection of the Middle Length Sayings (Majhima-Nikaya),* Vol. III, No. 140, "Discourse on the Analysis of the Elements."

7. The Chinese text for *The Parable of the Snake* can be found at the Web site http://www.jcedu.org/fxzd/ah/zb/4.htm#22. The Chinese *Agama* version of this text can be found in the *Ekottaragamma*, number 38 [0759c29]. The *Ekottaragamma* can be found at McRae (2003), the *Electronic Texts of the Chinese Buddhist Canon* Web site, T2, No. 125, located at http://www.indiana.edu/~asialink/canon.html. An English version, translated from the original Pali, can be found in Horner (1967), *The Collection of the Middle Length Sayings (Majhima-Nikaya),* Vol. III, No. 22, "The Parable of the Water Snake."

References

Ch'en, K. (1972). *Buddhism in China: A historical survey.* Princeton, NJ: Princeton University Press.

Conze, E. (1970). *Buddhist thought in India.* Ann Arbor: University of Michigan Press.

Horner, I. B. (Trans.). (1967). *The collection of the Middle Length Sayings (Majjhima-Nikaya), Vol. III: The final fifty discourses (Uparipannasa).* London: Luzac & Company.

Jie Zhuang Buddhist Educational Web Site. (n.d.). Available at http://jcedu.org/ index.php

Jordan, M. (1998). *Eastern wisdom.* New York: Marlowe and Company.

McRae, J. R. (2003). *Electronic texts of the Chinese Buddhist canon.* Available at http://www.indiana.edu/~asialink/canon.html

Rahula, W. (1962). *What the Buddha taught.* New York: Grover Press.

5

Daoism and Stress Management

The two fundamental texts of classical Daoism are the *Dao De Jing* and the *Zhuang Zi*. Unlike the teachings of Buddha, the teachings of the *Dao De Jing* and the *Zhuang Zi* do not provide the reader with a structured format such as the Four Noble Truths. Nonetheless, the concepts of a continually changing, integrated environment, adaptive problems, chronic stress, and a solution to the problem of chronic stress are clearly present. The focus, as with the teachings of Buddha, is on the solution offered by Daoism for resolving the issue of chronic stress.

This chapter examines the teachings of the *Dao De Jing* first and then follows with an examination of the *Zhuang Zi*. In Chinese scholarly tradition, the *Dao De Jing* is analyzed and explored utilizing commentaries to the text. The two most fundamental commentaries are those of He Shang Gong (traditionally, 2nd century BCE) and Wang Bi (226–249 CE).[1] Both of these commentaries are utilized in the analysis of the *Dao De Jing* presented here.

As does Chapter 4, on Buddhism, this chapter contains extensive translations from the Chinese of both the *Dao De Jing* and the *Zhuang Zi*. To get an in-depth understanding of classical Daoism and its solution to the problem of chronic stress, it is necessary to read the classic writings (albeit they are in English and subject to my interpretation).

Dao De Jing

Chinese tradition indicates that a man named Lao Zi, an older contemporary of Confucius (551–479 BCE), was the author of the *Dao De Jing*. According to this tradition, the text was written to address the tumultuous times during the latter part of the Spring and Autumn Period (770–476 BCE), when numerous kingdoms were battling each other for power and wealth. Scholarship, on the other hand, questions the existence of the man named Lao Zi and suggests that the text was written during the Warring States Period (403–221 BCE) to address the political, social, and spiritual chaos of the time (see Ames & Hall, 2003, pp. 1–10). The very name given by the Chinese themselves to this period, the Warring States, is indicative of an environment that was quite threatening to its inhabitants (see Gascoigne, 2003, p. 28). Numerous kingdoms, driven by their own greed to obtain as much wealth, land, and material goods as they could and their desire to control the behavior of others in order to maintain what they had acquired, continually fought among themselves.

Hucker (1975) notes that the Warring States Period was one of continual, confounding, hurried change that impacted upon almost all facets of living (pp. 37–40). Change itself is stressful, but the fact that it was confusing and rapid creates an environmental context that would appear to be a prime example for the development of allostatic load or chronic stress. Gernet (1999) described the Warring States Period as a time of tremendous, swift transformation at all levels of society (pp. 62–82). Again, this contextual upheaval is indicative of a stress-producing environment. It is clear from the context in which the *Dao De Jing* was written and from reading the text itself that chronic stress, across all levels of society, was a significant problem.

The Problem of War

The *Dao De Jing* makes it clear that warfare and battle create an environment that is quite stressful for all people. It is an environment that threatens their very survival. Chapter 30 states:

Where an army dwells, thistles and thorns are produced. Famine for years is what certainly follows an extended army.[2]

The commentary of Wang Bi (226–249 CE) to this passage in Chapter 30 is even more telling. The army and its warfare destroy life on all levels:

This means the army is a terrible and destructive thing. There is nothing which it helps, it is certainly harmful. It destroys the people and devastates the land. Thus it is said: Thistles and thorns are produced.

The physical environment is literally torn up. The people are confronted with the two most fundamental adaptive problems presented to all human organisms: those of safety and maintaining a regular source of energy (food). Warfare and battle so significantly compromise these adaptive challenges that the people are chronically starved and/or live in constant fear of being destroyed. This is certainly an example of allostatic load.

The concern with the apparent constancy of the warfare and its devastating results can be seen in Chapter 31 of the *Dao De Jing*. The *Dao De Jing* speaks to the ever-presence, and at times the necessity, of war and of the need to not take delight in the destruction of life:

> Weapons are utensils of misfortune. They are not the utensils of the ruler. When there is no alternative, they will be used. To be indifferent to fame and gain is the highest action. The vanquishing of others is not a pretty sight. To say it is a pretty sight is to take joy in the killing of men. Those who take joy in the killing of men will not attain satisfaction in the world.

The Problem of Government

The *Dao De Jing* points out that warfare and battle are not the only source of the people's famine and the destruction to the land. When the government and aristocracy are not concerned about the welfare of the people, the people will starve and the land will be damaged. The self-serving actions of the government and the aristocracy wreak havoc on the life of the people. In reference to the behavior of the government and the aristocracy relative to the consequence to the people, Chapter 53 states:

> Their courts are very clean. Yet the fields are very much overgrown with weeds. The warehouses are very empty, yet their clothes are patterned and colorful. Sharp swords are carried in their belts. They are satiated with food and drink. They have a surplus of wealth and commodities. This is called stealing and bragging.

Chapter 75 reinforces this notion of the inappropriate behavior by the government by noting:

> The people are starving because those above are eating them up with excessive taxes. That is why there is starvation.

The government creates taboos, commands, laws, demands, and expectations about the correct behavior of the people. The people are told how to think, feel, and act. Chapter 75 continues by focusing on the consequences of external, rigid control by the government on the people:

> The people are difficult to manage because those above try to control them. This is why they are difficult to manage. The people make light of death because those above demand too much of their lives.

When the government constantly interferes with the lives of the people, the people become stressed. In an environment where there is continual battle, killing, starvation, excessive taxes, ongoing external control of the lives of the people, incessant demands by the government, and unvarying expectations regarding norms for proper behavior, there is a significant toll on the physical and psychological well-being of the people. Chapter 58 clearly points this out:

> When the government is inspecting and scrutinizing, the people become defective and broken.

The commentary of Wang Bi to this chapter sheds light on the undermining, through the actions of the government, of the very nature of the people:

> It establishes performance, role, clear rewards, and punishments in order to examine for unfaithfulness and hypocrisy. Thus it is said it is inspecting and scrutinizing. These categories divide up the mind/heart of the people into contentiousness and fear. Thus it is said the people are defective and broken.

This ongoing division, by authority figures, of behavior into specified categories of appropriate behavior fragments the mind/hearts of the people such that they are chronically stressed, confused, and disorganized. Psychologically, they are dysfunctional. Their natural behavior becomes contrived, controlled, and reactive. The people have assimilated the values, standards, laws, expectations, desires, distinctions, roles, rituals, ceremonies, and educational processes that the ruling class has imposed on them to control their behavior. They have essentially accepted the worldview of those in authority. This worldview and contrived behavior results in a significant negative impact on the very stability of society and its people. Chapter 57 elucidates this quite clearly:

> When the world has too many taboos, the people will be very impoverished. When the people have too many sharp weapons, the State will be disorganized and confused. When the people have too many contrived skills and strategies, strange things multiply and rise up. When laws and commands are increased and made known, there will be more robbers and bandits.

The implementation, by the government, of external guidelines for the moral behavior of the people is an indication, from the perspective of the *Dao De Jing*, that the natural sense of being in harmony with the environment has been lost. The natural respect and kindness that people have for each other as human organisms has been replaced by contrived, artificial values that people are expected to learn, follow, and not question. Their behavior is being driven by fear, seeking rewards and avoiding punishment. They are focused on pleasing others in order to receive external praise and acceptance.

> When the extended *dao*[i] is lost, there will be benevolence and morally appropriate choices. When wisdom and intelligence are produced, there will be extended hypocrisy. When the six relationships are not in harmony, there will be filial piety and kindness. When the states are confused and disordered, loyal ministers will appear. (*Dao De Jing*, 18)

This move from concrete, natural reality (*dao*[i]) to the more superficial, artificial, contrived values (benevolence, morally appropriate choices, wisdom, intelligence, filial piety, and kindness) of the ruling class lays the foundation for a confused and disordered social structure. This structure creates an environment that is conducive to chronic stress.

> When the *dao*[i] is lost, virtue appears next. When virtue is lost, benevolence appears next. When benevolence is lost, morally appropriate choices appear next. When morally appropriate choices are lost, proper ritualistic behavior appears next. When proper, ritualistic behavior is lost, there is the superficiality of loyalty and trust, and the beginning of confusion and disorder. (*Dao De Jing*, 38)

Worldviews and the Problem of Language

During the time period that the *Dao De Jing* was compiled and written, there were numerous solutions offered by various thinkers to address the social and political instability among the various kingdoms. (See, for example, Fung, 1983, pp. 132–169.) The representatives of each of these solutions argued among themselves, trying to convince each other through rational argument and abstract concepts that their own perspective or viewpoint of the world was correct and that of their opponent was incorrect.[3] Their perspectives, as well as their thinking, were absolute and rigid.

From the perspective of the *Dao De Jing*, solutions to the problem of stabilizing and adapting to the environment that focus on absolute, abstract, ornate language are not adequate and are disconnected from the world wherein people actually live. To believe that through winning arguments and debates, the winner somehow has the correct solution to the adaptive problem is misguided. To assume that the more knowledge you display somehow means that you must truly understand the problem and are able to offer an acceptable solution is not realistic. The opening lines of Chapter 81 of the *Dao De Jing* state:

Flowery words are not authentic. Authentic words are not flowery. The expert does not argue. He who argues is not an expert. Those who know are not erudite. Those who are erudite do not know.

It is clear that the solution offered by the *Dao De Jing* to the problem of stabilizing and adapting to the environment does not involve flowery language, debate, argument, or parading about elevated levels of accumulated knowledge. It seems, for the *Dao De Jing,* that flowery language, debates, arguments, and accumulated knowledge result in a disconnect from the concrete world wherein people laugh, cry, and dance.

The *Dao De Jing* appears to suggest that words and names can take on a life of their own. These words and names start to define the various theories regarding the problem of stabilizing and adapting to the environment and the subsequent solutions generated from the theories. When theories, words, and names take on a life of their own, they are disconnected from the world wherein people live. They become, in a sense, actual, separate things. Individuals argue and debate about these theories, names, and words to the extent that these things become more real than the processes from which they emerged. Individuals argue for the correctness of their own theories, names, and words and the incorrectness of their opponents' perspective relative to their theories, names, and words.

As these individuals argue with each other , the arbitrator for right and wrong, truth and falsity, and good and evil becomes rationality. Rational argument and the subsequent logically consistent conclusions drawn from the rational argument determine the nature of right and wrong, truth and falsity, and good and evil. Rationality, through its theories, language, and arguments, defines reality and delineates the social structure.

From this perspective, the wise person or expert is the person who is successful in argument and debate. The intelligent person is the one who accumulates abstract knowledge. The ethical person is wise and intelligent relative to ethical theories, names, and words. These individuals believe that the rational world, made up of its language, theories, names, and rules, is unchanging. Words, names, terms become more real than the behavior they represent. Insofar as the rational world is believed to be unchanging, the participants assume they can clearly define right and wrong, good and evil, and so on. To the extent that they can clearly define the world, they believe they should, and in fact must, control individuals and their behavior in the social world.

Appropriate behavioral and ethical standards are defined and imposed externally onto the individual through the application of language within the context of rationality. Through this external controlling of behavior it is believed that the social world will be stabilized and people will be able to adapt to their environment.

When the focus of individuals is directed toward language, theories, names, and rationality, the natural, concrete, and spontaneous way of behaving in the world is lost. On the other hand, when this artificial framework is rejected, people behave in a natural, concrete, and spontaneous manner. Chapter 19 states:

> Reject sacredness, discard wisdom, the people will benefit a hundredfold. Reject human heartedness, discard right choice, the people will return to filial piety and compassion. Reject slyness, discard profit, there will be no robbers and thieves.

If the contrived, abstract, externally imposed framework is cast off, then the people will be able to act in a natural manner. Harmonious relations with others, filial piety, and compassion will be naturally and spontaneously generated from the people. The social structure will stabilize.

The *Dao De Jing* clearly rejects the external imposing of "truths" and values. Requiring people to learn, not to question, and to accept a set of artificial, contrived values, standards, needs, and "truths" is part of the cause, according the *Dao De Jing,* of political and social unrest. This is unmistakably pointed out in the opening lines of Chapter 3:

> Not honoring the worthy enables people not to contend. Not valuing goods difficult to obtain enables the people not to be robbers. Not looking at what may be desirable enables the people not to have a confused mind/heart.

The power brokers in society, through an abstract, artificial, contrived process, determine who is worthy to be honored, what goods difficult to be obtained should be valued, and what things should be desired by the people. The power brokers then externally impose their conclusions in these areas, through some process of education, onto the people. The people, having learned what being worthy means, who or what should be honored, what rare goods are valuable, and what needs and desires they should have, become confused, and begin to argue and steal.

That having to learn these artificial values is psychologically problematic for the people can be seen in Chapter 20:

> To be without chronic stress [*you*[a]] become disentangled from learning. How far apart are a prompt respectful answer and a groan? How far apart are good and evil? That which people fear it is not possible not to fear. How absurd! Will this never end!

This disentanglement is not to be construed as a blanket rejection of all learning. It is simply pointing out that people will be psychologically better off if they do not get entangled in the process of learning, accepting, and not questioning a set of absolute, abstract, artificial, and contrived standards, values, and needs to direct their behavior. To become entangled in this type of learning allows others and the affairs of the world to control one's actions (you must follow the learning of others and society's commands), and causes the individual to interfere with one's own actions (contrived doubt and fear, and so on, based on learning) and the actions of others (controlling their behavior to be consistent with what has been learned).

The very edifice of unchanging, absolute, conceptual truths, which an externally imposed set of standards, values, and needs rests upon, is dismantled in Chapter 2 of the *Dao De Jing*. Chapter 2 questions the very assumption of unchanging, absolute, independent names, words, and "truths" as it points out the relativity of language.

> When all in the world know beauty as beauty, there is ugliness. When all in the world know good as good, there is not good. Thus, space and form produce each other, difficult and easy complete each other, long and short form each other, above and below collapse into each other, tone and sound harmonize with each other, and front and back follow each other.

The *Dao De Jing* is obviously questioning and raising significant concerns with language itself and the impact it has on the social and political stability (chronic stress) of the environment in which it is applied. It is not, however, denying the use of language or terms to describe or communicate ideas and thoughts about the environment in which people live and dwell. The entire text uses language and terms to communicate about and describe many states of affairs, including how to adapt to the environment itself. It is important to realize, however, that language can only go so far. Once language starts becoming crystallized into absolute worldviews, thinking, judgments, values, norms, and standards, problems arise.

People argue, contend, and go to battle with each other over their absolute worldviews, ideas, value, norms, and standards. People mistake the map (language and all it generates) for the territory (the environment of simple, practical experience). This language-generated focus on endpoints, complexity, and differences pulls people out of the concrete present into an abstract, absolute realm that gives rise to chronic stress. From the perspective of the *Dao De Jing*, people must recognize the limitations of language. It has a practical, concrete function. When it moves past this practical, concrete function, people must not follow it. People must know when to stop. This concept of knowing when to stop is clearly stated in Chapter 32 of the *Dao De Jing*:

> The organization of the world begins with names. Names being established, people must know when to stop. As a result of knowing to stop, there is no danger.

Ames and Hall (2003), in their commentary to this section, note the importance of language and the practical, functional distinctions it provides. At the same time, however, they point out the dangers of language becoming crystallized.

> In order to function effectively in managing our environment, we need distinctions. These distinctions in themselves are functional and enabling, but once established, can take on a life of their own. We quickly fall into the trap of turning names into things, so that these names identify some more real "I-know-not-what" that stands independent of the now "superficial" way in which we actually experience any particular event. We misinterpret the persistence within process as some underlying foundation of our experience. Rational structures become institutionalized and, given enough time, petrified. The regimen of values they carry with them, empowering some against the others, become entrenched and uncompromising. What began as a convenience takes over, constraining the very experience it was created to facilitate, and in so doing, robs life of its creative vigor. (p. 127)

When language becomes a world of its own, the ruling class, the aristocracy, the intellectuals, and even the common people argue and contend over the absolute meaning of their perspectives, names, words, and terms. The intellectuals and ruling elite then impose upon the people their absolute meaning of names, words, and terms relative to commanding the people to behave in a manner that is consistent with the absolute meaning of the names, terms and words. The abstract, unchanging names, words and terms become the external standard that supposedly will stabilize and overcome the political and social unrest. For the *Dao De Jing,* these abstract, absolute perspectives, names, terms, and words are not the solution to stabilizing and overcoming the political and social unrest. In fact, these abstract, absolute perspectives, standards, values, names, terms, and words are a primary cause of the problem of social and political unrest.

The *Dao De Jing,* again, is not rejecting the use of language, names, words, and terms. It is, however, pointing out that language, names, words, and terms are relative and that any attempt to move beyond the normal, relative, descriptive, and communicative function of language will result in significant problems. In Chapter 70, the *Dao De Jing* clearly indicates that it uses words but also points out the connection of its use of words with the state of affairs from which the words emerged:

> My words are very easy to understand, very easy to practice. In the world no one is able to understand, no one is able to practice. Words have an ancestor. Interactions have a sovereign.

Chapter 70 is simply stating that the solution the *Dao De Jing* is offering focuses on simplicity, commonality, and beginning points. Its words are quite simple; anyone can understand and practice them. They are common to all. They have a beginning point, which is the here and now of existence itself. The here and now is the source or ancestor of words. The here and now is wherein all interactions occur. The here and now is self-sufficient and facilitates all.

The problem is that the world of the people is one of generated complexity, differences, and endpoints, and thus no one can understand or practice the teachings. This is because people in general are entangled in a worldview based on abstract, absolute language, names, words, and terms resulting in a disconnect from the ancestor: the ordinary, commonplace, yet very magical here and now. The present! The commentary of Wang Bi to this section states:

> It is possible to understand yet not leave the house or look out the window. Thus the saying "they [my words] are very easy to understand." Not interfering [*wu wei*ᵇ] yet successful. Thus the saying "they are very easy to practice." Confused by restless desires, thus the saying "they are not able to be understood." Enchanted by glory and wealth, thus the saying "they are not able to be practiced."

The commentary of Wang Bi clearly indicates that the reason people are not able to understand the words of the *Dao De Jing* and are not able to put them into practice is that their worldview is problematic. Because of their worldview, people are entangled in the affairs of the world. People are confused by their numerous desires and are captivated by glory and wealth. The worldview of the people, and thus of each individual, is made up of and controlled by absolute, rigid, inflexible, abstract values, standards, concepts, theories, and judgments.

The worldview of the people focuses on and is guide by complexity, differences, and endpoints. They are under the control of the map and are disconnected from the territory. This being the case, people compete, contend, and interfere for the purpose of controlling the behavior and property of other people. It is this worldview and the subsequent behavior generated from it that gives rise to the chronic stress for which the *Dao De Jing* offers a solution for managing and eliminating.

The Solution

The solution offered by the *Dao De Jing* for removal of both chronic stress and the disharmonious social structure is threefold: (1) still (*jing*ᶜ) and empty (*xu*ᵈ) the mind/heart of absolute, rigid, inflexible, abstract values, standards, concepts, theories, and judgments; (2) do not interfere with oneself or others (*wu wei*ᵇ); and (3) do not get entangled in the affairs of the world (*wu shi*ᵉ). All three of these components are interrelated and are based on a self-cultivation practice that requires individuals to nonjudgmentally observe and engage the environment in the present. By nonjudgmentally observing and engaging the environment in the present (*guan*[g]), individuals are able to experience existence as it is: a continually changing, noninterfering, nonentangled, supportive, and integrated process. This fundamental experience of existence results in the realization that the individual is part of this process of existence. This being the case, the individual is in harmony with existence. To be in harmony with existence is to be natural (*zi ran*[f]).[4] When people are able to be natural, society will be in harmony and chronic stress will be eliminated. The relationship between these concepts and the way they are enacted is presented in Table 5.1.

Table 5.1   Linking Basic Daoist Competencies

Concept	Meaning
jing[c]	Stillness, tranquility, quietude
	The mind/heart of the naturally integrated person/sage (*sheng ren*[o]) is still. The mind/heart is still because nothing can distract the sage.
	Being in harmony with the environment
xu[d]	Empty. Emptiness
	Because the mind/heart of the sage is still, it is empty of restrictions, limitations, absolute values, absolute concepts, and absolute perspectives.
	The mind/heart of the sage is nonjudgmental.
	Because the mind/heart of the sage is still, empty, and nonjudgmental, the sage is flexible, with unlimited potential.
	Being in harmony with the environment
guan[g]	A nonjudgmental observing of and engaging with the present
	Because the mind/heart of the sage is still and empty, existence can be observed/experienced without any limitations or restrictions.
	Being in harmony with the environment
wu wei[b]	Noninterference
	Not attempting to control, force, or coerce the behavior of other people
	Not getting in your own way. Not putting limitations, restrictions, or barriers in your own way. No moaning, complaining, whining, ruminating, criticizing, or blaming.

(Continued)

Table 5.1 (Continued)

Concept	Meaning
	Acting in a natural, open, flexible, adaptive, and healthy manner
	Continually creating environmental contexts that are conducive and supportive of growth and development for yourself and others
	Because the sage has a mind/heart that is still and empty, and is able to nonjudgmentally observe the present, the sage does not interfere. As there is no interference, there is no harm to the sage or others.
	Being in harmony with the environment
wu shi[e]	Not getting entangled in the affairs of the world. Not being controlled by the affairs of the world. Not becoming enamored with the affairs of the world. Not becoming attached to and controlled by situations, events, causes, objects, people, or other states of affairs.
	Because the sage has a mind/heart that is still and empty, is able to nonjudgmentally observe the present, and does not interfere, the sage will not get entangled in the affairs of the world.
	Being in harmony with the environment
zi ran[f]	Natural, spontaneous, flexible
	Thinking, feeling, and behaving in a natural, relaxed, centered, grounded, peaceful, and holistic manner.
	Because the sage has a mind/heart that is still and empty, is able to nonjudgmentally observe the present, does not interfere, and does not get entangled in the affairs of the world, the sage functions naturally.
	Because the sage functions naturally, the sage is in harmony with the environment.
	Being in harmony with the environment, the sage is not chronically stressed.

Stilling and Emptying the Mind/Heart (Jing *and* Xu)

According to the *Dao De Jing*, the process of self-cultivation requires the stilling and emptying of the mind and body of the thoughts, emotions, and behaviors that interfere with interacting with the here and now, the present. By stilling and emptying the mind/heart, the individual will be able to nonjudgmentally observe (*guan*g) and engage existence as it actually behaves.

Sincerely maintaining stillness [*jing*c], extreme emptiness [*xu*d] is reached. All things simultaneously acting together, I nonjudgmentally observe [*guan*g] their cycles. Things are numerous. All cycles return to their root. Returning to the root is called stillness [*jing*c]. This is said to be the cycle of destiny. The cycle of destiny is called the ordinary present. Being aware of the ordinary present is called letting the light shine forth [*ming*h]. Not to be aware of the ordinary present is to fall into darkness. Being aware of the ordinary present is to be open. To be open is to be impartial. To be impartial is to be linked. To be linked is to be with the natural environment. Being with the natural environment, then *dao*i. *Dao*i, then long lasting. To the end of the body there is no danger. (*Dao De Jing*, 16)

In his analysis of the term *guan*g, Cheng (2003) presents a lucid sense of a nonjudgmental engagement or observation of the environment wherein an individual acts. He suggests that this way of observing the environment is indeed a comprehensive experience of existence.

Guan involves an attitude of detachment and what can be described as tranquility and receptivity. It is a sense of seeking understanding and learning things without forcing any prior theoretical model onto nature and without being impeded by emotions and desires. . . . We may call *guan* phenomenological observation or a natural phenomenological method as opposed to either rational scientific methodology or the phenomenology of rationality. . . . Historically, *guan* as a method was cultivated in both the Confucian and the Daoist tradition. It was also adopted by Chinese Buddhists, who merged the meanings of comprehensive observation and inner meditation. (p. 518)

Chapter 16 provides the basis for self-cultivation that leads to the elimination of chronic stress. By maintaining stillness in feelings and thoughts, the individual will be empty of contrived absolute, judgmental, worldviews, thinking, and values. Controlling desires and feelings will be abandoned. The individual will be able to nonjudgmentally observe (*guan*g), without interference from desires, feelings, thoughts, judgments, and worldviews, that existence, including himself or herself, is a continually changing, cyclic, linked, integrated, and interrelated process.

Insofar as everything is subject to change and interrelated, the individual will have insight into the reality that a change in one area will result in a change in another area. This being the case, the individual will realize that nothing is fixed or predetermined. Every situation has many possibilities. The individual does not have to be locked into one way of thinking, feeling, behaving, or interrelating. By nonjudgmentally understanding and experiencing the process of change, the individual will come to the awareness that the many possibilities present in a situation can be altered by the individual's own behavior. By changing how one views and acts in the world, the individual can eliminate chronic stress.

Upon continual self-cultivation of stillness and emptiness, the individual will become more open and impartial in his or her thinking, feeling, behaving, and interacting in the world. The individual will realize that he or she has been disconnected from the natural environment, disconnected from being in harmony with the process of change. It is this disconnect or fragmentation from the natural environment, due to a faulty worldview, that fuels and maintains the chronic stress. For the *Dao De Jing*—for the human being, in fact—all things must be seen and experienced in relationship with the natural environment. There is no separation. This nonjudgmental relationship with the natural environment, with the process of change on all levels removes chronic stress.

The concept of *guan*^{g}, nonjudgmental observation, is further developed in Chapter 54 of the *Dao De Jing*. In this chapter, a hierarchy of cultivation, development, and progression is presented through which the individual first nonjudgmentally observes the body, then moves onto the family, the hometown, the kingdom, and finally to the entire world. In other words, puts into practice the Daoist model of beginning points, simplicity, and commonality.

That which is properly established cannot be uprooted. That which is properly embraced cannot be disconnected. Sons and grandsons presenting of offerings do not cease. Cultivated in the body, its gentle power [*de*^{j}] is real. Cultivated in the family, its gentle power [*de*^{j}] overflows. Cultivated in the hometown, its gentle power [*de*^{j}] is long lasting. Cultivated in the kingdom, its gentle power [*de*^{j}] is abundant. Cultivated in the world, its gentle power [*de*^{j}] is widespread. Therefore, nonjudgmentally observe [*guan*^{g}] the body as the body. Nonjudgmentally observe [*guan*^{g}] the family as the family. Nonjudgmentally observe [*guan*^{g}] the hometown as the hometown. Nonjudgmentally observe [*guan*^{g}] the kingdom as the kingdom. Nonjudgmentally observe [*guan*^{g}] the world as the world. How do I know the world is so? By this! (*Dao De Jing*, 54)

To nonjudgmentally observe (*guan*^{g}) the body as the body is to see and experience the body, in the present, as it is without any interfering preconceived biases, notions, values, filters, thoughts, or worldviews. This process results in the practitioner being rooted, established, engaged, linked, and connected. The practitioner has established a relationship, in the here and now, with the natural environment.

This relationship is rooted in stillness and emptiness and as such opens the individual to the natural power of *dao*[i], which in individuals or things is known as *de*[j] and is translated/interpreted here as "gentle power." It is that aspect of existence prior to the advent of distinctions, judgments, biases, value judgments, or worldviews. It is a power associated with being in harmony with the natural environment. It is the power of being natural, in harmony with the process of change, free from chronic stress and fully engaging the possibilities of existence.

The question remains, however. How does the practitioner still and empty the mind? How does the practitioner develop nonjudgmental observation (*guan*[g])? To examine this question, it is necessary to turn to Chapter 10 of the *Dao De Jing*.

> At the place where the body is managed and wholeness embraced, are you able to be without fragmentation? In relying on the breath [*qi*[k]] to deliver softness and yielding, are you able to be as an infant? In cleansing the mysterious [*xuan*[l]] vision, are you able to do it so there are no blemishes? In taking good care of the people and managing the kingdom, are you able to not interfere [*wu wei*[b]]? In the opening and closing of the sky gate, are you able to be the female? Clarity extended in all directions, are you able to be without contrived knowledge? Producing, nourishing. Producing and not possessing, acting and not having expectations, allowing growth and not restricting. This is called the mysterious gentle power [*de*[j]].

For the *Dao De Jing*, contrived desires and absolute thoughts, values, judgments, and worldviews fragment individuals from their own nature and their environment. Insofar as individuals are fragmented, they are chronically stressed. This fragmentation compromises the physical, psychological, and social functioning of individuals.

At the physical level, the most fundamental aspect of existence is compromised: that of breathing itself. When breathing is compromised, the body is out of harmony with itself and the environment of which it is part. The center or root is lost. Compromised breathing makes the body tense, rigid, exhausted, inflexible, unyielding, and open to all sorts of illness. The individual is not in the present or the here and now.

When the body is compromised, the mind/heart is compromised. When the mind/heart is compromised, the individual is subject to agitated thinking, the continual presence of ongoing thoughts, distractions, inability to focus, attending difficulties, rumination, difficulties processing information, problems with making decisions, memory difficulties, restricted choices, contrived desires and values, fear, depression, worry, anxiety, hostility, and so on. The center or root is lost. The individual is not in the present or the here and now. The individual is not whole and not integrated with the environment.

When the mind/heart is compromised, social interaction is compromised. When social interaction with others is compromised, individuals try to control others' behavior, are motivated by self-gain and benefit, interfere with others' behaviors, contend with others, are focused on winning and making others lose, are driven by attaining material goods and power, and are harmful to others and themselves. The center or root is lost. The individual is not in the present or the here and now. The individual is not whole and not integrated with the environment.

The first step, according to Chapter 10 of the *Dao De Jing*, is to get practitioners into or to focus on the present or the here and now. The fact that practitioners can bring their awareness to the here and now is an indication that they were fragmented from the ordinary present in the first place. It is too important to become aware that the body, mind, and environment are part of an integrated, continually changing process. The commentary of He Shang Gong to the first line of Chapter 10 states:

Managing the body is managing the mind and the body. As a result of being born a person has a mind and body that should be loved and nourished. Happiness and anger destroy the mind. Startle and fear damage the body. . . . Good wine and tasty meat deteriorates the liver and lungs. Therefore a mind that is stilled and committed to *dao*[i] is not confused. A body that is at peace attains long life and extends its years. This means if a person is whole there will be no fragmentation from the body. Thus the person will live a long time. Wholeness is that which *dao*[i] produced in the beginning. It is the great harmony of essential breath [*qi*[k]]. . . . Wholeness means a unified commitment. It is not a fragmentation/splitting into two.

The commentary presents a holistic approach to overcoming chronic stress. Individuals must manage both mind and body. It is clear from the commentary that an agitated mind, disturbed emotions, and an inappropriate diet can compromise the health of the mind and body of individuals. The practitioner who is in the here and now, has a stilled and focused mind/heart, is not overwhelmed by emotions, and has a healthy diet will be whole, at peace, and will live a long life. The question remains, however. How is this accomplished? The next step is focusing on the here and now, and to simply rely on the breath (*qi*[k]). It is to allow breathing to be natural. The commentary of He Shang Gong to the second line of Chapter 10 states:

Relying/allowing protects essential breath [*qi*[k]] and does not cause confusion. Thus the body is able to respond in a flexible and yielding manner. Able to be like an infant is internally to be without deliberation and externally to not force correctness in affairs. Thus essential spirit [*shen*^{m}] does not leave.

As the infant does not go through a deliberate, rationally structured, logically sequenced, rigid, inflexible, agitated, and overloaded decision-making process, the breathing of the infant is not compromised and is natural. The infant does not obsess, ruminate, or worry. As the infant does not try to coerce or force people to behave in an artificial, value-laden manner, the breathing of the infant is not compromised. The infant does not interfere in the behavior of others. With the breathing being natural, the infant is soft, flexible, unobstructed, and yielding. By allowing one's breathing to be natural and not interfered with by one's behaviors or thoughts, the practitioner will not be confused and will be able to respond in a flexible and adaptive manner. Not being confused, the mind/heart of the practitioner will be in the here and now, clear, still, and empty. There will be no chronic stress.

Given that the breath can be compromised by how an individual views, thinks about, feels, and acts in the various environmental contexts, the next step, according to the *Dao De Jing*, is to cleanse the mind/heart ("the mysterious vision"), which is naturally tranquil, still, and empty. The commentary of He Shang Gong to the third line of Chapter 10 states:

> You should wash your mind/heart allowing it to be clean and clear. The mind/heart resides in the place of profound mystery, observing and aware of all interactions. Therefore it is called the mysterious vision. There are no excessive or unhealthy thoughts that lead to illness.

When negativity, obsessions, ruminations, artificiality, rigidity, worry, and excessiveness are removed from the thinking/feeling process (mind/heart), the individual will be healthy, feel no chronic stress, and will be able to experience and fully engage existence or life itself. The here and now, the present! As long as there are restrictions or blemishes, the individual will not be able to fully engage life. The individual will remain chronically stressed.

The commentary of Wang Bi, to this same section of the *Dao De Jing*, further illustrates the necessity of removing the barriers of the mind/heart. When the barriers are removed, the individual will be able to fully observe, engage, and interact with the mystery or life itself.

> *Xuan*^{l} (mystery) is the ultimate of things. This means if you are able to wash away and eliminate the artificial, the superficial, and the contrived, reaching ultimate vision, not allowing things to compromise your brightness or blemish your spirit, then till the end of your life, you will be integrated with the mystery.

By removing the judgmental, restrictive, contrived, rigid, and artificial worldview, the individual will be able to clearly and fully experience the mystery and profoundness of the here and now. The individual will be able to experience existence as it is: a continually changing, integrated, interrelated process.

This experience also results in the realization that any viewpoint or perspective, concept, value, desire, intention, emotion, behavior, or interaction that runs counter to experiencing existence as a continually changing, noninterfering, supportive, integrated process may give rise to chronic stress and disharmony. Thus the importance, for the *Dao De Jing*, of changing how one views the world and eliminating the subsequent behavior derived from the problematic viewpoint.

Not Interfering (Wu Wei)

The second component of the approach of the *Dao De Jing* to managing stress is the practice of *wu wei*[b] or noninterference.[5] From the perspective of Daoism in general, all behavior (internal and external) is guided by *wu wei*[b] or noninterference. The practitioner of *wu wei*[b] does not interfere with himself or herself or interfere with others. At the level of the individual, the practitioner should, literally, not get in her own way. Do not let thoughts, self-imposed restrictions, desires, values, doubts, and criticism prevent you from acting in a natural, open, flexible, adaptive, and healthy manner. This is accomplished by disentangling (*wu shi*[e]) oneself from the world of contrived knowledge and learning.

> For learning, there is daily accumulating. For *dao*[i], there is daily decreasing. Decreasing and again decreasing arriving at noninterference [*wu wei*[b]]. Not interfering, there is nothing that is not done. (*Dao De Jing*, 48)

By not interfering with oneself, one will naturally not interfere with others. The commentary of He Shang Gong to the fourth line of Chapter 10, regarding behavior and *wu wei*[b], states:

> To manage the body take good care of the breath [*qi*[k]], then the body will be whole and integrated. To manage the kingdom take good care of the people, then the kingdom will be at peace. Managing the body is inhaling and exhaling essential breath [*qi*[k]] without letting the ear hear. Managing the kingdom is a distribution of gentle power [*de*[j]] without allowing those below [the people] to know it as such.

He Shang Gong examines the practice of proper breathing (see Table 5.2) in his commentary to Chapter 6 of the *Dao De Jing*. The phrases "inhaling and exhaling essential breath (*qi*[k]) without letting the ear hear" and "take good care of the breath" in the preceding quote should be clearer after examining the commentary of He Shang Gong on this chapter. Chapter 6 reads as follows:

> The valley spirit does not die. It is called the mysterious female. The gate of the mysterious female is called the root of the sky and the earth. Continuous as if it exists. It functions without effort.

Table 5.2   Fundamental Characteristics of Daoist Breathing

Characteristic	Description
One	Tongue lightly touches front roof of mouth. Inhaling and exhaling through the nose. Inhaling through the nose, exhaling through the mouth.
Two	Inhaling and exhaling is a continual cycle.
Three	Inhaling and exhaling is unbroken. There is no stopping or holding of the breath.
Four	Inhaling and exhaling is fine. Breathing is smooth without any coarseness or roughness.
Five	Inhaling and exhaling is subtle. Breathing should be without sound.
Six	Inhaling and exhaling should be long and slow. Breathing should not be rushed. Breathing should be deep, diaphragmatic, and abdominal.
Seven	Inhaling and exhaling should be relaxed. Breathing should not be labored or difficult. The mind/heart should be in the present and nonjudgmental. The mind/heart does not interfere with breathing.
Eight	Inhaling and exhaling heal. Breathing should preserve and restore existence.

He Shang Gong comments on the last three lines of this chapter, focusing on the meaning of "root," which he links to the nose and the mouth and the techniques of proper breathing.

> Root is origin. This means the gate of the nose and the mouth. This is the place where the original breath [*yuan qi*^{n}] that pervades the sky and the earth comes and goes. Breathing, inhaling and exhaling through the nose and the mouth, should be continuous, unbroken, fine, and subtle. Seeming

to be able to preserve and restore existence. Seeming to be nothing. Breathing should be relaxed and long. It is inappropriate for it to be rushed, difficult or labored.

By not interfering with the breath, the body and mind/heart will be naturally managed. By not interfering with the people, the kingdom will be naturally managed. The practice of *wu wei*[b] (noninterference) in managing the kingdom focuses on taking good care of the people by distributing gentle power or *de*[j] without the people being aware of it. This lack of interference (*wu wei*[b]) results in a kingdom being at peace. Chapter 3 of the *Dao De Jing* provides a more detailed presentation of what is meant by taking good care of the people through distributing gentle power or *de*.

Thus, the naturally integrated person [*sheng ren*[o]] manages by emptying their mind/hearts, filling their abdomens, weakening their wills and strengthening their bones. In the ordinary present, allowing people to be without contrived knowledge and contrived desires. He allows those with contrived knowledge not to dare to act. Acting by not interfering [*wu wei*[b]], there is nothing that is not managed.

The naturally integrated person engages others in the same manner that he or she engages in self-cultivation, through *wu wei*[b] or noninterference. The naturally integrated person creates an environment in which people are able to strengthen their bodies, find their centers, and empty their mind/hearts of contrived knowledge, values, and desires. An environment that is supportive, reinforcing, and allows people to work out their own destinies without any interference. The naturally integrated person does not attempt to control the behaviors of other people. In his commentary to Chapter 3, He Shang Gong states:

This says the naturally integrated person manages the kingdom and the body in the same manner. Gets rid of sensual desires [habits and desires] and is separate from confusion and irritation. Cherishing *dao*[i] and embracing one, the five spirits are protected. He is in harmony with softness, yielding and modesty, and does not dwell in the power of authority. He takes good care of his essence [*jing*], valuing its application. The marrow is full and the bones are solid. Return to simplicity and maintain the uncomplicated. Processes information deeply and does not speak without thinking. Not acting artificially, he acts by following natural patterns. Deeply influencing and transforming with the gentle power [*de*[j]] of kindness, the people are at peace.

Essentially, He Shang Gong is saying not to act in an artificial manner. Contrived values, knowledge, and desires are artificial, fragment the individual from the present, result in the individual interfering with and trying to control the behavior of others, create and maintain chronic stress, interfere with natural breathing, and in general result in physical, psychological, and interpersonal dysfunctionality. Wang Bi, in his commentary to this same chapter, notes:

> The mind/heart cherishes wisdom and the abdomen cherishes fullness. To be empty is to have wisdom and to be full is to be without contrived knowledge. Bones, considered as the tree trunk, are without contrived knowledge. The will is considered to produce confusion in one's affairs. The mind/heart being empty, the will is weakened. Maintain what is authentic. Those with contrived knowledge are said to act in a contrived manner.

To not interfere (*wu wei*^b) with the body and one's health, physical and psychological, requires the practice of proper breathing. Essential breath is breath that is not interfered (*wu wei*^b) with by thinking or feeling that is guided by rigidity, inflexibility, contrived values, artificial desires, absolute thinking, obsessions, worry, and so on. Through the practice of proper breathing, the mind/heart will still and empty. Being still and empty, the individual is open to all potentials and possibilities and will not attempt to interfere with or to control the behavior of others. The individual will be whole, naturally integrated, and free from chronic stress.

Not Getting Entangled in the Affairs of the World (Wu Shi)

The third component of the stress management program of the *Dao De Jing* is that of not getting entangled in the affairs of the world (*wu shi*^e). Not getting entangled in the affairs of the world means that when you do interact in various situations and events in the world, do not let the situations, events, and whoever populates them control or restrict your thinking, feeling, and behaving. Do not become attached to the events, situations, and whatever populates them. It means not being reactive, and thus entangled, such that you attempt to coerce or force other people to behave in a certain manner in your attempt to disentangle yourself from their grip. By not forcing or coercing others—in other words, not getting entangled—you reduce the probability of being harmed, physically and psychologically, by others, and you allow others the freedom to work through their own affairs and interactions in the world.

As noted earlier, not getting entangled in the affairs of the world (*wu shi*^e) also means not being controlled by contrived learning and knowledge. It means not being controlled by contrived, absolute, judgmental worldviews, thinking, and values. Not getting entangled in the affairs of the world is about being still, empty, and not interfering with oneself or others.

Essentially, not getting entangled in the affairs of the world is paradoxically about being naturally integrated with the environment. There are no barriers, restrictions, or obstructions. There is no separation or fragmentation. The individual has returned to the source. Chapter 48 of the *Dao De Jing* states:

> To become integrated with the world, do not become entangled in the affairs of the world [*wu shi*]. If you become entangled in the affairs of the world you cannot become integrated with the world.

Chapter 63 of the *Dao De Jing* integrates not becoming entangled with the affairs of the world (*wu shi*[e]), with noninterference (*wu wei*[b]), and with experiencing or tasting the world without relishing it (*wu wei*[q]). This combination is viewed by Wang Bi, in his commentary, as the ultimate of governing or healing. In his commentary, He Shang Gong views these three as being indicative of not being artificial, getting rid of troubles and simplifying matters, and tasting the essence of *dao*[i]. Chapter 63 states:

> In your actions do not interfere [*wu wei*[b]]. In your engagement with the affairs of the world, do not become entangled [*wu shi*[e]]. In your experiencing/tasting of the world, do not relish it [*wu wei*[q]].

The self-cultivation by the naturally integrated person or sage of *jing*[c], *wu wei*[b], and *wu shi*[e] allows the sage to be integrated with the world and to manage people such that they are able to cultivate themselves and work out their own destinies. This is demonstrated in Chapter 57 of the *Dao De Jing* and in the commentaries by He Shang Gong and Wang Bi to this chapter regarding the behavior of the naturally integrated person or sage (*sheng ren*[o]).

> By not being entangled in the affairs of the world [*wu shi*[e]], become integrated with the world. . . . I do not interfere [*wu wei*[b]] and the people transform themselves. I am fond of stillness [*jing*[c]] and the people do not let themselves go astray. I do not get entangled in the affairs of world [*wu shi*[e]] and the people enrich themselves. I am without contrived desires [*wu yu*[r]], and the people simplify themselves. (*Dao De Jing,* 57)

> By not becoming entangled in the affairs of the world [*wu shi*[e]] and by not interfering with it [*wu wei*[b]], the individual obtains ownership of the world. . . . Not interfering in their actions, the people transform themselves. The sage saying I am fond of stillness, not speaking and not teaching, the people themselves all center their mind/hearts not letting them go astray. In the affairs of the world, I do not force people to labor or draft them for work. The people are at peace in their trades. Thus all enrich

themselves. Without contrived desires, I get rid of the artificial. The people follow me becoming simpler in character. (He Shang Gong, Commentary to Chapter 57)

If that which I desire is only to be without contrived desire, the people moreover will be without contrived desires and simplify themselves. These four respect the root and extinguish the branches. (Wang Bi, Commentary to Chapter 57)

Summary of Discussion on *Dao De Jing*

The text and the commentaries make a clear distinction between natural, integrated behavior and artificial, fragmented behavior. Artificial, fragmented behavior is associated with complexity, endpoints, differences, chronic stress, and separation from the environment. Natural, integrated behavior is associated with simplicity, beginning points, commonalities, optimal health, and harmony or integration with the environment.

For the *Dao De Jing,* the conscious, focused, committed, and consistent practice of stilling and emptying the mind/heart, noninterference (*wu wei*[b]), and nonentanglement in the affairs of the world (*wu shi*[e]) lead to the elimination of chronic stress. These three components of the stress management program of the *Dao De Jing* are all oriented to returning the practitioner to thinking, feeling, and acting in a natural, holistic manner (*zi ran*[f]). To behave in a natural, holistic manner is to be integrated or in harmony with the environment.

Zhuang Zi

The *Zhuang Zi,* the second text of classical Daoism, was written in part by a man named Zhuang Zhou (early/mid-4th century BCE to early 3rd century BCE), who is also referred to as Zhuang Zi. Unlike the *Dao De Jing,* the *Zhuang Zi* is not concerned with teaching the ruler how to rule or establishing social and political harmony. The concern of the text is with freedom—freedom from all stimuli that compromise and interfere with the physical, psychological, interpersonal, and environmental well-being of the individual. In other words, the focus of the *Zhuang Zi* is on freedom from what we today call chronic stress. Chronic stress is not unique to modern times. The *Zhuang Zi* clearly paints a landscape wherein chronic stress is quite prevalent more than 2,000 years ago.

When people are asleep their spirits are knotted up. When they are awake their form is scattered. Interacting in the world creates entanglements.

Daily their mind/hearts battle: plodding, concealing, and tentative. Their small fears result in apprehensiveness. Their large fears result in being overwhelmed. In their judging of right and wrong their words shoot out as if an arrow was released from a bow. They hold onto their judgments as if they were sacred oaths. Guarding what they call their victory, they are executed like autumn moving into winter.[6] (3/2/10–12)

This section from the *Zhuang Zi* unmistakably presents an environment permeated with fear, anxiety, doubt, impulsiveness, impatience, control issues, and insecurity. In other words, the description is that of chronic stress (allostatic load). The people portrayed in this world are noticeably unhappy. This sense of unhappiness is further delineated in the following section of the *Zhuang Zi*:

That which is respected in the world is wealth, status, longevity and approval. That which is enjoyed is a comfortable life, tasty food, beautiful clothes, pleasant sights and sweet sounds. That which is not respected is poverty, dishonor, dying young and disapproval. That which is dissatisfying/ stressful is a life that is not comfortable, a mouth that does not have tasty food, a body that does not have beautiful clothes, eyes that do not have pleasant sights and ears that do not have sweet sounds. If these are not attained, there is chronic stress as well as fear. Those who treat the body in this way are indeed foolish. Now for those who are rich, the body is stressed and is made ill as they accumulate more wealth then they can possibly use. Those who treat the body in this manner are disconnected. Now those of status, day and night think about right and wrong. Those who treat their body in this manner are out of touch. People are born and all of life is a participation in anxiety/depression [chronic stress].[7] Those who seek a long life are of a confused mind. They are endlessly anxious/ depressed [chronically stressed] about death. Why do they bother? To treat the body in this manner is to be far away from it. (46/18/2–6)

This sense of chronic stress is even more evident in this passage, as the *Zhuang Zi* presents life as a participation in continual worry about not having wealth, honor, longevity, and approval from others. The people that the *Zhuang Zi* describes want, in fact, to demand that their senses be continually stimulated with only the finest materials, foods, sights, sounds, and tastes. They do not want their comfort compromised. Their perspectives of good and evil must be seen as correct. And last, but not least, these people fear death. They interfere in the lives of others and with their own lives in their quest to temporarily resolve their insatiable demands. For the *Zhuang Zi*, these are unhappy people. The *Zhuang Zi*, however, offers a solution to the problem of chronic stress. The solution is to be empty (xu^d).

To be empty is for the *Zhuang Zi* the defining characteristic of the Complete or Authentic Person. The Authentic or Complete Person is not chronically stressed. The Authentic or Complete Person is not entangled in the affairs of the world (*wu shi*^{e}), does not interfere with others or himself or herself (*wu wei*^{b}), does not attempt to control others (*wu wei*^{b}), and is not controlled by the world (*wu shi*^{e}). The Authentic or Complete Person is, essentially, free.

> Don't be the corpse of fame. Don't be the residence of schemes. Don't be controlled by interaction in the world. Don't be ruled by knowledge. Live your life in the endless and roam in the boundless. Use up that which you received from nature, yet do not see any attainment. Be empty [*xu*^{d}] that is all! (21/7/31–32)

How does one become empty (*xu*^{d}) such that the problem of chronic stress is removed? The *Zhuang Zi* offers a way of observing and engaging with the world called "mind/heart fasting" (*xin zhai*^{s}). What is required cognitively, affectively, and behaviorally to practice *xin zhai*^{s} such that this practice provides a solution for resolving the problem of chronic stress? In the next section of the chapter, we explore, cognitively, affectively, and behaviorally, this way of observing and engaging with the world. (See Table 5.3.)

Table 5.3   Three Levels for the Practice of *Xin Zhai:* Mind/Heart Fasting

Level	Practice
Cognitive	The will is unified. There is no distractibility. The mind/heart is nonjudgmental. The attention is engaged with and flexibly focused on the present. The mind/heart is still, empty, and clear. There is no confusion.
Affective/Emotional	The mind/heart is not moved by the affairs of the world. The words *good/bad* and *right/wrong* do not injure one's body or mind/heart. Death is accepted as a natural and inevitable part of the continually changing process called existence. Emotions are not excessive.
Behavioral	There is no entanglement in the affairs of the world. The individual is not controlled by nor enamored with the affairs of the world. There is no attempt to control, force, or coerce the behavior of other people. The individual does not put limitations, restrictions, or barriers in his or her own way.

Xin Zhai

Saso (1995, p. 24) notes that the pathway to healing the body and the community is through emptying oneself of judgments in the mind and self-ishness in the heart. This emptying is accomplished through the fasting of the mind/heart or *xin zhai*[s]. Jochim (1998, p. 52) describes *xin zhai*[s] as a technique of "mental stillness" that allows the practitioner to become aware of emptiness. Roth (2003, pp. 29, 32) states that mind/heart fasting is utilized to cultivate stillness and emptiness for the purpose of obtaining psychological freedom. Fox (2003, p. 217) describes *xin zhai*[s] as a way of removing restrictive thoughts, preconceptions, dogmatic beliefs and judgments, and the individual's "self-identification with them." Loy (1996, p. 53) argues that *x?n zhai* is about losing one's self.

Saso (1983, p. 146) points out that the function of *xin zhai*[s]—listening with *qi*[k]—is to allow the practitioner to open up to *dao*[i]. This is accomplished by emptying the mind/heart of all of its restrictions, limitations, contrived desires, contrived knowledge, and contrived values. He argues that this emptying of the mind/heart is the focus of Chapter 4 of the *Zhuang Zi*.

Before going any further, we must point out that in a number of instances the *Zhuang Zi* utilizes, in a satirical manner, Confucius and/or his favorite student Yan Hui to present the Daoist viewpoint. The section in Chapter 4 on *xin zhai*[s] or mind/heart fasting is one example.

This section begins with a discussion between Yan Hui and Confucius regarding Yan Hui going to the State of Wei to instruct the ruler on the proper way to govern his state. Yan Hui explains the problems with the current ruler and his lack of concern for the well-being of the people. Yan Hui says he wants to take all the ideas he has heard about governing and heal the State of Wei. Confucius tells Yan Hui that such actions would be dangerous and could lead to Yan Hui being punished.

Confucius tells Yan Hui that he needs to spend his time taking care of himself first before he goes off to encounter the ruler of Wei. Confucius then discusses the instability of Yan's *de*[j] (gentle power) and the manifestation of contrived knowledge. His *de*[j] is unstable because of the desire for fame, and with the desire for fame there is destruction. Contrived knowledge is made manifest because people argue, disagree, and contend with each other. Confucius describes both fame and contrived knowledge as lethal weapons and tells Yan Hui, as part of the process of taking care of himself first, to avoid them.

Confucius is attempting to get Yan Hui to examine himself. Why does he, Yan Hui, really want to go and correct the behavior of the ruler of Wei? Is it because he seeks fame? Does he desire to obtain this fame by parading his contrived knowledge in front of the ruler, demonstrating to the ruler that he, the ruler, is wrong in how he governs his kingdom? This behavior will lead to Yan Hui getting harmed.

Confucius asks Yan Hui to explain his plans for teaching the ruler of Wei how to rule in a correct manner. After Yan Hui offers his first plan, saying he will be upright and proper, yet humble, be committed and focused, he asks Confucius if it will work. Confucius says:

> No! It is not possible. To maintain this type of inflexible behavior is stress producing. One's color and expression is not stable. Ordinary people do not act contrary to this. Their feelings in reaction to others are suppressed as they seek to contain their mind/heart. (9/4/15–16)

Yan Hui then offers a second solution. He tells Confucius he will be internally upright and externally compliant, thus comparing his behaviors to the ancients and indicating he will be a follower who is a participator with *tian*^{t} (heaven). He then goes on to elaborate on the specifics of his approach. Once again Confucius says this behavior is unacceptable and will not work. Confucius tells him he has too many methods and ideas for governing. Confucius then tells Yan Hui that the reason he will not be successful with his approach is that he is still making his mind/heart his teacher.

> Yan Hui said, "I am unable to progress, may ask about your method?" Confucius (Zhong Ni) said, "Fast. I will then discuss it with you. Having a mind and acting, is it this easy? If you take it to be easy, then it is not appropriate for the sky to be bright." Yan Hui said, "The Hui family is poor. We have not drunk wine nor eaten meat for several months. Could this, thus, be consider fasting?" Confucius said, "This fasting is the fasting of sacrifices. It is not mind/heart fasting [*xin zhai*^{s}]." Hui said, "May I dare to ask about mind/heart fasting [*xin zhai*^{s}]?" Confucius (Zhong Ni) said, "Your will is unified. Do not listen with the ear, listen with the mind/heart. Do not listen with the mind/heart, listen with breath [*qi*^{k}]. Listening is stopped by the ear. The mind/heart is stopped by symbols. Breath [*qi*^{k}] is empty and is how one should deal with the affairs of the world. *Dao*^{i} is a gathering of empty space [*xu*^{d}]. To be empty [*xu*^{d}] is mind/heart fasting [*xin zhai*^{s}]. Yan Hui said, "Having not yet reached a point of applying this to myself, my self was real. Having applied it, I do not begin to have a self." Is it possible to call this emptiness [*xu*^{d}]?" Confucius (Fu Zi) said, "That is it!" (9/4/24–29)

Cognitive Exploration of Mind/Heart Fasting

The first step in *xin zhai*^{s} is to unify the will. It was the easily distractible will of Yan Hui that brought about the many varied solutions he offered to Confucius in regard to instructing the ruler of the State of Wei. It is these solutions and their entanglement with the affairs of the world that results in the confused mind/heart of Yan Hui. It is this confused mind/heart that seeks fame and self-importance. To seek for fame and self-importance is to judge others and contend with them about right and wrong, good and bad, acceptable and unacceptable, and so on. To contend with others is to argue that your perspective of the world is correct and their perspective of the world is wrong. This perspective develops artificial knowledge and reinforces a sense of separate, individual, unchanging self. It is this cognitive notion of a separate self and artificial knowledge to which the *Zhuang Zi* objects.

> *Dao*[i] is hidden by small achievements. Words are hidden by glory and splendor. Thus, there is the right and wrong of the Confucianists and the Moists. Each regards as right what the other regards as wrong. Each regards as wrong what the other regards as right. (4/2/25–26)

> Suppose you and I had a debate. You beat me. I did not beat you. Are you really right and am I really wrong? I beat you. You do not beat me. Am I really right and are you really wrong? Is someone right? Is someone wrong? Are we both right? Are we both wrong? If you and I are not able to know, then other people will certainly be in the dark. (7/2/84–87)

> Where there is life there is death. Where there is death there is life. Where there is possibility there is impossibility. Where there is impossibility there is possibility. The basis of right is the basis of wrong. The basis of wrong is the basis of right. Thus, the wise person does not follow this and is illumined by nature, which is, moreover, the basis of this. This moreover is that, that moreover is this. That moreover is one right and wrong. This moreover is one right and wrong. Is there really that and this? Is there really no that and this? This and that not attaining their mate is called the hub of *dao* [*dao shu*[u]]. When the hub attains its socket, the adaptations are endless. Right moreover is one endlessness. Wrong is moreover one endlessness. Thus it is said, there is nothing like using the light shining forth. (4/2/28–31)

Contending with others about your perspective based on artificial knowledge results in making one's *de*[j] (gentle power, empty space, or the *dao*[i] within) unstable. *De*[j] is then filled with contrived values, desires, and knowledge. Thus it is unstable. The consequence of an unstable *de*[j] is destruction both internally and externally. This is why Confucius tells Yan Hui he must stabilize his entire self first, before he goes to help others. This is why he warns Yan Hui of the danger of going to instruct the ruler of Wei.

It is the confused mind/heart of Yan Hui, filled with abstract, preconceived, inflexible, contrived, artificial knowledge, ideas, methods, and solutions, that Confucius refers to as the teacher of Yan Hui. Yan Hui is unable to progress any further because he relies on this contending, fame seeking, artificial knowledge-based, confused mind/heart as his teacher. Yan Hui is not in touch with the empty space within. Insofar as he is not in touch with the empty space within (*de*[j] or gentle power), he is separated from *dao*[i] or empty space. Yan Hui is not in the present.

The easily distractible will scatters the mind/heart in many outward directions and fills it with artificial, inflexible knowledge. Yan Hui is not focused, centered, rooted, or in the present. He is scattered. Whether the process for removing the easily distractible will is called "weakening the will," as in the *Dao De Jing,* or "unifying the will," the process is still the same. The mind/heart must be emptied of absolute, contrived, inflexible judgments, desires, values, perspectives, and knowledge. It is about eliminating the society-imposed and self-imposed teacher, which results in the individual contending, arguing, being confused, fragmented, and out of touch with *dao*[i]. It is about attending to the here and now, the present.

Thus, at the cognitive level, *xin zhai*[s] is concerned with being flexibly focused on the present and emptying of the mind/heart of artificial knowledge, values, perspectives, desires, and judgments that may be harmful to the individual. Judgments such as "right and wrong," "good and bad," and "beautiful and ugly" are considered problematic. *Xin zhai*[s] empties the mind/heart of the cognitive processes that may result in entanglement with the affairs of the world. *Xin zhai*[s] removes the artificial teacher.

Affective/Emotional Exploration of Mind/Heart Fasting

There is a clear link between the cognitive and affective/emotional levels throughout the *Zhuang Zi.* This link is clear for the practice of *xin zhai*[s]. When Yan Hui says he wants to take all the ideas (the artificial knowledge) he has heard about governing and heal the State of Wei, Confucius tells Yan Hui that such actions would be dangerous. Confucius continues, saying:

> It is not desirable to complicate the *dao*[i]. If it is too complicated the complications will result in trouble. Trouble results in worry and anxiety. Worried and anxious, you cannot be rescued. The complete man of the ancients first took care of his entire self and then afterward helped all others. (8/4/4–5)

Given this quote, it is clear that the *Zhuang Zi* is arguing that artificial knowledge and the complexity it generates disconnects the individual from the *dao*[i]. It is also argued that entanglement of artificial knowledge with the world results in emotional problems that appear irresolvable. In other words, artificial knowledge, which entails judging and arguing, results in emotional instability and thus harms the individual. This linking among the cognitive processes, feelings and emotions, and the harming of the body is further reinforced in the following passage:

> Hui Zi talking to Zhuang Zi said, "Is man originally without emotions?" Zhuang Zi said, "It is so." Hui Zi said, "If man is without emotions, how can you call him a man?" Zhuang Zi said, "*Dao*^{i} allows appearance, nature allows form, how can he not be called a man?" Hui Zi said, "Since he is already called a man, how can he be without emotions?" Zhuang Zi said, "Right and wrong is that which I call emotions. That which I call being without emotions is a man not using the words *good* and *bad* to internally injure his body, being in accord with the here and now, being natural [*zi ran*^{f}], and not adding on to his life." Hui Zi said, "Not adding on to his life, how can his body exist?" Zhuang Zi said, "*Dao*^{i} allows appearance, nature allows form, and not using good and bad to internally injure himself. Now you are outside of your spirit [*shen*^{m}] and straining your essence. Leaning on a tree and singing, holding your lute and shutting your eyes. Nature chose your form, and you cry out about hard and white." (14/5/55–60)

The emotions that the *Zhuang Zi* finds problematic are those linked to the cognitive process of judging. Judging based on contrived values, desires, and knowledge. Right and wrong and good and bad are judgments that the *Zhuang Zi* finds to be harmful to the inner aspects of the human being. This harm has been previously noted as anxiety, worry, being apprehensive, being overwhelmed, being uncomfortable, being physically ill, and fear. This is clearly a description of stress, and the context in which it is described is that of chronic stress or allostatic load.

Even with the issue of death, the *Zhuang Zi* makes it clear that individuals should not get stressed about death through their thinking and judgments. Death is natural and it is inevitable. It is simply another change in the continually changing process called life.

> Death and life are destiny. They are as ordinary as night and day. They are natural. They cannot be interfered with by people. They are the circumstances of all things. (16/6/20–21)

> Uncle Zhi Li and Uncle Hua Jie were nonjudgmentally observing [*guan*^{g}] Ming Bo Hills in the vastness of Kun Lun Mountains, the place where the Yellow Emperor rested. After a while, a willow tree grew out of the left elbow of Uncle Hua Jie. He was startled and expressed disgust. Uncle Zhi Li said, "Are you disgusted?" Uncle Hua Jie said, "It is gone. How can I be disgusted? Life is to borrow. To borrow is to live, life is dust and dirt.

> Death and life are night and day. You and I were nonjudgmentally observing [*guan*ᵍ] changes and now changes have caught up with me. Why should I be disgusted?" (46/18/19–22)

For the *Zhuang Zi*, any emotion, positive or negative, that is excessive and/or binds or entangles the individual in the affairs of the world is not acceptable. These are the types of emotions that are a manifestation of chronic stress or allostatic load. It is these types of emotions that harm the individual.

> I attained life because it was my time. Losing it, I will follow along. At peace during my time and managing by following along, sorrow and joy cannot enter me. This is what the ancients called freedom from restrictions/undoing the ropes. Yet people are not able to free themselves as they are bound by things. Moreover, nothing overcomes nature, why should I be disgusted? (17/6/52–54)

It is important to point out that emotions are normal. The *Zhuang Zi*, however, is concerned about and rejects emotions that harm the individual. The individual is harmed by emotions if (1) the emotions are excessive and (2) the emotions are generated through judgments that are based in artificial knowledge, which leads to entanglement in the world. In Chapter 18 of the *Zhuang Zi*, there is a section that discusses the reactions of Zhuang Zi to the death of his wife.

> The wife of Zhuang Zi died. Zhuang Zi was sitting on the floor, with his legs spread apart, beating on a basin and singing. Hui Zi said, "You have lived together, raised children, and grown old. That you do not weep is one thing. But beating a basin and singing, isn't that going too far?" Zhuang Zi replied, "Not so! When she first died, how could I alone not be like others? Examining her beginnings, she originally was without life. Not moving, without life, originally without form. Not moving, without form, originally without breath [*qi*ᵏ]. Undifferentiated! Suddenly, within the obscurity a change and there is breath [*qi*ᵏ]. *Qi*ᵏ [breath] changes and there is form. Form changes and there is life. Now, another change and there is death. This is the movement of the four seasons. Spring, autumn, winter and summer waiting on each other. She is presently lying down at rest in a gigantic room. Yet if I followed those who continually shouted and wept, I would consider myself as not understanding my destiny. Thus, I stopped!" (46/18/15–19)

In this section Zhuang Zi clearly acknowledges that he responded emotionally to the death of his wife. He goes on to point out, however, that he did not let his emotions overwhelm or control him. He expressed them and then stopped. To do otherwise would have resulted in harm to him, cognitively, emotionally, and physically. For the *Zhuang Zi,* emotions are as natural as four seasons. In reference to the authentic person (*zhen ren*[v]), the *Zhuang Zi* states, "Happiness and anger are linked like the four seasons" (15/6/10).

Thus, the practice of *xin zhai*[s] at the affective/emotional level is concerned with emptying the mind/heart of emotions that are harmful to the individual. Harmful emotions are generated by contrived judgments such as "right and wrong" and "good and bad." Harmful emotions are emotions that are excessive and ongoing. Harmful emotions are emotions that result in entanglement with the affairs of the world.

Behavioral Exploration of Mind/Heart Fasting

At the behavioral level, *xin zhai*[s] is concerned with not interfering with the affairs of the world. Entanglement with the affairs of the world leads to harm. The affairs of the world are linked with fame and knowledge. Confucius, in his discussion with Yan Hui, associated fame with destruction and knowledge with contending and arguing. He said that fame and knowledge were lethal weapons and should be avoided. Confucius was quite clear about this with Yan Hui when he told him that it would be dangerous for him if he went to instruct the ruler of Wei. It is quite likely that Yan Hui would become extremely stressed and harm himself.

This theme of chronic stress and harm associated with behavior that leads to entanglement with the affairs of the world is prevalent throughout the *Zhuang Zi.*

> Furthermore, a skillful wrestler begins with aggression and strength and often ends with passivity and weakness. At this extreme we rarely see skill. At ceremonies people drink wine. It begins with orderliness and often ends with confusion. At this extreme we rarely see pleasure. Everything is like this. Beginning with sincerity and ending with disdain. In the beginning we regard things as simple, in the end we make them complex. Words are wind and waves. Behavior is winning and losing. Wind and waves easily lead to movement. Winning and losing easily lead to danger. Likewise, anger is constructed from no other cause than deceitful words and biased phrases. It is a dying beast not choosing sounds, its breathing compromised, resulting in the production of a cruel mind/heart on both sides. This is hostility in its extreme. It is certainly an unworthy response from the mind/heart, yet we do not know that it is so. If we do not know this is so, who knows where it will end? (10/4/47–51)

In the previous passage, the *Zhuang Zi* shows how entanglement in the affairs of the world affects the individual at the cognitive, emotional, and behavioral levels. At the cognitive level the individual is confused, oblivious to what is happening to him or her, expresses disdain toward other people, and is concerned with winning while avoiding losing. At the emotional level the individual is angry, hostile, and rarely has pleasure. At the behavioral level the individual is cruel, turns simplicity into complexity, and engages in dangerous actions so that he or she is a winner and not a loser. This entanglement with the affairs of the world results in chronic stress (who knows where it will end?) that compromises the breathing of the individual and weakens his body. It is clear this entanglement in the affairs of the world harms the individual.

To avoid harm, the practice of *xin zhai*ˢ advocates not interfering in the affairs of the world. By not interfering in the affairs of the world, the individual will not be entangled and suffer from chronic stress.

> Zhuang Zi was fishing at Pu waters. The king of Chu sent an envoy of two senior officials who came before Zhuang Zi and said, "We wish for you to come and work for our kingdom." Zhuang Zi, holding the fishing pole and not turning around said, "I hear the Chu has a spiritual tortoise. It has been dead for over 3,000 years. The king conceals it in a basket and a cloth in the imperial temple. Would this tortoise prefer to be dead having its bones saved and honored or would it prefer to be alive dragging its tail in the mud?" The two senior officials replied, "It would prefer to be alive and dragging its tail in the mud." Zhuang Zi said, "Go away! I will drag my tail in the mud." (45/17/81–84)

For Zhuang Zi, to be honored, dressed in fine clothes, and working in the government is the same as being dead. He does not want to get entangled in the affairs of the world. A similar situation arises when Tian Gen asks the nameless man about governing the world. The nameless man does not want to be bothered by such a question, nor does he want to be harmed by becoming entangled in a discussion about the process of governing. Finally he relents but tells Tian Gen to not to interfere with the affairs of the world. He does this by telling Tian Gen that if he takes care of himself the world will be governed.

> Tian Gen was wandering through the land of Yin Yang and reached the banks of the Liao River. Happening to encounter a nameless man he said, "Excuse me, I wish to inquire about governing the world." The nameless man said, "Go away, you simpleton! How can you ask such an unpleasant question? I am about to participate in the creation of things. When I am tired of that, I will ride the bird of nonrestraint and insignificance by which I will be outside of the six poles, wander in the world where nothing really exists and dwell in the wild field of the boundless. How disturbed you are attempting to move my mind/heart by asking me about

governing the world!" Tian Gen asked again. The nameless man said, "Let your mind/heart wander in the distinctionless, join your breath [qi^k] with the vastness, be in accordance with the naturalness [$zi\ ran^f$] of things, do not contain a restrictive perspective and the world will be governed." (20/7/7–11)

Thus, the practice of *xin zhai*[s] at the behavioral level is concerned with not interfering *(wu wei*[b]) and not becoming entangled with the affairs of the world *(wu shi*[e]). If you do not interfere with the affairs of the world, you will not becoming entangled with it. By not interfering, the individual will not become chronically stressed and thus, not harmed.

The Practice of *Xin Zhai*

Once we have completed the exploration of *xin zhai*[s] at the cognitive, emotional, and behavioral levels, the next step is to determine what is entailed with the practice of *xin zhai*[s]. It is clear that the practice of *xin zhai*[s] requires the emptying out of the mind/heart. The question is, How is this accomplished?

Realizing that the desire of Yan Hui to travel to the State of Wei to instruct the ruler about good government is indicative of Yan Hui being entangled in the affairs of the world and of having a mind/heart that is confused by the desire for fame and knowledge, Confucius tells Yan Hui to fast. Yan Hui interprets fasting as giving up meat and wine. Confucius tells him this is incorrect and that he should practice *xin zhai*[s]. When Yan Hui asks about the meaning of *xin zhai*[s], he is told to unify his will. He is told to unify his will because his will is entangling him in the affairs of the world. His will is not focused and is easily distractible. His will is entangling him in the affairs of the world because his mind/heart is confused by contrived knowledge and the desire for fame. This unification of the will is then linked to his mind/heart being empty.

Mind/Heart Fasting (Xin Zhai)

As previously noted, Chapter 3 of the *Dao De Jing* indicates that the sage governs by emptying the mind/hearts of the people and weakening their will. The commentary of Wang Bi to this chapter links the will to, essentially, entanglement in the affairs of the world. Being entangled in the affairs of the world, the mind/heart is confused. To overcome the confusion and to disentangle the will from the affairs of the world, the mind/heart must be emptied. This being the case, how does the mind/heart become empty? For the *Zhuang Zi*, it is the practice of *xin zhai*[s] that empties the mind/heart. So how does the practice of *xin zhai*[s] lead to emptiness? The story of Carpenter Qing, in Chapter 19 of the *Zhuang Zi,* may shed some light on this process.

Carpenter Qing was carving wood to make a bell stand. After the stand was completed those who looked at it were startled as it appeared supernatural. Marquis Lu saw it and asking a question said, "Is there an art by which you make this?" Answering, Carpenter Qing said, "Your subject is a worker. What art could I have? However, there is one thing. Before I make a bell stand, I do not dare to scatter my breath [*qi*^k]. I must fast in order to still [*jing*^c] my mind/heart. After three days of fasting I do not feel compelled to think of approval, admiration, rank or salary. After fasting for five days, I do not feel compelled to think of not having a reputation, being skillful or clumsy. After seven days of fasting I am still. I forget about having four limbs and a body. At this moment, there are no official duties or royal court. I am focused on my skills and outside distractions disappear. After this I enter the mountain forest, nonjudgmentally observing [*guan*^g] with my natural instincts until a form appears such that I can see the completed bell stand. I then begin my work. There is nothing else. Thus take the natural to unite with the natural. That is the reason why people suspect the bell stand is spiritual. That is it!" (50/19/54–59)

According to the description of Carpenter Qing, the mind/heart is stilled and thus emptied through the practice of *xin zhai*^s. The mind/heart is emptied of judgments and the desire for approval, admiration, rank, salary, and reputation. There is no entanglement with the affairs of the world. This being the case, the will is weakened and unified by being empty and still. When the mind/heart is stilled and thus empty, there is a new way of seeing and interacting with the world. This new way of seeing, which is linked to emptiness and stillness, is called nonjudgmentally observing or *guan*^g. This linking among emptiness, stillness, and nonjudgmental observation is also found, as previously discussed, in Chapter 16 of the *Dao De Jing*. The chapter begins by stating:

Sincerely maintaining stillness [*jing*^c], extreme emptiness [*xu*^d] is reached. All things simultaneously acting together, I nonjudgmentally observe [*guan*^g] their cycles. Things are numerous. All cycles return to their root. Returning to the root is called stillness [*jing*^c]. This is said to be the cycle of destiny. The cycle of destiny is called the ordinary present. Being aware of the ordinary present is called letting the light shine forth [*ming*^h]. Not to be aware of the ordinary present is to fall into darkness. Being aware of the ordinary present is to be open. To be open is to be impartial. To be impartial is to be linked. To be linked is to be with the natural environment. Being with the natural environment, then *dao*ⁱ. *Dao*ⁱ, then long lasting. To the end of the body, there is no danger.

In addition to linking emptiness, stillness, and nonjudgmental observation in the mind/heart of the individual, emptiness and stillness are also associated with the very nature of all things, as all things return to emptiness and stillness. Thus, the emptiness and stillness of the individual is linked with the emptiness and stillness of the nature of reality itself. The commentary of Wang Bi to the first sentence of Chapter 16 provides further clarification of this linking.

> In other words, the genuine ultimate of things, is arriving at emptiness [*xu*^{d}]. The true correctness of things is the maintaining of stillness [*jing*^{c}].

This clarification is further established with the commentary of Wang Bi to the second sentence, which links, through nonjudgmental observation (*guan*^{g}), the emptiness and stillness of the individual with the emptiness and stillness of all things. The commentary states:

> With emptiness [*xu*^{d}] and stillness [*jing*^{c}] you nonjudgmentally observe [*guan*^{g}] the ongoing cycles. All things arise from empty space [*xu*^{d}]. Movement arises from stillness [*jing*^{c}]. Thus, although the 10,000 things interact together, in the end, they all return to empty space [*xu*^{d}] and stillness [*jing*^{c}]. This is the genuine ultimate of things.

When the mind/heart is still (*jing*^{c}) and empty (*xu*^{d}), the individual is able to nonjudgmentally observe (*guan*^{g}) the nature of reality, which is discovered to be still and empty. Thus the ultimate nature of the individual and the ultimate nature of reality are the same: still and empty. The Daoists refer to the still, empty space within as *de*^{j} (gentle power). *De*^{j} is the *dao*^{i} (still, dynamic, empty space) within the individual.

This appears to be the same process that Carpenter Qing discusses when he describes how he finds the correct tree to carve into a bell stand. Carpenter Qing practices *xin zhai*^{s} in order to still and empty his mind/heart. When the mind/heart is empty and still, he is able to nonjudgmentally observe and engage (*guan*^{g}) the environment such that he is able to find the appropriate tree to carve. He calls this taking "the natural to unite with the natural." His *de*^{j} (still, empty space within) or gentle power has united with *dao*^{i} or still, dynamic, empty space.

The emptiness and stillness within is the gentle power (*de*^{j}) of potentially. As much as *dao*^{i} (still, dynamic, empty space) is an unlimited potentiality nourishing and allowing all things to come into being and grow without any restrictions or limitations, the *dao*^{i} (still, dynamic, empty space) within or *de*^{j} has the same power to create, support, and nourish. Thus Carpenter Qing, through the practice of mind/heart fasting (*xin zhai*^{s}), stills and empties his mind/heart, releasing *de*^{j} or power, enabling him to nonjudgmentally observe the form of the bell stand in the appropriate tree. Insofar as he is without any restrictions or limitations, is not distracted or chronically stressed, and is not getting in his own way, he is still and empty. Being still and empty, he is in harmony with *dao*[i] and is able to tap into his natural, gentle power (*de*[j]).

Up until this point, the practice *xin zhai*[s] has been described as consisting of stilling and emptying the mind/heart. The stilling and emptying of the mind/heart unifies the will. The unified will is not entangled in the affairs of the world. Nonetheless, the question still remains. How is this accomplished?

Breathing From the Heels (Xi Yi Zhong)

After telling Yan Hui to unify the will, Confucius goes on to say that Yan Hui should not listen with the ear or the mind/heart. In both cases the ear/senses and the mind/heart distracts or creates the basis for desires in the individual. In both cases the mind/heart is constantly agitated and filled up with restrictions and limitations that compromise the ability of the individual to freely observe and engage the environment.

The ears or one's five senses are distracted by or desire a comfortable life, tasty food, beautiful clothes, pleasant sights, and sweet sounds. The senses become entangled in the world through the easily distracted and fragmented will, which is pulled by the senses. The senses provide a partial and thus restricted encounter with the world. The senses contribute to the restrictions of the mind/heart by constantly moving and filling it with contrived desires and distractions. Thus one should not listen with or be restricted by the ears or senses.

In addition to being moved by the senses, the mind/heart of the individual is moved by and filled up with contrived judgments and values such as good and bad, right and wrong, winning and losing, proper and improper, correct and incorrect, and ugly and beautiful. The mind/heart of the individual is filled up, agitated, and driven by its desire for power, control, fame, approval, acceptance, wealth, and contrived knowledge. The mind/heart becomes entangled in the affairs of the world through the easily distracted and fragmented will, which is directed by the mind/heart. The mind/heart, like the senses, provides a partial and thus restricted or limited encounter and engagement with the world. The mind/heart is thus filled with contrived desires, knowledge, and values. Therefore, the individual should not listen with or be restricted by the mind/heart.

As result of the desires and distractions of the senses and the mind/heart, the individual develops a false worldview that does not consider, see, or accept an interrelated, interdependent, relative environment that is continually changing. The world or environment is instead viewed as consisting of stable, disconnected, independent, and absolutely distinct components and things, material and immaterial, that can be possessed and maintained forever.

Because the mind/heart of an individual is easily agitated, moved, and filled up with these contrived desires and demands, and because the environment does not behave in accordance with the individual's false worldview, the individual becomes chronically stressed (allostatic load). The individual may be angry, depressed, anxious, overwhelmed, and fearful. Insofar as the individual recognizes that he will die, the individual fears death. All of this chronic stress, in turn, fills up and moves the mind/heart of the individual, resulting in a limited and partial encounter with the world.

In both cases—the sense and the mind/heart—the individual is not free. The individual is restricted, limited, moved by, controlled by, and filled up with contrived desires, demands, judgments, perspectives, and feelings. As a result the individual becomes entangled in the affairs of the world. Given the entanglement associated with the senses and the mind/heart, Confucius tells Yan Hui not to listen with either the ear (senses) or the mind/heart. Instead he tells Yan Hui to listen with breath (qi^k). Confucius tells Yan Hui that to listen with the breath (qi^k) is to be empty and is how one should deal with the affairs of the world. Confucius goes on to state that dao^i is a gathering of empty space (xu^d) and that, in fact, to be empty is the practice of xin $zhai^s$. So, how does one listen with qi^k or breath?

Qi^k is described by Ames and Hall (2003) as both the energy that animates and "that which is animated" (pp. 62–63). It is interesting to note, at this point, that a synonym for *animate* is *breathing*. Roth (1999) defines qi^k as "vital energy" or "vital breath" (pp. 41–42). In Roth's translation/interpretation of the xin $zhai^s$ section of Chapter 4 of the *Zhuang Zi*, he translates qi^k as "vital breath" (pp. 154–155). Roth argues that Confucius tells Yan Hui to focus (thus unifying his will) on his vital breath so that he will not be distracted by his senses and thoughts, and his mind will naturally become empty. Miller (2003) defines qi^k as the "breath of life" (pp. 54–55). This "breath of life" is further described as the natural rhythmic expansion and contraction, much like the process of breathing itself, of dao^i. The commonality between all these definitions of qi^k is an association with breath.

Is the method of emptying and stilling the mind—in other words, the practice of xin $zhai^s$—associated with breathing? In Chapter 6 of the *Zhuang Zi* there is a discussion of the Authentic Person ($zhen$ ren^v). (See Table 5.4 for a list of characteristics of the Authentic Person.) The Authentic Person is not entangled in the affairs of the world. He does not seek after fame and gain. He is not judgmental. He is not overwhelmed by his emotions. He is described as being empty. The question is, How did he become empty? There appears to be a link to a particular way of breathing. Deep breathing!

The Authentic Person [$zhen$ ren^v] of ancient times slept without dreaming, awoke without worry, ate without relishing and breathed very deeply. The Authentic Person breathes from the heels [xi yi $zhong^w$]. All other people breathe from their throats. Being restricted, the words in their throats are like retching, their desires longstanding and deep, and their essential nature is shallow. (15/6/6–7)

In this section, the *Zhuang Zi* makes a clear distinction between breathing deeply or from the heels (*xi yi zhong*[w]) and breathing that appears to be shallow or from the throat. Shallow breathing is associated with being restricted, retching of one's words, problematic desires, and, essentially, a

Table 5.4   Characteristics of the Authentic Person: *Zhen Ren*

Authentic Person: Zhen Ren	*Everybody Else*
Breathes from heels. Deep abdominal breathing.	Breathes from throat. Shallow, chest breathing.
Does not interfere with others or oneself.	Interferes with others and oneself.
Is not entangled in the affairs of the world.	Is entangled in the affairs of the world.
No sense of an individual, separate, independent, unchanging self.	Has an absolute sense of an individual self that is independent, separate, and unchanging.
Interacts with others by creating an environment that is supportive, nourishing, and conducive to growth and development.	Is self-centered, self-entitled, and narcissistic. Is driven by self-benefit and self-gain.
Mind/heart is open, still, flexible, not distracted, unrestricted, and empty.	Mind/heart is closed, agitated, inflexible, easily distracted, restricted, and full.
Nonjudgmental.	Judgmental.
Guided by naturalness.	Guided by artificiality.
Is in harmony with and recognizes the ever-changing, natural environmental process.	Fragmented and separate. Does not recognize an ever-changing, natural environmental process. Not in harmony.
Accepts one's death as a natural, inevitable part of the process of change.	Resists death. Does not accept one's death as a natural, inevitable part of the process of change.
Free, happy, and not chronically stressed.	Shackled, unhappy, and chronically stressed.

NOTE: *Zhen ren*[v] (authentic person), *sheng ren*[o] (naturally integrated person or sage), and *zhi ren*[af] (complete person) are all different names for the same person.

shallow nature. In other words, shallow breathing is linked with stress. On the other hand, deep breathing is associated with restful sleep, not worrying, and not taking excessive pleasure in anything. Deep breathing is associated with being relaxed.

Hoblitzelle and Benson (1992) also make a distinction between deep breathing and shallow breathing. Noting that breathing is normally a combination of deep and shallow, they recommend practicing deep breathing for stress management.

> An awareness of your breathing pattern is a first step in altering the physical, emotional, and mental effects of stress on your body. . . . There are two basic ways of breathing: the first is diaphragmatic or abdominal breathing; the second is chest or thoracic breathing. Normally, breathing is a combination of the two. . . .Though deceptively simple and subtle, the act of breathing diaphragmatically can offer control over some of the anxieties and tensions that contribute to stress-related physical symptoms. How remarkable that one of the important stress-management tools is as close as your own breath. (pp. 39–41)

In describing the relaxation response, a proactive technique used for managing stress, Benson (1975, pp. 162–163) discusses the relationship among breathing, awareness, rhythmic repetition, and having a passive or nonjudgmental attitude. He indicates that the passive or nonjudgmental attitude may be the most important aspect of practicing the relaxation response and associates it with emptying the mind of thoughts and distractions.

> The third element is a passive attitude. It is an emptying of all thoughts and distractions from one's mind. A passive attitude appears to be the most essential factor in eliciting the Relaxation Response. Thoughts, imagery and feelings may drift into one's awareness. One should not concentrate on these perceptions but allow them to pass on. A person should not be concerned with how well he or she is doing. (Benson, 1975, pp. 110–111)

Kabat-Zinn (2005) also contrasts shallow breathing and deep breathing. He notes that chest breathing is shallow and fast, while belly or diaphragmatic breathing is deep and slow. He points out that when people are aware of their diaphragmatic breathing in a nonjudgmental manner, the mind and body become calm and aware.

> In the stress clinic we generally focus on the feelings of the breath at the belly rather than at the nostrils or chest. . . . As you become more aware of your breathing pattern by focusing on your belly, you may find yourself breathing more this way naturally because it is slower and deeper

than chest breathing which tends to be rapid and shallow. If you watch infants breathe, you will see that diaphragmatic breathing is the way we all start out when we are babies. . . . Staying with the breath during meditation, no matter what, ultimately leads to deeper experiences of calmness and awareness. (pp. 52–53, 56)

Lewis (1997) points out that poor posture and chronic stress compromise diaphragmatic or deep natural breathing. When the individual does not breathe naturally, with diaphragmatic or deep breathing, he or she is subject to a host of physical disorders.

The diaphragm is . . . influenced by the health and mobility of the spine and the pelvis, and their associated muscles, and these in turn are influenced not just by our habitual postures, but also by our emotions and attitudes. On of the most adverse influences on the movement of the diaphragm is the unnecessary tension that many of us carry in our abdominal muscles and internal organs. Most of these tensions are the result of chronic stress, repressed emotions, and excessive negativity. . . . When the belly is overly contracted it resists the downward movement of the diaphragm. . . . Breathing based on such habits—habits in which the diaphragm is unable to extend through its full range and activate and support the rhythmical movements of the abdominal muscles, organs and tissues—has many harmful effects on the organism. . . . In short, such breathing weakens and disharmonizes the functioning of almost every major system in the body and makes us more susceptible to chronic and acute illnesses and "dis-eases" of all kinds. (pp. 40–43)

Lewis (1997) goes on to note that our habits, postures, and ways of thinking about, viewing, and behaving in our environments are so ingrained that we need to change how we experience ourselves and the world around us. He argues that we need to integrate with our environment and become whole.

It is . . . a matter of perceptual re-education, of learning how to experience ourselves in an entirely new way, and from an entirely new perspective. The etymology of the verb *to heal* is related to the verb *to make whole*. It is first necessary . . . to sense my dis-ease, to actually see and come to terms with my imbalance, my fragmentation, my illusions, my contradictions, and my incomplete sensation of myself. . . . It depends on discovering a dimension in myself of inner quiet, of inner clarity—a clear uncolored lens through which I can observe myself without any judgments, criticism or analysis. This inner clarity . . . is both a precondition and a result of working with sensation and breath. On of the very first steps of this work, therefore—a step that on no account must be skipped—is to learn how to "follow," to sense, the movements of our breath without interfering with them or trying to change them in any way. . . . Learning how to observe the mechanisms involved in breathing, as well as the various physical, emotional, and mental forces acting on them, depends in a large part on learning how to sense ourselves, to listen to ourselves. (Lewis, 1997, pp. 50–51)

Fried (1993) argues that it is clear that stress compromises breathing. He notes that the majority of the symptoms associated with stress and anxiety are also associated with hyperventilation or a decreased level of alveolar CO_2 (carbon dioxide). This decrease in alveolar CO_2 or hypocapnia results in restricted blood flow to the brain and the extremities and compromises the oxygen supply to all aspects of the body. Thus the symptoms! He also points out that the research indicates that these symptoms are reduced with stress management techniques that focus on breathing. Diaphragmatic breathing! He indicates his research efforts

have been based in large part on the substantial published research pointing to (1) the seemingly crucial effect of respiratory psychophysiology on brain functions; (2) the consistent reports of breathing-related symptoms in stress and anxiety; and (3) the reportedly successful treatment of these conditions with strategies centering on breathing. . . . In summary, the counterstress breathing relaxation strategies . . . typically reduce tension and anxiety, as well as the frequency and severity of psychophysiological disorders. Clients report that the strategies make them feel good, relaxed and in control, and that they have fewer symptoms as a result. Objective indices of counterarousal include decreased rate and predominantly abdominal mode of breathing, as well as normalization of alveolar CO_2. (Fried, 1993, pp. 308–309)

The relationship among stress, breathing, hyperventilation, and low levels of CO_2 is also addressed by Lewis (1997). He links hyperventilation with compromised functioning at cognitive, emotional, and behavioral levels, noting that many people hyperventilate without even being aware of it. He argues that as individuals become more aware of themselves they will be able to sense the connections between their breathing and their emotions.

Many of us, without even knowing it, habitually "hyperventilate"—that is, we take quick, shallow breaths from the top of our chest. These quick, shallow breaths sharply reduce the level of carbon dioxide in our blood. This reduced level of carbon dioxide causes the arteries, including the carotid artery going to the brain, to constrict, thus reducing the flow of blood throughout the body. When this occurs, no matter how much oxygen we may breathe into our lungs, our brain and body will experience a short-age of oxygen. The lack of oxygen switches on the sympathetic nervous system—our "flight or flight" reflex—which makes us tense, anxious, and irritable. It also reduces our ability to think clearly, and tends to put us at the mercy of obsessive thoughts and images. (Lewis, 1997, pp. 55–56)

Benson (1975), Kabot-Zinn (2005), Lewis (1997), and Fried (1993) all associate deep breathing with health, well-being, and the reduction of stress. All four approaches contrast shallow or chest breathing with deep or diaphragmatic breathing, indicating that shallow breathing is problematic for one's well-being. All four of these approaches are consistent with the behavior of the Authentic Person who is nonjudgmental and breathes deeply, from the heels (*xi yi zhong*[w]).

When Yan Hui is told by Confucius to not listen with the ears (senses), he is being told the ears (senses) are always full of distractions, moving about, restrictive, and judgmental. In other words, the ears (senses) are not still and are a stimulus for stress. When Confucius tells Yan Hui to not lis-ten with the mind/heart, Yan Hui is being told that the mind/heart is always full of distractions, moving about, restrictive, and judgmental. In other words, the mind/heart is not still and is a stimulus for stress.

As the senses and the mind/heart are very active, restrictive, easily dis-tractible, involved in judgments, stress producing, and entangle the individ-ual in the affairs of the world, Yan Hui is told to listen with the breath (*qi*[k]). To listen with the breath or *qi*[k] is to be empty, and is the manner, for the *Zhuang Zi,* in which one should deal with the affairs of the world. Confucius describes *dao*[i] itself as the "gathering of emptiness," and then directly links emptiness to the practice *of xin zhai*[s]. Yan Hui tells Confucius that before practicing *xin zhai*[s], he truly believed he had a substantial self or Hui. After practicing *xin zhai*[s], he realizes that he really does not have a self or Hui. Yan Hui then asks Confucius if is possible to call this emptiness.

Fu Zi said, "That is it! I say this to you. If you are able to enter and roam about in his cage without being moved by his importance/fame and he is receptive, then converse with him. If he is not receptive, then stop. Without barriers and without judgments, residing in a unified space, with-out distractions, you will be close. It is easy to disappear, to be without a trace is difficult. It is easy for the actions of man to be considered as fake. It is difficult for the actions of nature to be considered as fake. You have heard of flying with wings. You have not heard of flying without wings. You have heard of having knowledge and knowing. You have not heard of not having knowledge and knowing. Look upon everything as stopped/still. Empty [*xu*[d]] your chamber [mind/heart] giving birth to clarity. Good fortune will abide. However, not stopping is called galloping while sitting. Allowing your attention to be inwardly open and separate from the knowing mind/heart, spirits will come to dwell. How much more men? This is the transformation of all things. Bonding with Yu and Shun. It is that which Fu Zi and Ji Qu practiced until their end. Is this not strong enough reason for its distribution?" (9/4/29–34)

At this point, Confucius provides guidance for entering the world of affairs without getting entangled in them. He tells Yan Hui that, in order to avoid entanglement, he must not be controlled by the fame or the importance of the ruler of Wei. If the ruler is receptive to what you have to say, then converse with him. If he is not receptive, then don't converse with him. Confucius tells Yan Hui that by being without barriers, without judgments, without distractions, and unified, he will be close to the practice of *xin zhai*[s]. To really practice *xin zhai*[s], however, the mind/heart must be emptied and stopped/stilled. When the mind/heart is emptied and stilled, then the person will be able to see clearly. The mind/heart must, however, stay still and empty. In other words, the individual must listen with qi^k or breath.

Confucius tells Yan Hui that if he is unable to maintain the stillness and emptiness of his mind/heart, he will become entangled in the affairs of the world. It is the mind/heart that is full and racing around that leads to entanglements with the affairs of the world. It is this mind/heart that leads to harm of both the individual and others. Confucius referred to this mind/heart as "galloping while sitting."

So how does one still and empty the mind/heart so one does not become entangled in the affairs of the world, and once it is still and empty maintain it as such? By being nonjudgmental, not interfering (*wu wei*[b]), and not attempting to control others, the mind/heart will become still and empty, and the breathing of the individual becomes more natural or deeper. At this point, the individual is empty and listening with qi^k or breath. This is why Confucius tells Yan Hui that he must consciously, in the here and now, look upon everything as stopped/still and to empty his mind/heart. If he does so, he will see clearly. What he will clearly see is that all things are part of a process of continual change, and that the nature of everything, including the *dao*[i] and his own sense of self, is that of stillness and emptiness.

If Yan Hui is unable to still and empty his mind/heart, his mind/heart will continue to race, even if he is sitting still. He will interfere with himself and others, eventually becoming entangled in the affairs of the world. He will be chronically stressed. Being chronically stressed, he will be harming himself physically, psychologically, emotionally, and behaviorally. At the interpersonal level, he will harm himself and others.

Chronic stress is associated with shallow breathing. To be chronically stressed and thus breathing shallowly all of the time is not natural and is harmful to the individual. This is where nonjudgmental, deep breathing may enter the practice of *xin zhai*[s]. As noted earlier, the practice of nonjudgmental, deep abdominal breathing or breathing from the heels (*xi yi zhong*[w]) reduces chronic stress by relaxing the mind and the body. It stills and empties the mind/heart of stress-producing stimuli such as absolute, contrived judgments and artificial values.

The practice of *xin zhai*[s] is ultimately about having a mind/heart that is nonjudgmental (*guan*[g]), still (*jing*[c]), empty (*xu*[d]), and listens with *qi*[k]. This being the case, the individual will (1) not get entangled in the affairs of the world (*wu shi*[e]), (2) not interfere with himself or herself or others (*wu wei*[b]), (3) be at peace, (4) be healthy, (5) fully engage existence, (6) be natural, and (7) be in harmony or integrated with the environment and *dao*[i].

There are two integrated aspects in the practice of *xin zhai*[s] that lead to stilling the mind/heart so that it will be empty. The first aspect is to allow your attention to be inwardly open, clear, and not controlled by the external world and not controlled by the contrived knowledge of your mind/heart. The second aspect is nonjudgmental deep breathing. Both of these require lifestyle changes. To clear one's attention and be apart from the contrived knowledge of the mind/heart, the individual engages the present in a nonjudgmental manner. The individual practices being nonjudgmental in all aspects of his or her waking life. The individual does not contend or argue with other people. The individual does not make complex plans and schemes. The individual does not allow words such as *right* and *wrong*, *good* and *bad*, and *beautiful* and *ugly* to internally harm himself or herself. The individual is indifferent to fame, gain, honor, status, disapproval, approval, wealth, poverty, and knowledge itself. The individual realizes and accepts the world, including himself or herself as an organic, integrated, interdependent, continually changing process. Most of which he or she does not have control over.

The individual does not interfere (*wu wei*[b]) with himself or herself, other people, or with the affairs of the world (*wu shi*[e]). By being nonjudgmental, detached, and noninterfering, the individual will not be distracted by affairs of the world. Not being distracted by the affairs of the world, the emotional reactions of the individual will not be excessive. Because the individual is nonjudgmental, not distracted by the affairs of the world, and does not have excessive emotional reactions, his or her mind/heart is still and empty. When the individual's mind/heart is still and empty, the process of breathing naturally deepens. As the process of breathing naturally deepens, the individual is quiet, relaxed, and calm. Being quiet, relaxed, and calm the individual is not chronically stressed and thus not harmed.

The practice of deep breathing requires that the individual is focused on the breathing process of inhalation and exhalation. During this practice, there is a tendency for the mind/heart to get distracted and to make judgments on the distractions or make a judgment on the very fact that it got distracted in the first place. The practitioner must acknowledge that this is likely to occur, and when it does, not to make any judgments and to simply return to the practice of focusing on the process of breathing. Continuing in this manner will result in less distractions, fewer judgments, and deeper breathing. As the breathing deepens, the mind/heart will still and become empty. Being still and empty, the individual will be quiet, calm, and relaxed. Being quiet, calm, and relaxed, the individual is not chronically stressed and thus not harmed.

At the behavioral level, the practice of *xin zhai*[s] requires the individual to consciously practice deep breathing, being nonjudgmental, being noninterfering (*wu wei*[b]), and not becoming entangled (*wu shi*[e]) in the affairs of the world. This practice requires a continual—in the here and now—monitoring of one's thoughts, feelings, and actions. As the individual continues the practice, the mind/heart will more and more become still and empty. This behavioral, consciously directed practice in and of itself will reduce chronic stress.

For the *Zhuang Zi,* however, the continual practice, in the here and now, over a long period of time of *xin zhai*[s] eventually leads to an awareness and experiencing of the natural (*zi ran*[f]) stillness, emptiness, and mystery of the person and existence itself. At this point, *xin zhai*[s] is no longer a consciously guided behavioral practice. *Xin zhai*[s] is what is natural (*zi ran*[f]). Being in the here and now, being nonjudgmental, deep breathing, and not being entangled in the affairs of the world are all natural (*zi ran*[f]). The individual is in harmony with *dao*[i]. The emptiness and stillness within (*de*[j]) is gathered with the emptiness and stillness of *dao*[i].

Mind/Heart Like a Mirror (Xin Ruo Jing)

The *Zhuang Zi* also offers a more visual approach to the practice of *xin zhai*[s] by using the concept of a mirror as a metaphor for its practice. This practice as well requires a conscious effort on the part of the practitioner to be fully aware and engaged in the practice in the here and now. The individual is instructed to have a mind/heart that is like a mirror (*xin ruo jing*[x]). The mirror engages (reflects) all that appears before it. It does not judge, hold on to, interfere, or get entangled with whatever appears before it. The mirror is not moved by or controlled by whatever appears before it. The practice of *xin zhai*[s] is to not get distracted by nor get entangled with the affairs of the world. It is to be still and empty. To be still and empty is to be nonjudgmental and to not interfere in the affairs of the world. It is to be like a mirror.

Don't be the corpse of fame. Don't be the residence of schemes. Don't be controlled by interaction in the world. Don't be ruled by knowledge. Live your life in the endless and roam in the boundless. Use up that which you received from nature, yet do not see any attainment. Be empty [*xu*[d]] that is all! The complete person [*zhi ren*[af]] uses the mind/heart like a mirror [*xin ruo jing*[x]]. Neither leading nor welcoming. Responding, yet not storing. Thus, he/she is able to overcome things yet not harm them. (21/7/31–33)

Sitting in Forgetfulness (Zuo Wang)

The second approach for reducing chronic stress in the *Zhuang Zi* is the practice of sitting in forgetfulness (*zuo wang*[y]). Unlike *xin zhai*[s], which requires the individual to be fully engaged, in the present, with the environment, the practice of sitting in forgetfulness (*zuo wang*[y]) has an internal focus such that the individual's mind/heart becomes nonjudgmental, still, and absorbed in emptiness. Everything else, including the body and mind disappears. There is just awareness.

Benson (1975) presents sitting in forgetfulness (*zuo wang*[y]) as a Daoist example of his relaxation response. It is used as an example because it has the same fundamental characteristics, the resulting altered state of consciousness, and the benefits for stress reduction. He finds the relaxation response, and thus sitting in forgetfulness, to be similar to many meditative, relaxation, and stress-reduction practices in both Eastern and Western cultures.

In the section on sitting in forgetfulness from the *Zhuang Zi*, Confucius and his favorite student Yan Hui are once again utilized in a satirical manner to present the teachings of Daoism. Of particular interest is that the achievement of Yan Hui being able to sit in forgetfulness—requires not only the elimination (forgetting) of the body, the senses, form, and knowledge, but also the casting off (forgetting) of the fundamental Confucian values of *ren* (selfless love), *yi* (appropriate choice), *li* (appropriate behavior), and *yue* (ceremonial music).

From the perspective of the *Zhuang Zi*, these Confucian values contribute to the problem of chronic stress insofar as they are viewed as being judgmental, restrictive, interfering, and controlling relative to the behavior of individuals within various environmental contexts. The practice of sitting in forgetfulness minimizes the importance of the teachings of Confucianism, at least as understood by the *Zhuang Zi*.

Yan Hui said, "I succeeded." Zhong Ni (Confucius) said, "What do you mean?" Hui said, "I forgot *ren*[z] [selfless love] and *yi*[aa] [appropriate choice]." Confucius said, "That is possible, yet you are still not there." Later on, they saw each other again. Hui said, "I succeeded." Zhong Ni (Confucius) said, "What do you mean?" Hui said, "I forgot *li*[ab] [appropriate behavior] and *yue*[ac] [music]." Confucius said, "That is possible, yet you are still not there." Later on, they saw each other again. Hui said, "I succeeded." Zhong Ni (Confucius) said, "What do you mean?" Hui said, "I sit in forgetfulness [*zuo wang*[y]]." Zhong Ni, somewhat startled, said,

"What do you mean sit in forgetfulness?" Yan Hui said, "I let my body [limbs and trunk] fall away. I dismissed my senses. I separated from form and got rid of knowledge. I am the same as the great passageway. This is the meaning of sitting in forgetfulness." Zhong Ni (Confucius) said, "Being the same, thus you are without partiality. Transformed, thus without absolutes. The results are quite worthy." Qiu (Confucius) then requested to become his disciple. (19/6/89–93)

The practice of sitting in forgetfulness (*zuo wang*[y]) is an emptying out of all restrictions and limitations. Unlike *xin zhai*[s] or mind/heart fasting, however, the individual who is engaging in *zuo wang*[y] or sitting in forgetfulness is nonjudgmentally absorbed into the emptiness during the course of its practice. Upon completion of the practice, the individual emerges focused, rooted, centered, in the present, relaxed, refreshed, physically and psychologically strengthened, and ready to fully engage the environment.

In a very real sense, the practice of sitting in forgetfulness contributes to the development of *xin zhai*[s] or mind/heart fasting. The letting go and emptying out of all judgments, restrictions, partiality, absolutes, and barriers allows the individual to cultivate naturalness (*zi ran*[f]). The benefits of sitting in forgetfulness and cultivating naturalness spill over onto the practice of *xin zhai*[s], contributing to its further development.

While sitting in forgetfulness (*zuo wang*[y]) is a temporary withdrawal from the environment to center, nourish, and recharge the body and the mind/heart, *xin zhai*[s] or mind/heart fasting is to fully engage the ever-changing, interrelated, integrated environment in a nonjudgmental, noninterfering (*wu wei*[b]), noncontrolling, mirror-like manner through which the individual does not become entangled in the affairs of the world (*wu shi*[e]). The result of integrating both *zuo wang*[y] and *xin zhai*[s] into one's lifestyle is freedom, naturalness, and the elimination of chronic stress. It is, in the words of the *Zhuang Zi,* happiness!

A summary of the four techniques for stilling and emptying the mind/heart is presented in Table 5.5.

Happiness

Happiness is to see and experience the environment as it behaves. It is realizing that change is natural, continual, and applies to everything. It is accepting that you are part of this natural process and that no matter what you do, you and everything else will eventually disappear. It is coming to terms with the fact that you will die. Happiness is to fully experience and engage existence without interference from yourself or others. Happiness is to be natural and free! It is to enjoy your time in the present.

Happiness is not following another person's or society's perspective on what is good or not good. It is not behaving in a certain manner because

Table 5.5   Techniques for Stilling and Emptying the Mind/Heart

Technique	Description
Mind/heart fasting (*xin zhai*ˢ)	Flexibly focused, nonjudgmental observation of and engagement with the vastness of the present. Will is unified. There is no distractibility. Mind/heart is open and not subject to control by the senses or thoughts. Senses and thoughts are partial, limiting, and restrictive. Contact with the environment (internal or external) is based on qi^k (breath). Qi^k is rooted in emptiness. There is no sense of an individual, separate, independent, unchanging self.
Breathing from the heels (*xi yi zhong*ʷ)	Deep, abdominal breathing. Breathing is diaphragmatic. The goal is to make this type of breathing normal.
Mind/heart like a mirror (*xin ruo jing*ˣ)	The mind/heart is like a mirror. It simply reflects all that appears before it. It neither leads nor welcomes. Like a mirror, it does not judge, interfere, possess, or get entangled with anything that appears before it. It responds but does not store.
Sitting in forgetfulness (*zuo wang*ʸ)	Internal, nonjudgmental focus. Knowledge, thoughts, feelings, body, form, external and internal affairs, and the senses are out of awareness. Complete absorption into vast emptiness. Practiced with the eyes closed.

people previously have always behaved in that way. Happiness is not what society or custom defines or says it is. Happiness is not getting entangled in the affairs of the world. Happiness is not interfering with yourself or others.

Martyrs are seen by the world as good, but seeing them as good is not sufficient for them to live out their lives. I don't know if their commitment to goodness is good? Is not good? Although they acted in a good manner, it was not sufficient for them to live out their lives. Although I could consider their actions as not good, it was sufficient for others to live out their lives. It is therefore said, "If your sincere warnings are not listened to, withdraw and do not contend." Thus, Wu Zi Xu contended and his body was destroyed. If he did not contend, his fame would not have been achieved. Is there really something that is good or not? Now, that which people engage in by custom and is that which is their happiness, I do not know if the happiness is truly happiness or truly not happiness? I nonjudgmentally observe [*guan*ᵍ] that which, according to custom, happiness is. What the crowds hold up and desire, as if it is so and there is no alternative. And all say it is happiness. I am not happy moreover I am not unhappy. Is there truly happiness or not? I take noninterference [*wu wei*ᵇ] to truly be happiness. On the other hand, that which is the common practice is excessively bitter. Thus it is said, "Perfect happiness is without happiness. Perfect praise is without praise in the world." It is surely not possible to establish right and wrong. Nonetheless, noninterference [*wu wei*ᵇ] can establish right and wrong. Perfect happiness in life can only be found through noninterference [*wu wei*ᵇ]. Allow me to try these words, "The sky is clear because it does not interfere [*wu wei*ᵇ]. The earth is tranquil because it does not interfere [*wu wei*ᵇ]. Thus, these two join together in noninterferences [*wu wei*ᵇ] and all things are all able to change and transform!" How vast! How subtle! Not produced! How subtle! How vast! Formless! All things are flourishing. All produced through noninterference [*wu wei*ᵇ]. Thus it is said, the sky and the earth do not interfere, yet there is nothing that is not done. What person is able to achieve noninterference? (46/18/6–15)

Summary

Both the *Dao De Jing* and the *Zhuang Zi* clearly indicate that successful adaptation to the various environmental contexts is being compromised by what we today call chronic stress. Chronic stress is the fundamental human condition for which a solution is offered by both texts. From the perspective of these two texts, chronic stress is based on absolute, contrived, unchanging perspectives or worldviews that are guided by a focus on endpoints, complexity, and differences. The perspectives or worldviews and the subsequent behaviors derived from them need to be changed.

The solution offered by the *Dao De Jing* and the *Zhuang Zi* focuses on beginning points, simplicity, and commonality. Their solution is expressed by lifestyle changes that integrate being still (*jing*ᶜ), being empty (*xu*ᵈ), not interfering (*wu wei*ᵇ), not getting entangled in the affairs of the world (*wu shi*ᵉ), observing and engaging existence in a nonjudgmental manner (*guan*ᵍ), natural breathing, the unimpeded circulation of breath (*qi*ᵏ), the practice of sitting in forgetfulness (*zuo wang*ʸ), and the practice of mind/heart fasting (*xin zhai*ˢ). Ultimately, the solution offered by these two texts is concerned with freedom, happiness, and being natural (*zi ran*ᶠ).

The way of the sky is to circulate and not accumulate anything. Thus, all things are completed. The way of the emperor is to circulate and not accumulate anything. Thus the world returns. The way of the naturally integrated person [sage] is to circulate and not accumulate anything, thus all within the seas submit. The one who is clear about nature, united with the sages, united with the power [*de*ʲ] of the emperor which penetrates in all directions over the four seasons, in his own actions, although hidden, there is nothing that is not still [*jing^c*]. The sage is still [*jing^c*]. It is not said that stillness is good therefore he is still. The 10,000 things are not sufficient to distract his mind/heart, therefore he is still. Still water clearly illuminates the beard and eyebrows, and precisely centering on its levelness, the carpenter uses it as a model. If still water is so clear, how much more the essential spirit [*jing shen^{ad}*]. The mind/heart of the sage is still. It reflects the sky and the earth, it mirrors all things. Empty [*xu^d*], still [*jing^c*], indifferent to fame and gain, quiet and noninterfering [*wu wei^b*]. It is the level of the sky and the earth, and the completion of *dao^i* and *de^j*. This is where emperors and sages stop. Stopping, then empty [*xu^d*]. Empty [*xu^d*], then full. Full, then prepared. Empty [*xu^d*], then still [*jing^c*]. Still, then movement. Movement, then achievement. Stillness, then not interfering [*wu wei^b*]. Not interfering, then those responsible complete their tasks. Not interfering, then peacefulness. Those who are peaceful are not chronically stressed (depression [*you^a*] and anxiety [*huan^{ae}*] do not dwell in them). They live out a long life. Empty [*xu^d*], still [*jing^c*], indifferent to fame and gain, quiet and not interfering [*wu wei^b*], this is the root of all things. (33/13/1–7)

Important Terms

Dao^i (extended, still, dynamic empty space; the natural way)

De^j (*dao^i* within the individual; gentle power)

Dao De Jing (the text the *Classic of Dao and De*)

Guan^g (nonjudgmental observation)

He (harmony)

Jing^c (stillness)

Jing (essence)

Jing (a classic text: the *Dao De Jing)*

Qi^k (breath, life force, energy)

Shen^m (spirit)

Wu shi^e (not getting entangled in the affairs of the world)

Wu wei^b (not interfering)

Xin zhai^s (mind/heart fasting)

Xu^d (emptiness, empty space)

Yuan qi^n (original breath)

Zhong (centered)

Zhuang Zi (the text known as the *Zhuang Zi*)

Zi ran[f] (naturalness)

Zuo wang[y] (sitting in forgetfulness)

Exercises

For both the *Dao De Jing* and the *Zhuang Zi*, *wu wei*[b] or noninterference is a central concept of their teachings. *Wu wei*[b] means to not interfere with other people or yourself. I would like you to practice *wu wei*[b]. Stay in the present and be nonjudgmental.

A.   Pick a 24-hour period, say a Tuesday, and see if you can interact with other people without attempting to control their behavior. Do not attempt to criticize, manipulate, or coerce other people to satisfy your own needs and/or to get them to agree with your worldview about how people ought to behave. In your interactions with others be supportive and nourishing. If asked for your opinion, you may offer sincere and authentic suggestions to assist them in their growth and development. If they disagree or wish to argue with you about the suggestions, do not contend with them. Do not argue with them or try to convince them in any manner. Simply let it go and move on.

To practice *wu wei*[b] in your interactions with others, you need to be nonjudgmental and in the here and now. Observe how you feel when you practice *wu wei*[b]. What do you notice about yourself? About other people? Compare those observations with those that are generated from your behavior when you attempt to control (we all do) other people. What did you learn? Discover? Experience?

B.   Select another 24-hour period, say a Friday, and focus the practice of *wu wei*[b] on yourself. Regarding yourself, *wu wei*[b] means getting out of your own way. It means to stop ruminating, complaining, and whining. *Wu wei*[b] means to eliminate the self-imposed and society-imposed criticisms, restrictions, barriers, guilt, and doubt that prevent you from moving forward in a positive, growth-oriented manner.

Observe yourself, your thoughts, and your actions. How cluttered is your mind/heart with these negative barriers? What triggers the negativity? Are there certain events or situations? Is it habit? Is it your general worldview? How often do you interfere with yourself? How often do you hinder your own progress? How do you feel when you restrict yourself?

To practice *wu wei*[b] with yourself, stay in the present and be nonjudgmental. This will require a conscious effort on your part. If you are in the present and nonjudgmental, the negativity and limitations will fade away. They only stay around because you feed them with your judgments.

The negativity, doubts, and self-criticisms will rise up into your mind/heart—you have years of conditioning and practice—but they can only endure if you hold on to them with your judgments and thoughts. How do you feel when you practice *wu wei*[b]? What do you experience? Compare your observations to those when you do not practice *wu wei*[b]. What do you notice?

    C. Choose one more 24-hour period, say a Sunday, and see if you can practice *wu wei*[b] both with yourself and others. How do you feel when you practice *wu wei*[b] in this format? How does this combined practice of *wu wei*[b] differ from the practice of *wu wei*[b] directed solely toward yourself or others? How is it similar? What do you experience? Compare these observations to those when you do not practice *wu wei*[b]. What do you notice?

    How is *wu wei*[b] applicable in a counseling context? What benefit is *wu wei*[b] for the counselor? What benefit would it be to teach the client how to practice *wu wei*[b]?

Chinese Characters

a 憂	l 玄	w 息以踵
b 無為	m 神	x 心若鏡
c 靜	n 元氣	y 坐忘
d 虛	o 聖人	z 仁
e 無事	p 神	aa 義
f 自然	q 無味	ab 禮
g 觀	r 無欲	ac 樂
h 明	s 心齋	ad 精神
i 道	t 天	ae 患
j 德	u 道樞	af 至人
k 氣	v 真人	

Notes

1. For a comparison of these two commentaries, see Chan (1991, 1998).

2. All translations/interpretations of the *Dao De Jing* and the commentaries of Wang Bi and He Shang Gong are my own. The format *Dao De Jing, 18* refers to Chapter 18 of the *Dao De Jing.* The primary text utilized for this translation is the standard transmitted text with the Wang Bi commentary. This Chinese text can be found in Yang (1972). In addition, I also utilized Wang (1993) with the He Shang Gong commentary, and Wang (1972).

3. For an interesting perspective and analysis, see Graham (1995).

4. For a comprehensive discussion of being natural (*zi ran*[f]), see Liu (1998), pp. 211–228.

5. For an in-depth exploration of the concept of *wu wei*[b] and its relationship to government and establishing social harmony, see Slingerland (2003), pp. 77–117.

6. All translations from the Chinese are my own. The format of 3/2/10–12 indicates the page/chapter/lines in the *Harvard–Yenching Institute Sinological Index Series Supplement 20, A Concordance to Chuang Tzu* (1956). The text *Zhuang Zi Bai Hua Ju Jie* (1989) was used as a supplement for the translation/interpretation. Focus of the translation/interpretation is on inner chapters (1–7) and Chapters 13 and 17–22. For chapter authenticity, see Slingerland (2003), pp. 285–286. I consider Chapters 1–7 and Chapters 13 and 17–22 in the *Zhuang Zi* text to be representative of the teachings of the person Zhuang Zi.

7. The three components of this character (*you*[a]) represent, from top down: an old form for head, a heart, and walk slowly. Its meaning is that both the head and heart are moving slowly. Thus cognitive, affective, and behavioral aspects of the person are compromised. This is clearly an example of chronic stress, fear, anxiety, worry, sadness, and/or depression.

References

Ames, R. T., & Hall, D. L. (2003). *Dao De Jing: Making this life significant.* New York: Ballantine Books.

Benson, H. (1975). *The relaxation response.* New York: Avon Books.

Benson, H., & Stuart, E. M. (Eds.). (1992). *The wellness book: The comprehensive guide to maintaining health and treating stress-related illness.* New York: Simon & Schuster.

Chan, A. K. L. (1991). *Two visions of the way: A study of the Wang Pi and Ho-Shang Kung commentaries on the Lao-Tzu.* Albany: State University of New York Press.

Chan, A. K. L. (1998, Spring). A tale of two commentaries. In L. Kohn & M. La Fargue (Eds.), *Lao Tzu and the Tao Te Jing* (pp. 89–117). Albany: State University of New York. Available at http://plato.stanford.edu/archives/spr2002/entries/laozi/

Cheng, C. Y. (2003). Philosophy of change. In A. S. Cua (Ed.), *Encyclopedia of Chinese philosophy* (pp. 517–524). New York: Routledge.

Fox, A. (2003). Reflex and reflectivity: *Wu wei* in the *Zhuang Zi*. In S. Cook (Ed.), *Hiding the world in the world* (pp. 207–225). Albany: State University of New York Press.

Fried, R. (1993). The role of respiration in stress and stress control: Toward a theory of stress as a hypoxic phenomenon. In P. M. Lehrer & R. L. Woolfolk (Eds.), *Principles and practices of stress management* (pp. 301–331). New York: Guilford.

Fung, Y. L. (1983). *A history of Chinese philosophy, Vol. I.* Princeton, NJ: Princeton University Press.

Gascoigne, B. (2003). *The dynasties of China: A history.* New York: Carroll & Graff.

Gernet, J. (1999). *A history of Chinese civilization.* New York: Cambridge University Press.

Graham, A. C. (1995). *Disputers of the Tao.* La Salle, IL: Open Court.

Harvard–Yenching Institute. (1956). *Harvard–Yenching Institute Sinological Index Series Supplement 20: A Concordance to Chuang Tzu.* Cambridge, MA: Harvard University Press.

Hoblitzelle, O. A., & Benson, H. (1992). The relaxation response. In H. Benson & E. M. Stuart (Eds.), *The wellness book: The comprehensive guide to maintaining health and treating stress-related illness* (pp. 33–44). New York: Simon & Schuster.

Hucker, C. O. (1975). *China's imperial past: An introduction to Chinese history and culture.* Stanford, CA: Stanford University Press.

Jochim, C. (1998). Just say no to "no self" in Zhuang Zi. In R.T. Ames (Ed.), *Wandering at ease in the Zhuang Zi* (pp. 35–74). Albany: State University of New York Press.

Kabat-Zinn, J. (2005). *Full catastrophe living.* New York: Delta Trade Paperbacks.

Lewis, D. (1997). *The Tao of natural breathing.* San Francisco: Mountain Wind.

Liu, X. G. (1998). Naturalness (tzu-jan), the core value in Taoism: Its ancient meaning and its significance today. In L. Kohn & M. La Fargue (Eds.), *Lao Tzu and the Tao Te Jing* (pp. 211–228). Albany: State University of New York Press.

Loy, D. (1996). Zhuang Zi and Nagarjuna on the truth of no truth. In P. Kjellbert & P. Ivanhoe (Eds.), *Essays on skepticism, relativism, and ethics in the* Zhuang Zi (pp. 50–67). Albany: State University of New York Press.

Miller, J. (2003). *Daoism.* Oxford: One World.

Roth, H. D. (1999). *Original Tao.* New York: Columbia University Press.

Roth, H. D. (2003). Bimodal mystical experience in the qiwulun. In S. Cook (Ed.), *Hiding the world in the world* (pp. 15–32). Albany: State University of New York Press.

Saso, M. (1983). The Chuang-Tzu Nei-Pien. In V. Mair (Ed.), *Experimental essays on Chuang-Tzu* (pp. 140–157). Honolulu: University of Hawaii Press.

Saso, M. (1995). *The gold pavilion.* Boston: Charles E. Tuttle.

Slingerland, E. (2003). *Effortless action:* Wu wei *as a conceptual metaphor and spiritual ideal in early China.* New York: Oxford University Press.

Wang, H. (Zhu Shi). (1972). *Lao zi tan yi.* Taibei: Taiwan Shang Wu Yin Shu Guan.

Wang, K. (1993). *Lao zi dao de jing he shang gong zhang zhu.* Beijing: Zhong Hua Shu Ju.

Yang, J. L. (Zhu Bian). (1972). *Lao zi ben yi, Lao zi xin kao shu lue.* Taibei: Shi Jie Shu Ju.

Zhuang Zi. (1989). *Bai hua ju jie.* Hong Kong: Feng Hua Chu Ban Shi Ye Gong Se.

6

Confucianism and Stress Management

Confucius (551–479 BCE) lived during the end of the Spring and Autumn Periods (770–476 BCE) of the Zhou dynasty (1122–256 BCE).[1] He was married with two children, a boy and a girl, and held a position, which he left, as police commissioner/minister of justice in his home state of Lu. Essentially, though, Confucius was a wandering teacher who visited a number of kingdoms offering his teachings.

The period in which Confucius lived was a time of continual warfare between various kingdoms, political instability, and social change. (See Ames & Rosemont, 1998, and Hsu, 1965.) It was a time of chronic stress. The teachings of Confucius were offered as a solution to assist the ruler in ruling and to teach people how to live relative to establishing a harmonious and stable society. The focus of his teachings was on the interrelationships between people within the social context. His discussions and teachings regarding individual cultivation were always oriented toward the benefit of society as a whole.

Confucius taught people how to adapt and resolve their interpersonal challenges in various environmental contexts. He taught them how to manage the chronic stress that was generated because of problematic social skills and self-centeredness. Confucius believed that employment in government was contingent upon virtue, concern for others, relationships skills, and the competencies required for the particular position. One's position in the government—and in life, for that matter—should not be based on bloodline, power base, or connections. Everyone should earn his or her position and status based on demonstrated ability and achievement.

The teachings of Confucius are found in the *Lun Yu (Sayings and Discussions),* which is often translated as the *Analects.* (See Ames & Rosemont, 1998; Gardner, 2003; Lau, 1988; Legge, 1971; Van Norden, 2002;

and Waley, 1938.) This collection of sayings was compiled by the students and disciples of Confucius. He himself did not write anything.

As do the preceding two chapters, this chapter contains a significant number of translations. These translations from the *Lun Yu* will allow the reader to get a feel for the teachings of Confucius.

The Foundation of the Teachings of Confucius

There are two basic sources for the teachings of Confucius: history and the family. History meant, for Confucius, the time period of the traditional sage rulers of Yao, Shun, and Yu (middle-to-late 24th century to middle-to-late 23rd century BCE) and the beginning of the Zhou dynasty, especially under the guidance offered by the Duke of Zhou (11th century BCE). (See Fung, 1983, and Chan, 1973.)

History

The time period of Yao, Shun, and Yu was viewed as one of peace and harmony. Confucius used it as a model of the ideal society, where morality, positive relationships, concern for the well-being of the people, and filial piety were in the forefront. It was a time when merit, skills, competencies, and moral charisma, not bloodline, were the basis for promotion into positions of authority.

> The Master [Confucius] said, "How towering! Shun and Yu had the world, yet did not seek it." (*Lun Yu*, VIII-18)[2]

The Duke of Zhou was known for his administrative skills, loyalty, fairness, and the guiding of the Zhou dynasty in its earliest beginning. His nephew, the king, was a minor and the Duke of Zhou ruled in his place until the king became of age. This time period was also viewed by Confucius as an ideal model for social harmony.

> The Master said, "I have declined very much. For a long time I have not dreamt of seeing the Duke of Zhou!" (*Lun Yu*, VII-5)

> The Master said, "The Zhou dynasty examined two dynasties. How elegant their culture. I follow the Zhou." (*Lun Yu*, III-14)

Confucius also looked to the ancient classics for guidance. Two of the classics, the *Book of Songs/Poetry* (*Shi Jing*) and the *Book of History/Documents* (*Shu Jing*) provide a glimpse into the early Zhou dynasty. They offer insight into thinking, behavior, and the links among governing, the family, and social harmony.

The Master said, "The *Shi* [*Book of Songs/Poetry*] has 300 songs; it can be summed up in a single phrase, it is said, Thoughts do not wander from what is correct." (*Lun Yu*, II-2)

Someone once said to Confucius, "Why are you not active in governing?" Confucius replied, "The *Shu* [*Book of History/Documents*] says, 'Be filial [*xiao*[a]]! Strictly speaking being filial to your parents and being friends with your brothers is carrying out governing.' As this is also governing, why do you have to talk about being active in governing?" (*Lun Yu*, II-21)

The Family

For Confucius, it is in the family that appropriate thinking, feeling, and behaving begin and develop. It is in the family that relationships are discovered, managed, cultivated, and refined. The core relationship and value in Chinese culture and the heart of the Chinese family is that of *xiao*[a] or *filial piety*. *Xiao*[a] is the relationship between the children and the parents. It is a relationship in which the children demonstrate respect, reverence, attentiveness, loyalty, trust, commitment, compassion, and love toward their parents. The family is the context through which children learn about hierarchies and their place or position within the context of the familial hierarchy.

Meng Wu Bo asked about *xiao*[a] [filial piety]. The Master said, "Your father and mother only worry about you being ill." (*Lun Yu*, II-6)

The Master said, "If for three years you do not change from your father's *dao*[b] [moral path], it is possible to call you filial [*xiao*[a]]." (*Lun Yu*, IV-20)

The Master said, "In interacting with your parents admonish them gently. If you see they are not following your suggestions, be attentive. Do not be disobedient. Be persistent but do not complain." (*Lun Yu*, IV-18)

The second important relationship and value discovered, developed, and cultivated in the family is that of *fraternality* (*di*[c]). *Di*[c] is the relationship between the younger brother and older brother. *Di*[c] is also knowing your position in the hierarchical context. It is a showing of respect from the younger brother to the older brother.

For Confucius, *xiao*[a] and *di*[c] are fundamental values and behaviors that are applicable to all aspects of life. These relationships serve as the basis for interacting outside of the home and within the contexts of society and government.

You Zi [a disciple of Confucius] said, "It is rare for a person who is filial [*xiao*[a]] and fraternal [*di*[c]] to be fond of going against his superiors. You simply do not have someone who is not fond of going against his superiors starting a rebellion. The *jun zi*[d] attends to the root, the fundamentals. The root being established, the *dao*[b] [moral path] will grow. Being *xiao*[a] [filial] and fraternal [*di*[c]] are the root of *ren*[e]." (*Lun Yu*, I-2)

The Master said, "As a younger brother and son be filial [*xiao*[a]] when in the home. When outside of the home be courteous/fraternal [*di*[c]], cautious, trustworthy [*xin*[f]], full of fondness for all, and intimate with *ren*[e]. If you have any extra energy, then use it to study and cultivate yourself." (*Lun Yu*, I-6)

The Teachings of Confucius

As noted earlier, the teachings of Confucius were offered as a solution for resolving the political and social instability of the time. His teachings were presented to assist the ruler in ruling and the people in living their lives to the fullest. His teachings revolve around a set of core values and a model, the *jun zi*[d], who manifests these values in everyday life. The teachings of Confucius ultimately are about establishing social harmony. Although he speaks of self-cultivation, self-cultivation must always be seen in light of the individual's contribution to the betterment of society. Everything, I mean everything, that is done by the individual for self-improvement is always oriented toward social harmony. For Confucius, there really is no sense of individuality apart from society as a whole.

The fundamental values that serve as the beginning points for the teachings of Confucius, the establishment of good government, and social harmony are filial piety (*xiao*[a]), appropriate behavior (*li*[g]), appropriate choice (*yi*[h]), wisdom (*zhi*[i]), trust (*xin*[f]), attentiveness (*jing*[j]), doing your best/being authentic (*zhong*[k]), empathy (*shu*[l]), selfless interpersonal love (*ren*[e]), and the power of peace and tranquility (*de*[m]). All of these are cultivated, integrated, developed, refined, and manifested by the Confucian role model known as the fully integrated person (*jun zi*[d]). The *jun zi*[d] is often described as not being, for all intents and purposes, chronically stressed. The fragmented person, who makes up most of the population, is described as being chronically stressed. Thus, teachings of Confucius are oriented to eliminating the chronic stress in individuals so that the instability (chronic stress) of society can be eliminated.

The Approach of Confucius to Teaching and Learning

Confucius felt education was the manner in which the individual could develop, cultivate, and refine the virtues, values, skills, and competencies necessary for establishing social harmony. Education was the pathway to success in life. It was not, however, individual success that mattered but what the individual could do for the betterment of society.

Education was the way to eliminate self-centeredness and the dysfunctional thinking, feeling, and behaving associated with it. Confucius believed education should be open to all, without any discrimination. The potential student must, however, offer a token of appreciation, no matter how small, indicating commitment to learning and self-cultivation.

The Master said, "My teachings are for all without any discrimination." (*Lun Yu,* XV-39)

The Master said, "I have never refused instruction to anyone who has made even the humble offering of dried meat." (*Lun Yu,* VII-7)

In his teaching interactions, Confucius expected commitment and follow-through by his students. He expected them to be attentive, focused, and hard working. He was more than willing to open the door to learning, but he required the students to walk through the door on their own and bring back and apply what they discovered in their journeys. He was well aware that this journey would be at times challenging, frustrating, and troubling. If students were not fully engaged, committed to learning, and did not actively participate in the process of learning, he did not waste his time with them.

The Master said, "If they are not frustrated, I do not inspire them. If they are not troubled, I do not develop them. If I raise up a corner and they don't return the other three corners, I do not repeat it." (*Lun Yu,* VII-8)

Confucius looked to the ancients and the family as his foundation and for inspiration and guidance. He claimed to be merely a transmitter of ancient practices and methods. He did not view himself as creative or innovative.

The Master said, "I transmit not creating anything. I trust [*xin*^f] and am fond of the ancients, secretly comparing myself to old Peng." (*Lun Yu,* VII-1)

Although he claimed he was merely a transmitter, Confucius adapted the ancient teachings to make them applicable and functional in his current environmental context. To do this required a methodology for delivering the teachings. A fundamental technique in his tool kit was that of observational learning. Confucius stressed the importance of being attentive (*jing*^j) to your own behavior and the behavior of others. By being attentive to yourself and to others, you become aware of your strengths and weaknesses. Given this awareness and understanding, the individual is now able to make the appropriate changes necessary for self-improvement for the benefit of society. For Confucius, there really is no knowledge for the sake of simply knowing. Knowledge is for self-examination, application, and action. Confucius is concerned with continual self-improvement for the benefit of society.

> Ceng Zi [a disciple of Confucius] said, "I daily examine myself in three areas. In working for other people, have I not done my best/been authentic [zhong^k]? In interacting with my friends have I not been trustworthy [xin^t]? Have I not practiced what has been passed on to me?" (Lun Yu, I-4)

> The Master said, "Looking at their results, nonjudgmentally observing [guan^n] their reasons, and examining the place where they are at peace. How can they still be hidden? How can they still be hidden?" (Lun Yu, II-10)

> The Master said, "When traveling with three people, I will certainly have teachers. I will select that which is good and follow it. That which is not good, I will change it in myself." (Lun Yu, VII-22)

Confucius did not want his students simply to gather information and learn about it without reflecting on its validity, meaning, and application. He did not want his students to simply discuss and reflect without learning. He wanted his students to process information on a deeper level. This was for the purpose of being able to appropriately apply what one had learned to various environmental contexts in order to establish social harmony.

> The Master said, "To learn and not reflect upon it, is to deceive yourself. To reflect yet not learn, is to endanger yourself." (Lun Yu, II-15)

It was important for Confucius that his students fully understood what they studied. If they truly understood what they were studying, then they could apply their learning to the various environmental contexts for the purpose of developing, establishing, and maintaining social harmony. There was the potential, however, for significant negative consequences if the students claimed that they knew and understood, when in fact they did not, and then attempted to apply their lack of knowledge to the social context. Knowledge for Confucius was not only understanding that you knew something when you in fact did know, but also understanding that you knew you did not know something when in fact you did not know.

> The Master said, "You [a disciple of Confucius]! Shall I teach you about wisdom [zhi^i]? To say that you know when you do know and to say that you don't know when you don't know, this is wisdom." (Lun Yu, II-17)

For Confucius, the process of education, the learning process itself, was the shaping, cultivating, and refining of the raw primitive stuff of the human being. Confucius pointed out that it was important to understand that the civilized, compassionate, empathic, authentic, self-confident, relaxed, nonstressed individual, the *jun zi*^{d}, was an integration of the raw primitive stuff of the human being and the patterns of culture and practical learning. Excess on either side, being too physical or too refined or intellectual, was problematic and not conducive to harmony and balance.

> The Master said, "If one's primitive stuff/physicality overwhelms refinement/ culture [*wen*°], then there is unruliness. If refinement/culture overwhelms one's primitive stuff/physicality then there is a parading of one's learning. Refinement/culture and the primitive stuff/physicality must be equally distributed. Then there is the *jun zi*^{d}." (*Lun Yu*, VI-18)

As the process of being educated is an integration, so to is the process of teaching. To teach effectively, the teacher must integrate the old and the new. As everything is a process of continually change, individuals must learn to adapt to the changes in the environment. An integrative approach to education and teaching facilitates this adaptation.

> The Master said, "Review the old and learn the new, then it is possible to be a teacher." (*Lun Yu*, II-11)

It is important once again to point out that for Confucius education was about the practical application of what one has learned in various social contexts. It is about contributing to and establishing social harmony. It is about eliminating stressful interpersonal situations. Confucius was not concerned with flowery language, rhetoric, or gathering knowledge simply for the sake of saying you knew something. He learned through his own experiences that you must observe the behavior of people. Through their behavior or lack of behavior you will come to understand them.

> Zai Yu [a disciple of Confucius] was sleeping during the day. The Master said, "You cannot carve rotten wood. A wall of clods of manure cannot be troweled. Regarding Zai Yu, why punish him?" The Master said, "In the beginning when I interacted with people, I listened to their words and trusted they would act accordingly. Now in my interactions with others, I listen to their words and nonjudgmentally observe [*guan*^{n}] their actions. This change is because of Zai Yu." (*Lun Yu*, V-10)

Given the practical, integrative, and observational approach, rooted in tradition and the family, of Confucius to education, teaching, and learning, it is now time to examine the fundamental components of his solution for establishing social harmony and eliminating chronic stress. Although the components are presented individually, they must be seen as part of an integrative whole.

Confucian Relationship Virtues

Confucius's solution is ultimately about changing how one views, thinks about, feels, and behaves in the world. It is about developing a worldview that sees society as a whole and the relationships with others that weave its tapestry together as the primary focus. It is a worldview that focuses on eliminating self-centeredness and the dysfunctional thinking, feeling, and behaving that is generated from it.

Appropriate Behavior (*Li*)

The character *li*^{g} has such meanings as ritual, ceremony, rites, manners, propriety, and etiquette. It is formal, contextually appropriate behavior. For Confucius, however, all interactions between people and institutions are governed by appropriate behavior (*li*^{g}). Depending upon the status or role of the individuals in the interaction and the context, there are appropriate behaviors or *li*^{g} for each situation.

> Lin Fang [a disciple of Confucius] asked about the root of *li*^{g}. The Master said, "Great question! In ceremonies rather than be extravagant, be frugal. In mourning rather than being unassuming, it is better to grieve." (*Lun Yu,* III-4)

It is important to note that *li*^{g} is not just empty, rote behavior. It is behavior that facilitates relationships, reverence, and respect. It is the behavior that holds society together. It is the behavior that articulates the roles that are performed by the members of the social structure. It is the vessel that allows appropriate attitudes and feelings to be expressed.

> The Master said, "Reverence without *li*^{g} [appropriate behavior] results in exhaustion. Being cautious without *li*^{g}, results in fear. Being courageous without *li*^{g}, results in confusion. Being straightforward without *li*^{g}, results in entanglement. The *jun zi*^{d} being sincere with his parents, the people will promote *ren*^{e}. Not leaving behind old friends, the people will not be distant." (*Lun Yu,* VIII-2)

Appropriate behavior or *li*^{g} is what allows trusting, respectful, empathic relationships to develop and be maintained. *Li*^{g} are behaviors that are focused on harmonious relationships between people and institutions in various social contexts. Individuals must see themselves in the context of their relationships with other people. If people are self-centered and out for their own benefit and gain at the expense of others, their behavior will be contrary to *li*^{g}.

If the person's behavior is contrary to appropriate behavior (*li*^{g}), then that person's actions that are contrary to appropriate behavior reinforce his or her self-centered worldview. As long as their worldview is continually shaped by self-centeredness, they will be fragmented and not in harmony. This being the case, they will be chronically stressed. This is why it is important for Confucius that people do not engage in any interactions that are contrary to appropriate behavior.

For Confucius, to truly practice and engage in appropriate behaviors (*li*^{g}), people must see themselves, and in fact identify themselves, in their relationships with other people. They must eliminate their self-centeredness, selfishness, and self-absorption. If people eliminate self-centeredness, recognize and choose appropriate contextual behavior in their relationships with others, then society will come together and people will not be chronically stressed.

> Yan Yuan [a disciple of Confucius] asked about *ren*^{e}. The Master said, "Overcoming your self-centeredness and returning to *li*^{g} is *ren*^{e}. If for one day you overcome your self-centeredness and return to *li*^{g}, then the whole world would come together in *ren*^{e}. This is because *ren*^{e} is due to the self. How could *ren*^{e} be due to anything else?" Yan Yuan said, "May I ask about what this entails?" The Master said, "If it is not appropriate behavior [*li*^{g}], do not look. If it is not *li*^{g}, do not listen. If it is not *li*^{g}, do not speak. Do not anything contrary to *li*^{g}." Yan Yuan said, "Although I am not very smart, I will engage in what you have said." (*Lun Yu*, XII-1)

Appropriate Choice (*Yi*)

Yi^h is the choosing of appropriate behavior or *li*^{g} for any context. *Yi*^{h} is appropriate choice. The context and the individuals populating it determine the *li*^{g} that are appropriate for interpersonal behavior. Selecting and acting on the *li*^{g} for a given context is appropriate choice (*yi*^{h}).

Yi^h is choosing *li*^{g} that are conducive to the betterment and benefit of society. *Yi*^{h} or appropriate choice of *li*^{g} is always within the context of developing and maintaining social harmony. There is no sense of personal bias, self-interest, self-absorption, or self-centeredness in making appropriate choices.

> The Master said, "In his interactions in the in the world, the *jun zi*^{d} is without bias. He makes appropriate choices [*yi*^{h}] by comparing and contrasting." (*Lun Yu*, IV-10)

> The Master said, "The *jun zi*^{d} is guided by appropriate choice [*yi*^{h}], the fragmented person is guided by personal gain." (*Lun Yu*, IV-16)

Wisdom (*Zhi*)

Given that the context and the people that populate it generate which behaviors (*li*^{g}) need to be selected (*yi*^{h}) to develop and/or maintain social harmony, it is important to be able to have the wisdom to be able to choose the appropriate choices and actions. *Zhi*^{i} is wisdom. It is important to understand, however, that wisdom is always involved with action or behavior. You cannot really talk about wisdom without behavior in a specific context. The wisdom and the behavior, of course, are always related to relationships with others and to establishing social harmony.

> Fan Chi [a disciple of Confucius] asked about wisdom [*zhi*^{i}]. The Master said, "Making appropriate choices [*yi*^{h}] in your interactions with the people, and being attentive [*jing*^{j}] to the spirits while keeping them at a distance may be called wisdom [*zhi*^{i}]." He then asked about *ren*^{e}. The Master said, "Regarding *ren*^{e}. First resolve that which is troublesome/distressful, and then afterward obtain success. This may be called *ren*^{e}." (*Lun Yu*, VI-22)

> Fan Chi asked about *ren*^{e}. The Master said, "Love people." He asked about wisdom. The Master said, "Know and understand people." (*Lun Yu*, XII-22)

For Confucius, the wisdom (*zhi*^{i}) necessary for making appropriate choices (*yi*^{h}) relative to context specific behaviors (*li*^{g}) in order to develop, establish, and maintain social harmony begins, is cultivated, and is applied in the family. The core Confucian virtue of *xiao*^{a} or filial piety, respect for one's parents and/or elders, originates in the family. The family is where the child is educated and learns about social relationships, authority, hierarchies, roles, status, working together as a unit, the importance of focusing on the group rather than the individual, social harmony, managing and governing people, and culture.

Within the family context the child learns about trust, honesty, sincerity, respect for others, feelings, the appropriate expression of feelings, context-specific behaviors, choosing context-appropriate behaviors, the process of change, understanding the feelings of others or empathy, and doing your best or being authentic. It is in the family that the child expresses and learns about love. It is here that the child begins to know and understand other people.

It is in the family context that the child is taught to apply that which was learned to the outside world. The child is taught functional behavior that allows for adaptation both within the family and in the environment outside of the family. It is here where wisdom begins! This is why the family is so important in Chinese culture.

The application of that which was developed in the family to the outside world is further cultivated by Confucius as he instructs his students about the teachings of the ancient rulers. This instruction is oriented to preparing individuals to administrate kingdoms and government agencies for the benefit and welfare of the people. The wisdom developed in the family is further developed in the educational environment provided by Confucius: an educational environment directed toward teaching others how to respectfully and empathically interact with each other for the over-all benefit of society. The wisdom (zhi^i) developed in the family and the Confucian educational environment serves as the basis for the ability to appropriately choose (yi^h) the proper behavior (li^g) and act accordingly given the demands of a specific environmental context.

Confucius was teaching people how to functionally adapt to an environmental context by allowing for the elimination of interpersonal stress and the establishment of social harmony. This is the wisdom Confucius sought to nurture in others.

Attentiveness (*Jing*)

One of the most fundamental skills and competencies for social interaction is that of attentiveness: the ability to be focused and to maintain that focus when distractions present themselves. *Jing*[j] is about being in the present, the here and now, in all activities. For Confucius, *jing*[j] means the individual needs to be totally engaged to the extent that there is a reverence, a sense of awe, if you will, toward having the opportunity to connect with life. This presence and reverent engagement or *jing*[j] can be seen in his response to a statement about sacrificing to the spirits.

> To sacrifice as if present, is to sacrifice to the spirits as if they were present. The Master said, "If I do not participate in the sacrifice, it is as if there is no sacrifice." (*Lun Yu*, III-12)

For Confucius, if he is not fully present and reverently engaged in the sacrificial ceremony, it is as if the ceremony did not take place. While traditionally the sacrificial ceremony to the spirits was focused on some individual gain or benefit from the spirits or ancestors, for Confucius the sacrificial ceremony was about self-cultivation. It was an opportunity to be fully engaged in the present. It was about cultivating and refining attentiveness (*jing*[j]).

Jing[j], for Confucius, is one of the fundamental self-cultivation practices of the fully integrated person (*jun zi*[d]). It serves as the basis for calming other people insofar as the (*jun zi*[d]) needs to be attentive, in the present, and fully engaged with others in order for them to be relaxed, tranquil, and stress-free.

> Zi Lu [a disciple of Confucius] asked about the *jun zi*[d]. The Master replied, "They cultivate themselves by being attentive [*jing*[j]]." Zi Lu said,

> "Is that it?" The Master replied, "They cultivate themselves by calming other people." Zi Lu said, "Is that it?" The Master replied, "They cultivate themselves by calming all people. Cultivating themselves by calming all people, even Yao and Shun would find this difficult." (*Lun Yu*, XIV-42)

Being attentive (*jing*[j]) is being attentive in all interactions. It is being in the here and now with all of your senses. It is not enough to engage in the appropriate behavior (*li*[g]) for a given context. The individual must be fully present and engaged, in other words be attentive (*jing*[j]) while performing the appropriate contextual behavior (*li*[g]). This is why Confucius said, "If I do not participate in the sacrifice, it is as if there is no sacrifice." Participation is to be attentive, in the here and now, to the appropriate behavior for performing the sacrifice. If a person is not attentive, is not fully engaged and present, then the *li*[g] are nothing more than ritualistic, internally dead, empty motions in space.

> The Master said, "Why would I want to nonjudgmentally observe [*guan*[n]] a person, who in holding a position of authority, is not open and flexible, is not attentive [*jing*[j]] while engaging in appropriate behavior [*li*[g]], and does not grieve at the time of mourning?" (*Lun Yu*, III-26)

In all relationships with people, it is of utmost importance that the person is attentive (*jing*[j]). Being attentive means to really listen to the other person. Being attentive means acknowledging the other person as a human being.

> The Master said, "Yan Ping Zhong is kind in his relationships with other people. He is always attentive [*jing*[j]]." (*Lun Yu*, V-17)

Trust (*Xin*)

Another fundamental concept that is important for Confucius is *xin*[f] or trust. The character *xin*[f] consists of two components. On the left-hand side is the character *ren*[u] or person. On the right-hand side is the character *yan*[p] or word. The picture presented is that of a person standing by his or her word. A person who can be relied on to faithfully act upon his word, in other words, a person who can be trusted. It is trust between people that allows relationships to be established, cultivated, and to grow. Trust is a fundamental aspect of a harmonious society.

> Ceng Zi [a disciple of Confucius] said, "I daily examine myself in three areas. In working for other people, have I not done my best/been authentic [*zhong*[k]]? In interacting with my friends have I not been trustworthy [*xin*[f]]? Have I not practiced what has been passed on to me?" (*Lun Yu*, I-4)

The Master said, "A person whose word cannot be trusted [xin^f], I do not know if he/she is worthy of anything. A large cart without a linchpin, a small cart without a pin, how would they be able to go?" (Lun Yu, II-22)

The Master said, "Let zhong^k [doing one's best/being authentic] and xin^f [trustworthiness] be your guide. Do not have friends not equal to yourself. If you make a mistake, do not be afraid of changing." (Lun Yu, IX-25)

Empathy (Shu) and Authenticity (Zhong)

The focus of the teachings of Confucius is on establishing trusting, mutually respectful relationships in which individuals in the relationship are sincerely acknowledged as human beings and seen as contributing to and working together for the overall well-being of society as a whole. For this to occur, each individual in the relationship must understand the other person or persons in the relationship from his or her own perspective. In other words, people need to be *empathic*. Each individual needs to be attentive to the cues, be they visual, auditory, or behavioral, of the other people in the relationship in order to help them adapt to and solve their environmental challenges.

In these relationships people need to be open and flexible. They need to present themselves in a manner that will allow the others in the relationships to understand their perspectives. People need to be *authentic*. Being authentic, they will be able to do their best toward solving their adaptive problems and contributing to social harmony.

For Confucius, empathy and doing your best or authenticity is the thread that runs through all of his teachings. Empathy (shu^l) and doing your best or authenticity (zhong^k) are the ultimate foundation of attentiveness (jing^j), appropriate behavior (li^g), appropriate choice (yi^h), trust (xin^f), and wisdom (zhi^i). Doing your best/authenticity (zhong^k) and empathy (shu^l) are the foundation for establishing social harmony. All actions and interactions are guided by doing your best/authenticity (zhong^k) and empathy (shu^l).

The Master said, "Zeng [a disciple of Confucius]! My dao^b uses a single thread." Zeng Zi said, "So it does." The Master left. The disciples asked, "What did he mean?" Zeng Zi said, "The way of the Master is zhong^k [doing your best/being authentic] and shu^l [being empathic]. That is it!" (Lun Yu, IV-15)

The character zhong^k consists of two components. On the top is the character zhong^v, meaning center or middle. On the bottom is the character xin^q or mind/heart, which is indicative of thinking and feeling being intertwined. Given the Confucian focus on practical application, the combination suggests one's actions coming from the center of the mind/heart; in other words, being real or authentic. To come from the center of your mind/heart, to be real or authentic, is suggestive of doing your best.

> Duke Ding asked, "How should the ruler employ his subjects? How should the subjects serve the ruler?" Kong Zi (Confucius) said, "The ruler should employ his subjects through appropriate behavior [*li*[g]]. The subjects should serve their ruler by doing their best/being authentic [*zhong*[k]]." (*Lun Yu*, III-19)

The character *shu*[l] consists of two components. On the top is the character *ju*[r], meaning similar or alike. On the bottom is the character *xin*[q], or mind/heart, which is indicative of thinking and feeling being intertwined. Given the Confucian focus on practical application, the combination suggests having a similar heart/mind, which is essentially the definition of *empathy*. This empathy or *shu*[l] is at times expressed in the negative in its concern for the well-being of others.

> Zi Gong [a disciple of Confucius] asked, "Is there one word, which one can practice throughout one's life." The Master said, "It is *shu*[l] [empathy]. What you do not desire, do not impose on others." (*Lun Yu*, XIV-24)

The thread that holds the teachings of Confucius together are empathy (*shu*[l]) and authenticity (*zhong*[k]). As long as your behavior is directed by *shu*[l] and *zhong*[k] you will not go astray. Your thinking, feeling, and behavior will not wander from what is correct. What is correct is empathy and authenticity.

Selfless Interpersonal Love (*Ren*)

For Confucius, the integration and expression of filial piety (*xiao*[a]), fraternality (*di*[c]), empathy (*shu*[l]), doing your best/authenticity (*zhong*[k]), attentiveness (*jing*[j]), appropriate choice (*yi*[h]), trust (*xin*[f]), and wisdom (*zhi*[i]) through appropriate behavior (*li*[g]) relative to the demands of various environmental contexts for the purpose of establishing social harmony is *ren*[e] or selfless interpersonal love. *Ren*[e] or selfless interpersonal love is concerned with the well-being of the people and the society as a whole. This selfless interpersonal love is expressed in human relationships. *Ren*[e] does not exist without human relationships. It can only be found in human relationships.

> Zhong Gong [a disciple of Confucius] asked about *ren*[e]. The Master said, "When you are away from home it is like meeting with an important guest. Employ the people as if you were carrying out a great sacrifice. That which you do not desire, do not impose on other people. In the city there will be no resentment. In one's family there will be no resentment." Zhong Gong said, "Although I am not very smart, I will engage in what you have said." (*Lun Yu*, XII-2)

Fan Chi [a disciple of Confucius] asked about *ren*ᵉ. The Master said, "In your home be respectful, in managing your affairs be attentive [*jing*ʲ], and when interacting with others do your best/be authentic [*zhong*ᵏ]. Even if you were among the barbarian tribes, it is not possible to abandon these." (*Lun Yu*, XIII-19)

The character *ren*ᵉ consist of two components. On the left-hand side is the character *ren*ᵘ or person. On the right-hand side is the character *er*ʷ or the number two. The combination is suggestive of a relationship between at least two people. This relationship is the most important concept in the teachings of Confucius.

These Confucian relationship virtues are easily related to Western counseling. The relationship virtues of attentiveness, respect, authenticity, empathy, and trustworthiness are the foundation of counseling. Confucius's focus on behavior, behavioral change, choosing contextually appropriate behaviors, and developing the knowledge base to functionally apply these behaviors in the appropriate contexts is, essentially, the core process of contemporary counseling. Both Confucius and Western counseling are concerned with relationship issues. (See Table 6.1 for a comparison of Confucian relationship virtues with Western counseling skills.) The core difference is that Confucius defines the individual in relationship to others and society. Thus, his goal is social harmony. Western counseling defines the individual relative to himself or herself. Thus, the goal of Western counseling is the strengthening of the self, personality, or ego. A self-centeredness! With a strengthened sense of self, personality, or ego, the individual is believed to be better equipped to address relationship issues. From the perspective of Confucius, this focus on individuality and self-centeredness is not adequate, and in fact contributes to the problem of dysfunctionality. It is Confucius's focus on being in harmony with the social structure that can enhance and inform Western counseling.

The *Jun Zi*

The *jun zi*ᵈ or fully integrated person is the individual who is able to successfully assimilate and apply the teachings of Confucius in social contexts for the purpose of establishing social harmony. The *jun zi*ᵈ does not seek personal gain or benefit. The *jun zi*ᵈ is the ideal or role model for Confucius.

The Master said, "The *jun zi*ᵈ cherishes *de*ᵐ [the power of peace and tranquility]. The fragmented person cherishes property [land]. The *jun zi*ᵈ cherishes the methods of peace and tranquility. The fragmented person cherishes personal gain." (*Lun Yu*, IV-11)

Table 6.1   Confucian Relationship Virtues Compared to Counseling Skills

Basic Confucian Relationship Virtues	Basic Counseling Skills
Jing[j]: Attentiveness to and awareness of oneself, others, and the environmental context. Fully integrated in the here and now.	Awareness of and attentiveness to the client's presence and needs.
Xiao[a]: Filial piety. Respect shown to one's parents and elders.	Respecting the client as a person.
Xin[f]: Presenting oneself as being trustworthy. Establishing a trusting relationship between oneself and others.	Trust is a fundamental aspect of the counseling relationship. Client's trust of counselor is a significant component for client behavioral change. Counselor presents himself to the client as trustworthy.
Li[g]: Appropriate contextual behavior. Behavior that facilitates functional and successful interpersonal relationships. Behaviors that are conducive to establishing social harmony.	Counselor facilitates client behavioral change relative to addressing client's problems, needs, issues, and concerns.
Yi[h]: Choosing appropriate contextual behavior.	Assisting client in developing and exploring appropriate choices and behavioral options relative to client's problems, needs, issues, and concerns.
Zhi[i]: Knowledge and wisdom base for choosing appropriate contextual behavior (*yi*[h]).	Counselor's knowledge and wisdom base for selecting and applying appropriate techniques and strategies relative to assisting client in addressing client's problems, needs, issues, and concerns.
Shu[l]: Empathy. Understanding another person from his or her perspective. Not doing unto others what you do not want done unto yourself. Foundation of *jing*[j], *xiao*[a], *xin*[f], *li*[g], *yi*[h], and *zhi*[i].	Counselor understands client from client's perspective (empathy). Empathy and establishing a trusting relationship between counselor and client are the two most fundamental counseling skills.
Zhong[k]: Being authentic. Doing one's best. The application of *shu*[l] in various interpersonal contexts.	Counselor is authentic in relationship with client.
Ren[e]: Integration and expression of *jing*[j], *xiao*[a], *xin*[f], *yi*[h], *zhi*[i], *shu*,[l] and *zhong*[k] through *li*[g] relative to the demands of various environmental contexts for the purpose of establishing social harmony. Selfless interpersonal love. Highest Confucian virtue/character strength. Is only found in human relationships.	Counselor assists client in developing appropriate interpersonal competencies relative to resolving client's problems, needs, issues, and concerns.

The Master said, "Behaviors that are based on self-gain result in much resentment." (*Lun Yu,* IV-12)

The Master said, "The *jun zi*^{d} is guided by appropriate choice [*yi*^{h}], the fragmented person is guided by personal gain." (*Lun Yu,* IV-16)

This fully integrated person or *jun zi*^{d} is psychologically calm and at peace. The *jun zi*^{d} is relaxed and free from chronic stress, while the majority of humanity is chronically stressed. Given the status of the fully integrated person (*jun zi*^{d}), there is, nonetheless, no arrogance or need to be recognized. The *jun zi*^{d} is at ease in all interactions.

The Master said, "The *jun zi*^{d} is calm and at ease, the fragmented person is always stressed [sad, worried, anxious, sorrowful, distressed]." (*Lun Yu,* VII-37)

Si Ma Niu [a disciple of Confucius] asked about the *jun zi*^{d}. The Master replied, "The *jun zi*^{d} has neither sorrow nor fear [not chronically stressed]." Si Ma Niu said, "If he has neither sorrow nor fear, how can he be called a *jun zi*^{d}?" The Master said, "Finding neither fault nor illness within himself, why should he be worried or fearful?" (*Lun Yu,* XII-4)

The Master said, "The *jun zi*^{d} is peaceful and is not arrogant, the fragmented person is arrogant and is not peaceful." (*Lun Yu,* XIII-26)

The *jun zi*^{d} understood that in order for there to be social harmony people must be able to communicate with each other. They must understand each others' words, terms, and social roles. These words, terms, and roles, however, must not be seen as something independent of action and behavior. There is no real separate knowledge base independent from behavior in the various environmental contexts. For example, the word and the role of "father" must always be seen in light of context, interpersonal relationships, activity, behavior, and performance.

Duke Qing of Qi asked Confucius about governing. Kong Zi (Confucius) said, "The ruler is the ruler, the minister is the minister, the father is the father, and the son is the son." The Duke said, "Very good. If the ruler didn't act as the ruler, the minister didn't act as the minister, the father didn't act as the father, and the son didn't act as the son, although there was grain, and I attained it, would it be nourishing?" (*Lun Yu,* XII-11)

The *jun zi*^{d} recognized that lack of communication about terms, roles (*li*^{g}), and responsibility was clearly a problem not only in interpersonal relationships but also in the government relative to administrating in an effective and efficient manner. People must know and understand their roles and act accordingly. Communication difficulties about roles, terms, and words were unmistakably a source of chronic stress and social instability.

> Zi Lu [a disciple of Confucius] asked, "If the ruler of Wei needed you to govern, what would you do first?" The Master said, "Surely make names correct [*zheng ming*^{s}]." Zi Lu said, "Why this? It does not seem practical. What is this making correct [*zheng*^{t}]?" Confucius said, "How unrefined you are. The *jun zi*^{d}, from his place of not knowing about something will overcome his deficiency. If names are not correct, then what is said will not be appropriate. If what is said is not appropriate then affairs will not be completed. If affairs are not completed, then ceremony [*li*^{g}] and music will not thrive. If ceremony and music do not thrive, then punishment will not be applied consistently. If punishment is not applied consistently, people will be without a place for either hand or foot [they won't know what to do]. Therefore what the *jun zi*^{d} names one is certainly able to speak appropriately about it. When it is spoken one is certainly able to practice it. From his words, the *jun zi*^{d} is confident [without nervousness and desperation]." (*Lun Yu*, XIII-3)

Lack of understanding of roles or positions in government, the parameters of these roles and positions, and the responsibilities associated with each of the roles and positions leads to people interfering in areas where they do not belong. This interference contributes to social instability and chronic stress. Thus Confucius was clear about staying out of areas you did not know about or did not, by one's social position, belong in.

> The Master said, "If you do not hold a position in that office, do not make plans for its governing/management." (*Lun Yu*, VIII-14)

The *jun zi*^{d} is always seeking self-improvement for the purpose of establishing social harmony. The *jun zi*^{d} seeks the benefit of all that is a Confucian ideal, while the common person or fragmented person seeks their own personal gain. For Confucius, seeking personal gain is the lowest path through life.

> The Master said, "The *jun zi*^{d} reaches for the highest, the fragmented person reaches for the lowest." (*Lun Yu*, XIV-23)

Thus, the *jun zi*^{d} is the individual who integrates and applies the teaching of Confucius with a focus on establishing social harmony. For Confucius, it is the *jun zi*^{d} who should be administrating the government and acting as a role model for all of the people. This is the case, for Confucius, primarily because the *jun zi*^{d} is not motivated by self-gain, is not likely to be biased, is concerned about the welfare of the people, and seeks to establish social harmony.

The Master said, "The *jun zi*[d] who has broad learning from culture and controls his conduct by *li*[g] [appropriate behavior], is not likely to be biased." (*Lun Yu,* VI-27)

The Master said, "The *jun zi*[d] takes appropriate choice [*yi*[h]] as the substance, takes *li*[g] as the action, takes the results as what is put forth, and takes trust [*xin*[f]] as the completion. Such is the *jun zi*[d]!" (*Lun Yu,* XV-18)

The Master said that Zi Chan [a minister in the State/Kingdom of Zheng] had four ways of the *jun zi*[d]. "In his actions he was respectful, in his interactions with his superiors he was attentive [*jing*[j]], in nourishing/supporting the people he was kind, and in employing the people he made appropriate choices [*yi*[h]]." (*Lun Yu,* V-16)

De and *Dao*

For Confucius, *de*[m] is the charismatic power that emanates from an individual who has successfully integrated and applies the teachings of the ancients, the family, and Confucius. As this individual who manifests *de*[m] is centered, focused, in the present, peaceful, tranquil, and stress-free, people gravitate to this person. It is the person of *de*[m] (the power of peace and tranquility) who is, for Confucius, the ideal administrator.

When people all know their roles and responsibilities and act accordingly, the administrator is simply centered, present, and manifests the confidence and assurance of peace and tranquility. The administrator sincerely plays the role of the administrator. The administrator does not move from the center. There is no interference. Everyone turns toward the center and completes their roles and tasks.

The Master said, "To use the center is *de*[m] [power of peace and tranquility]. This is the highest you can get! Among the people this has been rare for the longest time." (*Lun Yu,* VI-29)

The person who manifests *de*[m] is at the center, balanced, and not biased. People are pulled toward this person. Confucius uses the metaphor of the pole star to present his picture of *de*[m] being manifested.

The Master said, "To govern by *de*[m] [power of peace and tranquility] is to be like the pole star. It resides in its place [not moving] and all the stars together face toward it." (*Lun Yu,* II-1)

For Confucius, not cultivating *de*[m] is one of his greatest worries. Along with not monitoring and critically examining what he has learned, knowing what the appropriate choices are and not making them, and not changing behaviors that are not functional, not cultivating *de*[m] is a major concern.

The Master said, "Not cultivating *de*[m] [power of peace and tranquility], not examining what I have learned, hearing which choices are appropriate and not following them, not able to change what is not good/skillful, this is what I worry about." (*Lun Yu,* VII-3)

For Confucius, *dao*[b] refers to the path or way that is concerned with the overall well-being of the people and society as a whole. (See Table 6.2 for a comparison of *de* and *dao*.) The *dao*[b] is about social harmony. It is the learning and accumulation of all the appropriate teachings and applications of the ancient traditions, the family, and of Confucius himself. It is the path to resolving challenges and successfully adapting to the environment. It is the path to eliminating chronic stress. When society is in harmony with the well-being of its people and social harmony is the focus, the *dao*[b] is present. The *dao*[b] or path is extended by people working together with the same goal of social harmony. The *dao*[b] does not extend or broaden the people. It is the activity of people that creates results. For Confucius, if people do not have the same *dao*[b] or path, they cannot work together.

The Master said, "It is the person that is able to extend the way/path [*dao*[b]]. It is not the way/path [*dao*[b]] that extends the person." (*Lun Yu,* XV-29)

The Master said, "If the way/path [*dao*[b]] is not the same, then you cannot work together." (*Lun Yu,* XV-40)

Table 6.2   Confucian Concepts: *De* and *Dao*

Concept	Meaning
De[m]	The charismatic power that emanates from an individual who has successfully integrated and applies the teachings of the ancients, the family, and Confucius. The individual expression of *dao*[b]. The power of peace and tranquility.
Dao[b]	Path or way that is concerned with the well-being of the people and society as a whole. Social harmony. It is the path to developing and expressing *ren*[e]. A society can be said to have and express *dao*[b].

For Confucius, ultimately, if the individual experiences the pleasure and enjoyment of learning and appropriately applying, with no self-interest, what one has learned for the betterment of society, they are on the Confucian Path or *dao*[b].

The Master said, "If in the morning you hear the *dao*[b], in the evening you may die." (*Lun Yu,* IV-8)

Summary

The approach of Confucius clearly falls within the parameters of (1) adaptive problems in the environment (social instability), (2) chronic stress (the fragmented person), and (3) stress management (a solution for stabilizing society and removing chronic stress). The perspective of Confucius can also be easily placed in the model of beginning points (ancient tradition and family), simplicity (interpersonal relationships), and commonalities (empathy, authenticity).

The solution offered by Confucius for stabilizing society and removing chronic stress focuses on changing how one views and acts in various environmental contexts. For Confucius, a worldview that is based on self-centeredness and guided by personal gain (the fragmented person) at the expense of others generates interpersonal behavior that is detrimental to the individual and to the society as a whole.

Confucius's solution, stress management approach if you will, is to change how you view the world and act accordingly. He focused on repairing interpersonal relationships as the path toward removing chronic stress and the social instability that resulted from it. He used ancient tradition and the family unit to teach and guide individuals to focus on social harmony, not personal gain and self-centeredness, as the basic worldview. People must see themselves as part of a social process. Who you are is that social process. You are not separate from it. To view yourself as somehow separate and independent leads to chronic stress and social instability.

This is not to say that everyone is equal and should be treated exactly the same. For Confucius society was hierarchical and paternalistic. No matter your status or role, however, respect, empathy, and authenticity are mutually manifested in the relationship. The degree to which is determined by the context and the participants. Confucius is clear that if a person is engaged in behavior that is not conducive to social harmony, that person will be treated differently.

Somebody said, "What are your thoughts on responding to resentment/ grudges with *de*^{m} [power of peace and tranquility]?" The Master said, "How would you respond to *de*^{m}? Use straightforwardness to respond to resentment/grudges and use *de*^{m} to respond to *de*^{m}." (*Lun Yu*, XIV-34)

Confucius is saying people need to start being concerned about other people instead of whining and complaining (chronic stress) about their own self-centered, narcissistic sense of self-entitlement.

The Master said, "Do not worry that other people do not know you, worry that you do not know other people." (*Lun Yu*, I-16)

The Master said, "Do not worry about not having a position [in government]. Worry about that which is required for such a position. Do not worry about not being known. Seek to behave in a manner that may be knowable." (*Lun Yu*, IV-14)

The Master said, "Do not worry that others do not know you, worry that you do not have the abilities and skills to be known." (*Lun Yu*, XIV-30)

If people were attentive, authentic, and empathic in their interpersonal relationships—in other words, actually cared about their fellow human beings—society would be in harmony. Being focused, present, and caring for other encourages them, according to Confucius, to be attentive, authentic, and do their best.

Ji Kang Zi [from the State/Kingdom of Lu] asked, "How can you encourage and bring about attentiveness [*jing*[j]] and doing your best/being authentic [*zhong*[k]] in the people?" The Master said, "Be serious when you interact with them and they will be attentive [*jing*[j]]. Be filial [*xiao*[a]] and compassionate, and they will be authentic and do their best [*zhong*[k]]. Promote those who are skillful, and teach those who do not have the skills, this will encourage them." (*Lun Yu*, II-20)

Important Terms

Dao[b] (the social way)

Di[c] (brotherly/fraternal love)

De[m] (the power of peace and tranquility)

Jing[j] (attentiveness)

Jun zi[d] (fully integrated person)

Li[g] (appropriate behavior)

Lun Yu (*The Analects*)

Ren[e] (selfless interpersonal love)

Shu[l] (empathy)

Xiao[a] (filial piety)

Xin[f] (trust)

Yi[h] (appropriate choice)

Zhi[i] (wisdom)

Zhong[k] (authenticity/doing one's best)

Exercises

A. Think of the Confucian concepts of *jing*[j] (attentiveness), *shu*[l] (empathy), and *zhong*[k] (authenticity/doing your best) within the context of your own interpersonal encounters during the past week. Were you attentive, empathic, and authentic? Did the context influence your actions relative to being attentive, empathic, and authentic? Did the person or persons influence your actions relative to being attentive, empathic, and authentic? Remember, for Confucius, being attentive, empathic, and authentic is expected behavior in all interpersonal encounters.

B. Select a 24-hour period, say a Thursday, and attempt to be attentive, empathic, and authentic in all of your interpersonal encounters. What reactions (cognitive, emotional, and behavioral) do you notice in the other person? In yourself? In the encounter or relationship itself? Can you feel the encounter?

C. How can being attentive, empathic, and authentic help you as a counselor? How can teaching a client to be attentive, empathic, and authentic help the client?

Chinese Characters

[a] 孝	[i] 知	[q] 心
[b] 道	[j] 敬	[r] 如
[c] 弟	[k] 忠	[s] 正名
[d] 君子	[l] 恕	[t] 正
[e] 仁	[m] 德	[u] 人=
[f] 信	[n] 觀	[v] 中
[g] 禮	[o] 文	[w] 一
[h] 義	[p] 言	

Notes

1. Exact dating of time periods varies somewhat depending on the sampling of information utilized. See Ames and Rosemont (1998); Cua (2003); Gascoigne (2003); Hsu (1965); Roberts (2000); and Van Norden (2002).

2. All translations/interpretations of the *Lun Yu* and are my own. The format of VIII-18 refers to the Book (8) and Section (18) of the *Lun Yu*. The Chinese texts utilized for this translation can be found in Yang (1972) and Hong (1973). Recommended English translations with introductions are *Confucius: The Analects (Lun Yu)* by Lau (1988) and *The Analects of Confucius: A Philosophical Translation* by Ames and Rosemont (1998).

References

Ames, R. T., & Rosemont, H. (Trans.). (1998). *The Analects of Confucius: A philosophical translation.* New York: Ballantine.

Chan, W. T. (Trans.). (1973). *A source book in Chinese philosophy.* Princeton, NJ: Princeton University Press.

Cua, A. S. (Ed.). (2003). *Encyclopedia of Chinese philosophy.* New York: Routledge.

Fung, Y. L. (1983). *A history of Chinese philosophy: Vol. 1.* Princeton, NJ: Princeton University Press.

Gardner, D. K. (2003). *Zhu Xi's reading of the Analects: Canon, commentary, and the classical tradition.* New York: Columbia University Press.

Gascoigne, B. (2003). *The dynasties of China: A history.* New York: Carroll & Graff.

Hong, C. H. (Xiao Zhe). (1973). *Si shu shou ji, zhu xi shou ji.* Taibei: Hua Lian Chu Ban.

Hsu, C. Y. (1965). *Ancient China in transition: An analysis of social mobility, 722–222 B.C.* Stanford, CA: Stanford University Press.

Lau, D. C. (Trans.). (1988). *Confucius: The Analects.* New York: Penguin Books.

Legge, J. (Trans.). (1971). *Confucius: Confucian Analects, the great learning, the doctrine of the mean.* New York: Dover.

Roberts, J. A. G. (2000). *A concise history of China.* Cambridge, MA: Harvard University Press.

Van Norden, B. W. (Ed.). (2002). *Confucius and the Analects.* Oxford, UK: Oxford University Press.

Waley, A. (Trans.). (1938). *The Analects of Confucius.* New York: Vintage.

Yang, J. L. (Bian Ci). (1972). *Lun yu zhu shu bu zheng.* Taibei: Shi Jie Shu Ju.

PART III

Integration and Application of Culturally Diverse Approaches to Managing Stress

The integration and application of the wisdom of Buddhism, Daoism, and Confucianism to individuals in a counseling context is guided by the Daoist teachings of beginning points, simplicity, and commonalities. These Daoist teachings allowed for the creation of a bamboo bridge, constructed from the knowledge of evolutionary theory and evolutionary psychology, stress and the stress response, and stress management, from which one can view human psychological difficulties as chronic stress generated by an inability to functionally solve adaptive problems in their environmental contexts. Since the root of the problem is chronic stress, the solution is to manage the stress. From the perspective of the bamboo bridge, Buddhism, Daoism, and Confucianism clearly provide culturally diverse approaches to managing stress.

Part III briefly examines the integration and application of Buddhism, Daoism, and Confucianism to rapport, thinking, feeling, behaving, interpersonal relationships, and spirituality. A specific example is provided in each chapter. It is imperative that the counselor practice each of the examples prior to attempting to utilize them with clients. It is also imperative that the counselor determine the appropriateness for and amenability of the client prior to the implementation of each example. For each example, it is assumed that the counselor has explained the exercise to the client and the client has agreed to engage in the exercise. Although each of these areas is addressed in a separate chapter, it is important to remember that the separation is artificial and that individuals must be seen and engaged in a continually changing, interdependent, and integrated environmental process.

The focus of this text has been on beginning points, simplicity, and commonalities in order to create a bamboo bridge that allows for the teachings of Buddhism, Daoism, and Confucianism to expand, inform, and enhance Western counseling and psychotherapy. Nonetheless, there are fundamentally different cultural assumptions underlying Western counseling and psychotherapy on the one hand, and Buddhism, Daoism, and Confucianism on the other hand. It is necessary to examine these assumptions to be able to best utilize the contributions of Buddhism, Daoism, and Confucianism when assisting individuals in functionally adapting to their environmental contexts in a manner that is free from chronic stress. The first chapter of Part III explores these underlying assumptions.

7

Underlying Cultural Assumptions

While the previous chapters in this text have been concerned with establishing a common ground, a bamboo bridge, to allow the teachings of Buddhism, Daoism, and Confucian to inform, expand, and enhance Western counseling and psychotherapy, it is, nonetheless, important to address the cultural assumptions by which classical Chinese teachings and Western counseling and psychotherapy differ. Given the relevancy to the counseling context, the three most fundamental areas of difference, which are intimately intertwined, are the nature of knowledge and knowing, the nature of reality, and the sense of self.

The cultural assumptions of Western counseling and psychotherapy are, ultimately, based on and derived from Western philosophy, religion, and science. Philosophy, religion, and science provide solutions for adapting to various environmental contexts. On the most basic level, the solutions attempt to reduce the chronic stress associated with the perception of uncertainty, meaninglessness, purposelessness, lack of control, and individual death.

Philosophy

The history of Western philosophy can be seen, in one sense, as a search for certainty. What is the nature of reality? What and how do we know? What is the self? Its foundation in this search can be found in the teachings of Plato and Aristotle. Its movement into the modern era regarding this search can be found in the teachings of Descartes.

The Pre-Socratics offered various explanations for the ultimate nature of reality. Probably the most relevant to current thinking were those of Democritus (circa 460–370 BCE), who argued that reality consisted of various configurations of indivisible, unalterable atoms moving about in empty space. Everything could be explained by and reduced to these atoms.[1] Through Plato, Aristotle, and then, much later, Descartes, the focus expanded to include a stronger focus on knowledge, knowing, and the sense of self.

Plato (circa 427–347 BCE) was influenced by the dialectic-based, essence-focused teachings of his mentor Socrates (469–399 BCE) and the mathematical- and mystical-focused teachings of the Pythagoreans. Both approaches sought abstract, certain knowledge or truth.

Socrates utilized an approach that came to be known as the *Socratic method* to seek out certainty regarding the meaning of various concepts and terms. In this method, Socrates would ask a question about the meaning of a concept or term; for example, "courage" (*Laches*) or "friendship" (*Lysis*).[2] The students provide answers that are used to establish a possible definition or hypothesis regarding the meaning of the term or concept. Socrates would then ask those who put forth the potential definitions a series of questions, eventually leading either to a contradiction in the definition or to an agreed-upon definition. If an agreed-upon definition is found, then a claim for certainty can be made regarding knowledge of the term or concept.

What is being sought are not individual examples of "courage" or "friendship," but instead the abstract *essence* of the term or concept. What is the unchanging, abstract, absolute truth or essence of "courage" and "friendship" that everyone can clearly see and agree upon? The essence is not found through the senses, as the senses deal with the world of change, and nothing can ever be known with any certainty about something that is always changing. Essences can only be apprehended through rationality. It is only through the rational mind that the individual can discover the unchanging, absolute truths or essences.

The Socratic method reinforces the Greek perspective of a world that consists of discrete objects waiting to be investigated, examined, and categorized.[3] This method clearly gives rise to and supports exploring, analyzing, and debating individual perspectives and opinions. The Socratic method is consistent with and reinforcing of an independent and separate sense of self.

Pythagoras (circa 580–500 BCE) viewed the world through mathematics and religion.[4] They were, for him, two sides of the same coin that were linked by harmonious relationships. Pythagoras's view of reality was dualistic, with the physical, changing world being apart from and inferior to the unchanging, abstract world of numbers. Numbers, for Pythagoras, had a magical and mystical quality. The realm of numbers was reality! The realm of numbers, nonetheless, shape and structure the physical world. For Pythagoras, the physical world could only be understood through numbers. The harmonious relationship between numbers! To understand the physical world was to understand numerical harmony. This could only be accomplished by rationality, as the senses were considered to be inferior, inadequate, and unable to access the realm of numbers.

Pythagoras believed in an immortal rational soul that went through the process of transmigration. Thus, self-cultivation, which denied the trappings and desires of the physical world of change, was practiced until the individual was purified and thus in harmony. Once harmony and purification occurred, the soul would no longer be reborn and would ascend into the realm of the gods.

Both the teachings of Socrates and the Pythagoreans offered a perspective where the changing physical world was inferior to an unchanging realm of abstract truths. A realm based in rationality lying outside of or beyond the world of senses and change. A realm wherein one could discuss certain knowledge and provide ultimate meaning regarding the nature of existence.

Clearly influenced by both the teachings of Socrates and the Pythagoreans, Plato posited (in the *Republic*) two separate worlds: the world of abstract, distinct forms or ideas and the physical world of change.[5] The world of abstract, unchanging, absolute *forms* was ultimate reality and was separate and independent from the physical world. The world of the forms existed beyond the physical world. They were the essences of which the physical world was mere shadows. For everything in the physical world there was a corresponding form. Certain knowledge, truth, and reality was only found in the world of forms.

As the physical world continually changes, the senses are unable to apprehend any certain knowledge. For that matter, the senses could only provide beliefs. Knowledge, for Plato, was knowledge of the forms. The forms could only be apprehended by reason. As knowledge could not be obtained from the changing physical world, the question arose regarding how knowledge was obtained. Plato answered this question by arguing that an immortal soul remembered the world of forms where it previously dwelled. Through the process of reason, the soul was able to turn away from the physical world and gaze upon the unchanging forms that influenced and shaped the changing, physical world.

Aristotle (384–322 BCE) was a student of Plato. Unlike his teacher, who was greatly influenced by mathematics, Aristotle was more influenced by biology. Aristotle disagreed with Plato's separation of the world of forms from the physical world and with his methodology, which turned away from the senses and the changing, physical world toward reason and the abstract, unchanging, realm of distinct forms.

For Aristotle, the forms or universals are not separate from the physical world. Each individual distinct entity, such as a person or a cow, is a substance that consists of both form and matter (*Metaphysics*).[6] The form cannot really be separate from matter. In a statue of a dog made of clay, the statue would not exist if either the form of the dog or the clay was not present.

His methodology, unlike Plato's, begins with the senses attending to distinct, separate objects in the changing, physical world. This then leads to the production of memory, then experience, and finally to the apprehension, by reason, of the unchanging, abstract forms/universals/principles (*Metaphysics*). Certain knowledge!

Aristotle makes it clear that the senses cannot provide wisdom, as they can only tell the individual that, for example, fire is hot. They cannot tell the individual why the fire is hot. It is only knowledge of the forms/universals/principles that provides the why. It is, ultimately, only through reason that knowledge of the forms/universals/principles occurs and wisdom is gained (*Metaphysics*). Certain knowledge!

Aristotle also focused on the importance of observation, classification, and categorization. Consider by many to be the first biologist, he is credited with developing the first systematic method for classifying life forms, which reinforces the notion that that the changing physical world is made up of distinct objects. He provided the first formal study of logic (*Organon*) with his introduction of the syllogism (*Prior Analytics*).[7]

As the Greeks were fond of debate, the use of logic, in demonstrating that an opponent's argument regarding a particular topic was not valid and/or was contradictory, would be beneficial for an individual who wanted to win a debate. This strong focus of logic on the form of the argument reinforces a perspective that is not contextual in nature. (See Nisbett, 2003). The focus on debate and the use of logic reinforces a sense of self that is separate from an environmental context.

Descartes (1596–1650), believing that the philosophers before him had not found certainty, continued the search for absolute certain knowledge. Like Plato and Aristotle, his approach was, ultimately, based on reason. Like Plato, he was guided in his quest by mathematics. Mathematical truths demonstrated certainty. He invented analytical geometry, linking algebra and physics, and believed all of the physical world could be explained and measured. Using this as a foundation, and his methodology of objective, nonjudgmental, clear and distinct ideas (*Discourse on the Method, Part, II*),[8] he eventually established—at least he believed he did—the certainty of his own existence with his *cogito ergo sum* or "I think therefore I am" (*Discourse on the Method, Part IV*). He argued that this was an idea that was so clear and distinct, he could not doubt it.

Given the starting point of his own certain existence, Descartes went on to establish the existence of God, innate ideas, and the physical world. He made a clear distinction between mind/reason and the physical world, which included his own body. Mind is associated with thinking/reason, and the physical world, including the human body, is associated with extension (*Principles of Philosophy, Part Two, Principle IV*). The two are completely separate.

Descartes argued that the separate and distinct body should be viewed, like the rest of the physical world, as a machine. In the same sense that the cause of a watch not working or running is due to broken parts, when a person dies, it is because certain parts of the body are no longer functioning correctly. For Descartes, the human body is certainly nothing more than a machine (*The Passions of the Soul, Articles V, VI, VII*).

In addition to knowledge gained through reason, Descartes allowed for some knowledge to be gained from or through the senses. He noted, however, that there is very little that is gained with any certainty through or by the senses. He stated that the senses were placed in his body by God and God would not provide him with deceptive tools (*Meditations on First Philosophy, IV*). Nonetheless, he noted that, he often made mistakes by relying on his senses. He argued that the basis of his mistakes was that he did not have clear and distinct ideas. In those cases, he deferred to reason to provide clear and distinct ideas.

Religion

The Judeo-Christian teachings, which have greatly influenced Western thought and behavior, also create a dichotomy between mind/soul/self and body; the physical world and an unchanging absolute world that was superior; and reason and the senses. The tradition argued for an absolute or immortal soul. While the tradition is extremely rational, ultimately it rests in faith.

According to this tradition, God, an absolute, all-knowing, unchanging state of affairs, created the universe and all that is in it (Genesis I:1–25). (See Ebor, 1970.) God created man and woman in his own image (Genesis I:26–28; II:7–8, 21–25) and gave them dominion over the physical world (Genesis I:28–31). Clearly we have in the book of Genesis a distinction between humans and the rest of the world. The humans have a spark of the divine in them. They are in fact made in the image of God. The physical world is clearly inferior and is presented as the playground, if you will, in which human beings may do as they so please. There is a definite basis for a sense of separation and individuality.

This sense of individuality is further developed in the book of Exodus (XX:1–21), when the Ten Commandments are passed down to Moses. Individuals are expected to behave in a certain manner or they will suffer the consequences. A single God is raised up above all others. Only this God can be worshipped. Only through this God is truth discovered. The sense of a separation between the physical world and the world of God or heaven is further reinforced as God tells Moses to tell the people that he spoke to him from heaven (Exodus XX: 22–23).

In the Gospel of Matthew, the separation between the physical world and the world of God is further developed and reinforced. In the Sermon on the Mount (Matthew VI:19–21), there is a talk on the difference between the kingdom of heaven and the physical world. Jesus indicates that individuals must make a choice, as they cannot fully participate in both worlds (Matthew VI:24–34). He lectures the audience on how they ought to behave if they desire to enter the kingdom of heaven, and he further establishes the basis for a personal, individual relationship with God (Matthew VII:1–14).

The Christian tradition, filtered through Greek thought, ends up with an absolute separation between the physical world and the world of God. The individual is separate and distinct from the physical world. The individual's immortal soul, the spark of divinity, is separate and distinct from the body.

The eventual development of the Christian tradition through the church resulted in it defining what could be talked about and what could not be talked about. What could be examined and not examined. It defined what methodologies were or were not acceptable. The absolute control of the church defined reality. It defined knowledge. Anything that was consistent with its interpretation of reality, which was ultimately based in faith, was considered good. Anything that was not consistent with its interpretation was considered evil.

Ultimately though, the Judeo-Christian tradition is about eliminating the chronic stress, the uncertainty, the threat, and the fear that death is the complete and total end to one's individual, distinct existence. An end, if it was the case, that would make life meaningless and purposeless. Jesus (in John VI:22–71) eliminates the chronic stress, the uncertainty, the threat, and the fear of death by offering eternal life in heaven. It is about being victorious over death. Life on earth now has purpose and meaning because it is about believing in and having faith in Jesus. It is about practicing the teachings of Jesus. The belief, the practice, the turning away from the continually changing realm of the flesh, the physical world, and turning toward the unchanging, eternal, absolute realm of heaven overcomes the chronic stress associated with one's individual death and provides the believer with a distinct sense of separate, individual salvation.

Science

The church's absolute control of the interpretation of reality and knowledge, of what could be examined or not examined, talked about or not talked about, and what methodologies were acceptable or not acceptable, eventually gave way to a new authority that wielded similar control and power. Science!

Following its predecessors, science defines reality, knowledge, and the acceptable ways of gaining knowledge. It sets the parameters of what can be examined and not examined, talked about or not talked about. It sets the guidelines for the process of inquiry and what methodologies are acceptable and not acceptable. It looks for certainty.

Like it predecessors, science has a hidden world of reality lurking behind the physical world of change. A world of absolute, unchanging, abstract laws! Looking to Aristotle, science begins with observation of a physical, changing world consisting of distinct and separate objects. Following in the footsteps of Pythagoras, Plato, and Descartes, science utilizes reason and mathematics in an objective and nonjudgmental manner to uncover these laws, and explain, describe, make predictions about, and determine the causes of the observations.

Science uses observations as its starting point but employs reason and mathematics and statistics to quantify them. The observations are quantified so the scientist can draw objective conclusions and make knowledge claims of varying degrees of certainty.

Given the power of science, the medical field has made many discoveries that have contributed to the health and well-being of humankind. The forte of Western medicine is in the area of acute disorders. Its advances in surgery and pharmaceuticals are stunning.

Western medicine has been guided by a model that separates mind and body, is mechanistic and reductionistic. This model has worked well for acute disorders. The focus is on the body (mind and body are separate) where some body part or system is not working or is compromised (mechanistic) and can be repaired by simply addressing the part or system with surgery and/or drugs (reductionistic).

The problem arises, however, when the disorders are chronic. Remember that in Chapter 2 we mention that Benson noted that approximately 60 to 90 percent of all office visits to doctors are stress related and involve a mind/body interaction. The individual is essentially having adaptive problems regarding resolving a demand from his or her various environmental contexts. While the symptoms are real, the utilization of the medical model is unable to detect a physical cause. A solution cannot be found applying a mechanistic, reductionistic model that ignores the contribution of the mind and the environment to the problem.

A Comparison of Cultural Assumptions

Given that Western philosophy, religion, and science all operate from a set of similar underlying cultural assumptions regarding the nature of reality, knowledge, and the self, it is not unreasonable to assume that those same cultural assumptions guide the common man and woman through life. There will, of course, always be exceptions, but for the majority the following assumptions appear to be the case. The classical Chinese perspective, based on the examination of **Buddhism, Daoism,** and **Confucianism,** is provided in **bold** for each assumption. The classical Chinese perspectives of Buddhism, Daoism, and Confucianism should not be confused with later developments in each of these areas.

• From the perspective of Western cultural assumptions, there is an independent physical world that consists of distinct, separate objects that behave, for all intents and purposes, like machines. **From the perspective of classical Chinese cultural assumptions, all of existence is an interrelated, interdependent, relative, continually changing, integrated process. There is no separation.**

• Lying hidden from view behind the physical world, if you will, is a set of unchanging, absolute, abstract laws that can explain the mechanistic behavior of the physical world, and/or there exists a God, living in heaven, who created the physical world and its laws. **There is no hidden world.**

• The individual is separate and independent from the physical world, which is his to use as he sees fit with no perceived consequence to himself. **The individual is not separate from the physical world. There is a clear understanding that her actions on the physical world are essentially actions on herself.**

• There is a separation between mind and body. They do not affect each other. **There is no separation between mind and body. They do affect each other.**

• Reason, logic, and science and/or faith are the final arbitrators for determining knowledge about and truth regarding occurrences in the physical world and the hidden world behind it. **For Buddhism and Daoism, direct experience is the final arbitrator. For Confucianism, reason and direct experience are the final arbitrators. There is no hidden world.**

• Individuals look to overcome change and establish a sense of stasis and certainty allowing them to control, grasp, possess, and accumulate the distinct objects in the physical world. **Individuals seek to be in harmony with the continually changing world, realizing that, ultimately, they cannot control, grasp, possess, and accumulate the continually changing processes in the world.**

• Individuals have an independent, separate, context-free sense of self-identity. The majority believe they will overcome death and live forever in the unchanging world of heaven. Death is something to resist and overcome. **Individuals have an interdependent, integrated, contextual sense of self-identity and view death as nothing more than a normal part of the ongoing process of change. Death is inevitable and should be accepted.**

A summary of the differences between Chinese and Western counseling or psychotherapy because of differing cultural assumptions is presented in Table 7.1.

Table 7.1   Some Fundamental Differences Between Chinese Thought and Western Counseling

Chinese Thought	*Western Counseling/Psychotherapy*
Problem is universal in nature. It applies to everyone. Everyone's behavior is compromised by suffering, dissatisfaction, or unhappiness.	The paradigm in counseling/psychotherapy is that the problem is individual in nature. Not everyone has problems with hostility, anxiety disorders, mood disorders, substance abuse disorders, alcohol abuse disorders, and so on.
Cause of problem is interactive in nature. A person's perspective on how existence behaves and the actual behavior of existence (including the people that populate it) are inconsistent or not in harmony. The individual, the environment, and their relationship are of equal importance.	The paradigm in counseling/psychotherapy is that the cause of the problem is in the person. The medical model espoused by the American Psychiatric Association and the American Psychological Association is that anxiety disorders, mood disorders, substance abuse disorders, and so on are diseases in the person, diseases of the brain. Although there are many other counseling/psychotherapy explanations for the cause of the problem, the majority of these explanations still view the problem as being, one way or another, within the individual.
The sense of self is seen as being part of the problem. A sense of an absolute, independent, separate self must be eliminated. The self must be experienced as being relative, interdependent, and part of the continually changing environment.	The sense of self has been weakened by the disease (medical model), the irrational thinking (cognitive), and so on. An individual sense of self that is absolute, independent, and separate from the environment must be strengthened.
Focus is directed toward the relationship between mind, body, and environment. They all must be experienced as being part of the continually changing process called existence.	Focus is directed, primarily, toward the brain/mind.
Intervention/treatment is primarily experiential in nature.	Intervention/treatment is primarily drug-based, reason-based, or a combination of drugs and rationality. Reason, logic, and science, in most cases, are the final arbitrators.

Summary

Given the Daoist teachings of beginning points, simplicity, and commonality; the bamboo bridge of evolutionary theory and evolutionary psychology, the stress response and stress management; and the cultural assumptions noted in this chapter, it is important to remember to approach each counseling context and client as being unique. It is important to understand clients in the framework of their world and shape the counseling process to the needs of the client relative to assisting them in resolving their challenges for the purpose of functionally adapting to their various environmental contexts.

In the rest of the chapters in this book, the teachings of Buddhism, Daoism, and Confucianism are integrated and applied to the areas of rapport, thinking, feeling, behaving, interpersonal relationships, and spirituality, to help the counselor in shaping and implementing the counseling process and facilitating the client's return to adaptive health and well-being.

Exercises

A. Think about what kind of assumptions you make about the nature of counseling. What are they? Where did they come from? How are these assumptions linked to your own culture?

B. Western counseling and psychotherapy are supposedly based on the scientific method. Science is considered to be an objective, independent, and universal approach to understanding the underlying truth about reality and the behavior of its animate and inanimate objects. Is it? Ask yourself, What assumptions are made by the scientific approach? What is truth? How do you know that you know? Is there an independent reality? What does it mean to be objective? Independent? Universal? Is Western science based on a set of cultural assumptions?

C. One more question to ponder: Is Western science culturally insensitive? From the perspective of Western science, if something cannot be defined and operationalized to the extent that it can be measured and quantified using the tools and methodology of the scientific method (random assignment, controls groups, and so on), then it does not really exist.

For the Chinese, the geography of the body is somewhat different. It also contains *meridians*. Acupuncture is based on understanding and stimulating these meridians. The Chinese have a more than 2,000-year history of using acupuncture for healing. It is still used today because it works for the Chinese. From the perspective of Western science, these meridians do not exist because they cannot be operationalized to the extent that they can be measured using Western scientific methodology and tools. Is this being culturally insensitive? Is Western science the source of all truth?

Notes

1. See Jones (1969), pp. 74–107. For a brief history of philosophy with a specific focus on psychology, see Hergenhahn (1997).

2. *Laches* and *Lysis* are the names of dialogues by Plato. See Hamilton and Cairns (1971).

3. See Nisbett (2003) for an in-depth analysis and comparison of classical Greek and classical Chinese thinking. See also Callicott and Ames (2001), pp. 1–17, for an analysis and comparison of the Judeo-Christian tradition, Western philosophy, and Asian philosophy regarding the environment.

4. For a brief account of Pythagoras, see Cornford (1974), pp. 65–70. See also Jones (1969), pp. 31–39, and Hergenhahn (1997), pp. 28–30.

5. The *Republic* is a dialogue by Plato. See Hamilton and Cairns (1971).

6. The *Metaphysics* is a treatise by Aristotle. See McKeon (1941).

7. The *Organon* refers to Aristotle's collected works on logic. The *Prior Analytics* is a treatise in the *Organon*. See McKeon (1941).

8. *Discourse on the Method, Parts I* and *II*, are philosophical works by Descartes. See Haldane and Ross (1970).

References

Callicott, J. B., & Ames, R. T. (Eds.). (2001). *Nature in Asian traditions of thought: Essays in environmental philosophy.* Albany: State University of New York Press.

Cornford, F. M. (1974). *Before and after Socrates.* London: Cambridge University Press.

Ebor, D. (Chrm.). (1970). *The New English Bible with the Apocrypha.* London: Oxford University Press and Cambridge University Press.

Haldane, E. S., & Ross, G. R. T. (Trans). *The philosophical works of Descartes: Vol. I.* London: Cambridge University Press.

Hamilton, E., & Cairns, H. (Eds.). (1971). *The collected dialogues of Plato, including the Letters.* Princeton, NJ: Princeton University Press.

Hergenhahn, B. R. (1997). *An introduction to the history of psychology.* Pacific Grove, CA: Brooks/Cole.

Jones, W. T. (1969). *A history of Western philosophy: The classical mind.* New York: Harcourt, Brace & World.

McKeon, R. (Ed.). (1941). *The basic works of Aristotle.* New York: Random House.

Nisbett, R. E. (2003). *The geography of thought: How Asians and Westerners think differently and why.* New York: Free Press.

8

Rapport

The relationship between the client and the counselor is an integral, if not *the* integral, component in a counseling context. *Rapport* is the simple beginning point of an authentic therapeutic relationship in which counselor and client share a commonality in understanding and perspective. For change to occur, the client must feel safe and supported. If the client feels safe and supported in the counseling relationship, then the client is more likely to take risks on the path to developing more functionally adaptive behavior. Rapport is not just established, however, by the client feeling safe and supported. A psychoeducational component is necessary. Clients need to have an understandable, contextual explanation of their symptoms and/or general distress. This explanation needs to provide and link the cause of their symptoms or general distress with the solutions for their removal. The explanation also needs to link to the environmental context. Clients need to see and understand their symptoms and/or general distress and solutions within their own worlds.

Given the explanation, the client needs to believe it is correct and that the solutions offered will work. The client also has to believe that the counselor believes the solutions will work. It is important that the client perceives and feels that the counselor is empathic, respectful, and as committed as the client to resolving the adaptive problems. Frank and Frank (1993) argue that the explanation and the solution offered by a therapist may be viewed as "myth" and "ritual," respectively, as the theory that generated the explanation and solution cannot be substantiated with empirical evidence. Nonetheless, a shared belief in the myth and ritual establishes a therapeutic bond between the counselor and the client that, they argue, is essential for a successful outcome. They note:

Despite differences in specific content, all therapeutic myths and rituals have functions in common. They combat demoralization by strengthening the therapeutic relationship, inspiring expectations of help, providing new learning experiences, arousing the patient emotionally, enhancing a sense of mastery or self-efficacy, and affording opportunities for rehearsal and practice. (p. 44)

All of these components are necessary for a successful treatment outcome. In fact, the evidence seems to support the primacy of the relationship over any specific theoretical approach. Wampold (2001), in arguing for a contextual model of counseling and psychotherapy that stresses shared aims, notes:

The scientific evidence overwhelmingly supports a model of psychotherapy that gives primacy to the healing context, to the understanding of one's difficulties, to the faith in the therapy, and to the respect for the client's worldview. . . . The contextual model emphasizes the commonalities among therapies. All therapies involve the relationship of a client and a therapist, each of whom believes in the efficacy of the treatment. The therapist provides the client with a rationale for the disorder and administers a procedure that is consistent with the rationale. (p. xii)

For rapport to develop and be maintained, it is of utmost importance that the worldview of the client is understood and respected. Pedersen (1996) argues, given the client's worldview, the manner in which rapport is established is contingent upon understanding the client's cultural context. Each client must be viewed as unique. Pedersen notes:

Although a loving, trusting and genuine relationship of rapport is important in all counseling, the way the rapport is established will reflect the complex and dynamic cultural context of each client. The right approach in one cultural context my well be the wrong approach in a different cultural context. Multiculturalism is more than an emphasis on technique; the focus must always be on competence in an effective therapeutic relationship, which will be assessed differently in each cultural context. . . . Respect for the client, genuineness, and empathic understanding are themselves products of a cultural context, and they will need to be interpreted differently in each complex and dynamic cultural situation even among those for whom these goals are primary. (p. 236)

Pedersen's (1996) perspective reinforces the importance of addressing and integrating the commonality, noted by Wampold (2001), of respecting the client's worldview. This commonality contributes to rapport being established.

Integration and Application

The Buddhist concept of mindfulness, the Daoist concept of mind/heart fasting (*xin zhai*[a]), and the Confucian concept of being attentive (*jing*[b]) all emphasize the importance of being in the present without judging. By being nonjudgmentally in the present, the counselor will be able to fully and authentically (*zhong*[c]) engage and contact the client.

The Buddhist, Daoist, and Confucian perspectives all view individuals as being part of a continuous, continually changing, interrelated, interdependent process. Clients must be understood as being part of this process. In other words, clients must be viewed from the perspective of their various environmental contexts. The Four Noble Truths of Buddha provide a clear explanation of an adaptive problem, its cause, the goal of the treatment, and the treatment plan. All components are clearly linked together. Similar explanations are offered by Confucius and the teachings of Daoism. All three explanations are consistent with Wampold's (2001) commonality requirement of providing a rationale for the problem and the linking of the treatment to the rationale.

The Confucian, Buddhist, and Daoist perspectives all emphasize the importance of relationships. It is in the relationship that people are complete and fully integrated. For Confucius, the relationship is focused on other people and the social structure. Confucius emphasized being respectful (*xiao*[d]), being empathic (*shu*[e]), being authentic (*zhong*[c]), creating a climate of trust (*xin*[f]), and choosing/engaging (*yi*[g]) in contextually appropriate behaviors (*li*[h]) as the foundation for establishing mutually considerate relationships. For Buddha, the relationship is focused on realizing you are part of an interdependent, impermanent, and nonsubstantial process. For Daoism, the relationship is essentially a mind, body, and environment integration.

For all three perspectives, there is no separate, independent, individual sense of self. There is no sense of self-entitlement or self-centeredness. There is no fragmentation. Who you are is always seen in the context of a relationship.

Buddhism, Daoism, and Confucianism are all focused on alleviating chronic stress. They all clearly see the negative impact of chronic stress on physical, psychological, emotional, behavioral, and interpersonal functioning. Their focus is on creating a healing environment.

While Buddhism, Daoism, and Confucianism do not really talk about rapport or a counseling context, nonetheless, their focus on being nonjudgmentally in the present, being seen and understood as part of continually changing environmental contexts, providing a clear explanation of the problem, its causes, and its solutions, the focus on relationships, the elimination of self-centeredness, and the creation of a healing environment are all important components for establishing rapport. The teachings of Buddhism, Daoism, and Confucianism are also consistent with the requirements of Wampold (2001) and Pedersen (1996) relative to establishing a healing counseling context.

Example

If an individual is happy, in control, without problems, and functionally adapted to the environment—in other words, not chronically stressed—it is unlikely that there will be a need for counseling services. In general, a client that enters therapy or counseling is chronically stressed. Given this state of affairs and the need for establishing a mutually trusting relationship (rapport) relative to a successful counseling outcome, a technique that integrates the teachings of Buddhism, Daoism, and Confucianism may be a first step in establishing rapport. It is a technique that must be practiced ahead of time by the counselor. The counselor must be experienced in and feel comfortable using the technique. It is called the *Basic Breathing Exercise* and can be used, on an as-needed basis, during any counseling session.

Toward the start of the first counseling session, the client is asked if he or she would like to practice a simple breathing exercise that will likely be of assistance in reducing the symptoms that are currently being experienced and in helping the client address the presenting problem. Assuming the client is amenable, he is asked if the breathing exercise will compromise any preexisting conditions. Given clearance, the exercise is explained to the client.

The client is told, first of all, simply to smile. The counselor asks the client how he feels while smiling. The client is then asked to smile while doing the breathing exercise that the counselor is about to explain. The client is told to slowly inhale and exhale through the nose. On each exhalation, the client silently counts. On the first exhalation, the client says, "One." On the next exhalation, the client says, "Two," and so on. The client is told that the exercise is not a race and not a contest to see how far the client can count. The client is informed that if the client gets distracted, his mind wanders, and he loses count, he is not to make any judgments; simply return to the breathing and begin again with number one. Inform the client that this exercise will take a few minutes (3–5 minutes is a good beginning point) and the client will be told when to stop. The client is told that counselor will do the exercise with the client.

Although it is advisable for the exercise to be done with the eyes closed (fewer distractions), it can be effectively performed with the eyes open. The client is asked to sit up straight, smile, and slowly inhale, and upon exhaling to begin counting. After the time period has elapsed, the client is told to stop. The client is asked to describe his experience. What did he feel?

If the client follows instructions, the client will have a sense of being relaxed, centered, focused, in control, and not stressed. The client should be able to approach the presenting adaptive problem more objectively. The client is told that he is responsible for the change in feelings. This simple exercise gives the client a sense of control and empowerment and provides the client with a technique to assist in addressing the feelings associated with chronic stress.

This technique integrates both the Buddhist and Daoist use of breathing exercises, Buddhist mindfulness, Daoist mind/heart fasting, and Confucian attentiveness. It also utilizes the Confucian concept of correct form/appropriate behavior (li^h), as the breathing exercise requires the individual to sit up straight. Sitting up straight (proper form/appropriate behavior) makes the breathing exercise more effective and efficient.

The technique is clearly consistent with the commonalities of chronic stress and stress management. This technique addresses the "new learning experience," "self-efficacy," and the "opportunity to practice" components noted by Frank and Frank (1993) for establishing a bond between the client and the counselor. Help has been provided. It will help establish a belief in the expertise of the counselor and the effectiveness of the approach. It has the potential of being beneficial in establishing rapport.

Chinese Characters

[a] 心齋	[e] 恕
[b] 敬	[f] 信
[c] 孝	[g] 義
[d] 孝	[h] 禮

References

Frank, J. D., & Frank, J. B. (1993). *Persuasion and healing: A comparative study.* Baltimore: Johns Hopkins University Press.

Pedersen, P. (1996). The importance of both similarities and differences in multicultural counseling: Reaction to C. H. Patterson. *Journal of Counseling and Development, 74,* 236–237.

Wampold, B. E. (2001). *The great psychotherapy debate: Models, methods and findings.* Mahwah, NJ: Lawrence Erlbaum.

9

Thinking

Buddhism, Daoism, and Confucianism all link difficulties in adapting to various environmental contexts, and the chronic stress that may be generated and maintained, to the individual's worldview. They argue that the individual's worldview is not consistent with the behavior of the various environmental contexts. When individuals have expectations about how existence and all of its components ought to behave, and existence does not behave accordingly, the individual's worldview may be threatened. If it is threatened, the threat is likely to be maintained as a result of individuals not changing their worldviews. They continue to think in the same manner. Their cognitive schemas remain the same. Their assumptions about existence and its behavior remain unaltered. This being the case, chronic stress is generated and maintained, and the health of individuals is compromised physically, cognitively, emotionally, behaviorally, and interpersonally.

Frank and Frank (1993) argue that counseling and psychotherapy is about changing and modifying assumptions, attitudes, and meanings—assumptions, attitudes, and meanings individuals have about their various environmental contexts. They note, "The aim of psychotherapy is to help people feel and function better by encouraging appropriate modifications in their assumptive worlds, thereby transforming the meanings of experience to more favorable ones" (p. 30).

Frank and Frank (1993) also argue that illness is directly linked to problems in functionally adapting to various environmental contexts. Problems in adapting are connected to ineffective coping mechanisms and an inconsistency between the individual's worldview and the behavior of the components of the various environmental contexts. In addition, they point out that the assumptive world or worldview is quite resistant to change. If the coping mechanisms do not work or are maladaptive and the assumptive world or worldview remains intact, the individual becomes "demoralized" or, in the context of this text, chronically stressed.

> All illness can be viewed as a failure of adaptation, an imbalance between environmental stress and coping capacity. The ability to cope is determined by constitutional vulnerability and strengths on the one hand and by favorable or unfavorable meanings persons attribute to events on the other. These meanings are determined by an organized set of assumptions, attitudes, or beliefs, about the self and others that we have determined the assumptive world. . . . Unhealthy assumptive systems are internally conflictual and do not accurately correspond to circumstances. They lead to experiences of frustration, failure, and alienation that paradoxically increase a person's resistance to changing in response to new experiences, such as those provided by psychotherapy. People protect the stability of their assumptive worlds by means of avoidance and confirmatory bias. Persistent failure to cope resulting from maladaptive assumptive systems leads to demoralization. (Frank & Frank, 1993, pp. 50–51)

Integration and Application

The Buddhist Perspective

For Buddhism, *dukkha* or chronic stress is due to ignorance and craving. Ignorance refers to a worldview or an assumptive system that understands behavior in the various environmental contexts to be permanent, substantial, and independent. This being the case, the individual craves to obtain, possess, and maintain a wide range of objects in the various environmental contexts. When the behavior of the components of the various environmental contexts is not consistent with the individual's worldview and/or the individual is not able to obtain, possess, or maintain the objects that are craved, *dukkha* is present.

To eliminate *dukkha,* the individual needs to think about and experience the world differently. The worldview or assumptive system needs to change to be consistent with the actual behavior of the various environmental contexts, which are impermanent, nonsubstantial, and interdependent. The solution to thinking about and experiencing the environmental contexts differently is found in the Eightfold Path.

The Buddha realized that reason, logic, authority, the written word, and belief were not adequate to change a worldview. For people to truly understand the various environmental contexts as impermanent, nonsubstantial, and interdependent, they had to experience them as such on a regular basis and across many situations. In other words, understanding required a lifestyle change based in direct experience.

The primary component of this lifestyle change is the practice of mindfulness. Mindfulness is a flexibly focused, nonjudgmental engagement with the present. It is a nonjudgmental, direct experience in the present. For Buddha, it is only through the regular and consistent practice of mindfulness that individuals can change their worldviews and eliminate *dukkha* or chronic stress.

The change in worldview also requires individuals to consciously change behavioral patterns. The Eightfold Path is quite clear in this area, as it asks the individuals to change their speaking, actions, and livelihoods such that they do no harm and are consistent with a worldview of impermanence, nonsubstantiality, and interdependence. Thus the worldview is changed by integrating mindfulness with behavioral change.

The new worldview of thinking about and experiencing the various environmental contexts, including one's own self, as being impermanent, nonsubstantial, and interdependent is consistent with the behavior of the environmental contexts. The individual's total behavior (cognitive, emotional, physical, and interpersonal) is consistent with the behavior of the environmental contexts. There is no sense of a separate, independent self. This being the case, *dukkha* or chronic stress will eventually be eliminated.

The Daoist Perspective

For the Daoist, a worldview that is based on absolute, contrived, unchanging values, judgments, and desires and denies change as being the nature of reality leads to getting in one's own way, controlling the behavior of others, being controlled by others, and being controlled by a variety of affairs in various environmental contexts. In other words, it leads to chronic stress.

This problematic worldview is changed through the practice of mind/heart fasting (*xin zhai*[a]), noninterference (*wu wei*[b]), and nonentanglement in the affairs of the world (*wu shi*[c]). Mind/heart fasting is experiencing the present with a nonjudgmental, still, and empty mind/heart. With the mind/heart being nonjudgmental, stilled, and emptied, individuals will experience the various environmental contexts and all that makes them up as a continually changing, integrated, interrelated process. This includes the sense of self. There is no separate, disconnected self.

The mind/heart will be like a mirror. Still and empty. Nonjudgmental! Neither controlling nor controlled. Not holding on to anything. Simply reflecting what is present. When what is present leaves, it is no longer reflected. It is gone!

The experience of mind/heart fasting allows individuals to clearly see that the contrived, absolute values, judgments, and desires are in fact barriers created by humans, are subject to change, and are relative. This experience will allow the individual to address and change the problematic worldview.

To change the worldview and eliminate chronic stress not only requires the practice of mind/heart fasting, it also requires the individual to consciously not interfere (*wu wei*[b]) with themselves and others and not get entangled in the affairs of the world (*wu shi*[c]). By consciously engaging in the behaviors of not interfering and not getting entangled in the affairs of the world, and practicing mind/heart fasting, the problematic worldview and chronic stress will be eliminated.

The Confucian Perspective

For Confucius, the problematic worldview that leads to chronic stress is a result of seeing the self as being separate from other people and separate from the various social contexts that people populate. This problematic worldview is due to self-centeredness, self-entitlement, and narcissism. Self-centeredness results in and is maintained by a perspective that is motivated by self-benefit and self-gain. The focus on self-benefit and self-gain at the expense of others results in chronic stress. If everyone is motivated by self-benefit and self-gain, then there will obviously be disagreement, conflict, disrespect, lack of trust, fear, and the perception of threats. All of this leads to chronic stress.

To change this problematic worldview, Confucius focuses on relationships. People need to understand themselves not as separate, disconnected individuals. They must understand themselves as part of a larger group. Who they are, their identity, can only be truly found in relationships with others.

Individuals must, first and foremost, be attentive (*jing*[d]) in all of their relationships. By being attentive they will be able to mutually focus on each other. They need to understand the other person from the other person's perspective. What are the needs of the other person? They need to practice empathy (*shu*[e]).

To practice empathy, people need to be authentic/do their best (*zhong*[f]). When interacting with other people, individuals need to be considerate and respectful. They need to mutually acknowledge each other as fellow human beings contributing, in varying degrees, to the overall well-being of the social structure.

For Confucius, the problematic worldview is replaced with a worldview that focuses on understanding oneself and the various environmental contexts from the perspective of relationships. It is a worldview that is guided by empathy (*shu*[e]), authenticity/doing one's best (*zhong*[f]), respect (*xiao*[g]), and trust (*xin*[h]). This worldview, however, is meaningless unless it guides the individual's behavior in the various contexts. Without appropriate action or behavior (*li*[i]), nothing will change. Individuals must engage in behavior that is conducive to establishing a positive, mutually respectful environment for human interaction. The behavior of individuals must change from being self-centered and narcissistic to being selfless and group focused. The individual must move from worldview to behavior through appropriate choice and engagement (*yi*[j]). Ultimately, however, it is only through practice that change will occur.

Example

At some point in the counseling process, when the counselor is discussing cognitive processes and/or overall worldviews, the counselor will indicate to the client there is an exercise that would be beneficial in helping the client address and resolve his or her particular problem. The client is informed that the exercise has a preparation component and four parts. The preparation component is the *Basic Breathing Exercise,* which will help center and focus the client. Part 1 explores the client's worldview relative to the particular adaptive problem. Part 2 explores the perspectives of the other people involved in the client's adaptive problem from the client's perspective. Part 3 compares and contrasts the worldviews. The final part integrates and applies the first three parts to the client's adaptive problem. The client is asked about engaging in the exercise. Assuming the client says yes, the *Basic Breathing Exercise* is completed. The client is then asked to select a relationship relevant to the adaptive problem.

The client is asked about her worldview. What are her values? Are they subject to change? Can they be questioned? What are her needs? Are they being met? The client is then asked about expectations. How do you expect the world to behave? How does the client expect the people in her various environmental contexts to behave? The counselor and client explore the answers.

Regarding the worldview of the other individuals involved in the adaptive problem, the client is asked about how these individuals, one at a time, view the client and the problem. The client is asked to present the perspectives, nonjudgmentally, of the other people, one at a time, in the relationships pertinent to the client's problems. What are their values? Are they subject to change? Can they be questioned? What are their needs? Are they being met? How do they view the world? What expectations do they have regarding the client? The counselor and client explore the answers.

The third part of the exercise is to compare and contrast the worldview of the client with the worldviews of the other individuals involved in the adaptive problem. The client is the asked to explore the relationships she has with these various individuals relative to the adaptive problem. Having finished the first relationship, depending on time, of course, the focus can move, one at a time, to all other relevant relationships. Having examined the various relationships, ask the client if she sees any commonalities in her worldview and the worldviews of others across all of the relationships. The counselor and client explore the answers.

The final step is to ask the client if she sees anything about her worldview in relationship to others that may be contributing to the problem. If so, what is it and how can it be changed? The client is then asked about her behavior toward the other people in the relationship. What impact do these behaviors have on the other people in the relationship? Is there anything she could change?

The focus of the exercise is to attempt to modify the client's worldview by having the client see herself from a different perspective: that of relationships, as opposed to individuality. It is hoped that the change in perspective will broaden the client's understanding of the problem.

Chinese Characters

[a] 心齋	[f] 忠
[b] 無為	[g] 孝
[c] 無事	[h] 信
[d] 敬	[i] 禮
[e] 恕	[j] 義

Reference

Frank, J. D., & Frank, J. B. (1993). *Persuasion and healing: A comparative study.* Baltimore: Johns Hopkins University Press.

10

Feeling

All human being have feelings or emotions. Emotions are part of the evolutionary package that assists humans in surviving, reproducing, maintaining their gene pool, and adapting to various environmental contexts. Emotions assist human beings in solving adaptive problems. Emotions are normal.

Pert (1999), in her discussion of Charles Darwin and his text *The Expression of the Emotions in Man and Animals,* Richard Dawkins and his text *The Selfish Gene,* and emotions, argues that there is a commonality in the presence of emotions across humans and animals. She indicates that this commonality is integral to assisting animals and humans in surviving, noting that Darwin felt it was a fundamental component for survival.

> For example, a wolf baring its fangs uses the same facial musculature as any human being does when angry or threatened. The same simple physiology of emotions has been preserved and used again and again over evolutionary eons across species. On the basis of the universality of this phenomenon, Darwin speculated that the emotions must be key to the survival of the fittest.... If emotions are that widespread across both human and animal kingdoms, they have been proved, evolutionarily, as crucial to the process of survival, and are inextricably linked to the origin of the species.... I must tell you that the experts ... disagree about many things including whether feelings are the same as emotions.... They do agree, however, that there is now clear scientific experimental evidence that facial expressions for anger, fear, sadness, enjoyment and disgust are identical whether an Eskimo or an Italian is being studied. (Pert, 1999, pp. 131–132)

Emotions are important for survival, thus the commonality, because they communicate information to the individual and to other people. Emotions alert individuals about possible threats in their environment.

Emotions stimulate and motivate individuals to act or behave, to approach, avoid, stay still, or withdraw.

It is important that emotions be understood as occurring within various environmental contexts (internal and external) and as attempts to assist the individual in solving problems for the purpose of adapting to those environmental contexts. Nesse and Williams (1996) note:

> Emotional capacities are shaped by situations that occurred repeatedly in the course of evolution and that were important to fitness. Attacks by predators, threats of exclusion from the group, and opportunities for mating were frequent and important enough to have shaped special patterns of preparedness, such as panic, social fear and sexual arousal. Situations that are best avoided shaped aversive emotions, while situations that involve opportunity shaped positive emotions. Our ancestors seem to have faced many more kinds of threats than opportunities, as reflected by the fact that twice as many words describe negative as positive emotions. (p. 210)

In the same sense that normal, functional emotions are considered processes that assist human beings in solving problems and adapting to the environment, abnormal, dysfunctional emotions must also be seen, nonetheless, as processes that attempt, albeit in a maladaptive manner, to assist human beings in solving problems and adapting to the environment. In other words, by understanding the problematic emotion from the perspective of what it does for the person, rather than from a disease perspective, the counselor will be better able to assist the client in discovering the adaptive problem and in generating functional solutions.

For example, given a client with anxiety problems, the counselor can ask a series of questions to ascertain the function of the anxiety for the client and the adaptive problem the client is attempting to address with the anxiety. For instance, "What does your anxiety do for you?" "What does your anxiety allow you to avoid?" "What does your anxiety get for you?" "What threat does your anxiety allow you to avoid?" "What fear does your anxiety allow you to avoid?"

The important point is that the dysfunctional emotions need to be understood as having a function, albeit a maladaptive one. This is why Nesse and Williams (1996) feel it is important to link the maladaptive expression of the emotion back to its normal adaptive function. Normal anxiety is functional and assists individuals in adapting to the environment in many ways. Normal anxiety is the result of the activation of the fight-or-flight response or stress response (allostasis) relative to addressing and solving a problem in the environment. Once the problem is resolved, the fight-or-flight response is turned off and the anxiety disappears.

> Maladaptive extremes of anxiety, sadness, and other emotions make more sense when we understand their evolutionary origins and normal adaptive

functions. . . . Knowledge about the normal functions of emotions would provide, for psychiatry, something like what physiology provides for the rest of medicine. Most mental disorders are emotional disorders so you might think that psychiatrists are well versed in the relevant scientific research, but no psychiatric training program systematically teaches the psychology of emotions. This is not as unfortunate as it seems, since research on the emotions has been as fragmented and confused as psychiatry itself. In the midst of ongoing technical debates, however, many emotions researchers are reaching a consensus on a crucial point: our emotions are adaptations shaped by natural selection. . . . If our emotions are subunits of the mind, they can be understood, just like any other biological trait, in terms of their function. (Nesse & Williams, 1996, pp. 209–210)

As noted previously, Nesse and Williams (1996) believe that "most mental disorders are emotional disorders" and should be viewed as dysfunctional attempts to resolve an adaptive problem in the environment. Maladaptive emotions are a manifestation of a chronically activated stress response (allostatic load) that is attempting to address and resolve problems in the environment. As the stress response is unable to assist in resolving the problem, the adaptive problem remains and the normal emotional responses become chronic and maladaptive.

The paradigm, however, in psychiatry—and unfortunately more and more in psychology (witness its attempts to obtain the authority to write drug prescriptions[1])—is that psychological and/or mental disorders are diseases. Diseases that can be individually and independently classified, categorized, and investigated. Nesse and Williams (1996) argue:

By trying to find the flaws that cause disease without understanding normal functions of the mechanisms, psychiatry puts the cart before the horse. Research on the anxiety disorders exemplifies the problem. Psychiatrists now divide anxiety disorders into nine subtypes, and many researchers treat each as a separate disease, investigating its epidemiology, genetics, brain chemistry, and response to treatment. The difficulty is, of course, that anxiety is not itself a disease but a defense. (p. 230)

Integration and Application

Buddhism, Daoism, and Confucianism all view emotions as being normal. They all agree, however, that if emotions are held on to or maintained, and are not allowed to follow the continually changing, natural process they will become chronically excessive. This chronic excessiveness results in significant adaptive problems. All three perspectives understand these maladaptive emotions to be linked to a worldview that is fragmented and disconnected from the actual behavior of the environment. A worldview that is supportive of a separate, independent sense of self. They are all clear that attempts to solve adaptive problems in the environment with a fragmented, disconnected worldview that is supportive of an alienated sense of self results in the generation of chronic stress and maladaptive emotions.

The Buddhist Perspective

For Buddhism, these problematic, excessive emotions are *dukkha* or chronic stress. Buddhism addresses these dysfunctional emotions through the practice of mindfulness. By being nonjudgmentally present with the dysfunctional emotion, the emotion will be seen for what it really is: impermanent, nonsubstantial, and interdependent. As the emotion is not fed by judgments, it will dissipate. The insight gained by the practitioner is that his or her thoughts and worldview hold on to and maintain the maladaptive emotion. This insight is not gained through reason, logic, or faith; it is gained through the direct experience of being nonjudgmentally present with the emotion. The problem, of course, is that unless the overall worldview is modified or changed, the chronic stress and maladaptive emotions will be continually generated as the individual attempts to resolve adaptive problems in the environment.

The Daoist Perspective

For Daoism, chronic stress is generated by believing in, contending over, and arguing about absolute, contrived, unchanging worldviews, perspectives, values, standards, and judgments relative to addressing adaptive problems in the environment. The maladaptive emotions are an expression of this chronic stress. Emotions associated with and linked to absolute, contrived, dichotomies such as right and wrong, good and bad, and beautiful and ugly are maladaptive and excessive and disconnect the individual from the continually changing, integrated, interdependent process of existence.

Daoism addresses these maladaptive emotions and thus chronic stress through the practice of mind/heart fasting and sitting in forgetfulness. In both cases, the mind/heart is stilled and emptied through the practice of being nonjudgmental. In the case of mind/heart fasting, the practitioner is fully engaged with the present. The practitioner is able to nonjudgmentally observe existence as a continually changing, integrated, interrelated process.

Still and empty like a mirror, there is no holding on to or possessing of anything. As the practitioner continues to practice, the insight arises that the continually changing process occurs in emptiness or empty space. It is the same emptiness or empty space within the individual. It is the empty space that allows, without interference (*wu wei*[a]) or entanglement (*wu shi*[b]), everything's passage. Everything arises from and returns to empty space. There is, however, no object of empty space.

This insight is not based on reason, logic, or faith. It is based on the direct experience of being nonjudgmentally in the present. There no longer is a separation or disconnect. The worldview has changed. The chronic stress and negative emotions are gone.

Sitting in forgetfulness differs from mind/heart fasting. There is no linking to the external world. The eyes are closed. It is more of an absorption experience. By simply focusing, nonjudgmentally, on the breathing, the conceptual, emotional, and physical worlds, including the body, are forgotten. The experience deepens so there is no longer a focus on even the breath. The internal world disappears. The practitioner dwells *in* empty space but not *on* empty space. There is no object of empty space. The experience deepens even further until there no longer is a practitioner practicing. Everything is forgotten. Chronic stress and negative emotions are long gone. However, this is only a temporary reprieve from the adaptive problem generating the emotion and chronic stress. While the continual practice is beneficial physically and psychologically, and is stress reducing, the practitioner still needs to confront and address the adaptive problem through mind/heart fasting. The overall worldview needs to be changed.

The Confucian Perspective

For Confucius, maladaptive emotions and chronic stress are a result of a worldview that is disconnected, fragmented, and grounded in self-gain and self-benefit. The well-being of others is of no concern unless it benefits the individual. There is a clear sense of self-entitlement and narcissism. This self-entitlement and narcissism clearly disconnects the individual from the social environment.

Confucius addresses this alienation by focusing on reestablishing respectful, trusting, and empathic human relationships. When individuals focus on the well-being of others without any self-serving strings attached, they become fully integrated with their environment. There is no alienation. With the well-being of the family, the group, and the society as a whole as the focus, the maladaptive emotions disappear. There is no self-centeredness and sense of entitlement to generate and maintain them.

Example

Although the practice of mindfulness must be seen as a lifestyle change and not merely as one technique among many other techniques, its effectiveness is, nonetheless, readily apparent when applied to a maladaptive emotion. Consider a client who is having a problem with anger. Being with the emotion, in the present, in a nonjudgmental manner, the client will notice the anger will dissipate. The anger dissipated because the client is not feeding it with any thoughts or judgments. If it is not fed, it cannot be maintained. The life, if you will, is drained out of it.

There are a number of insights to be gained by the client. First is that emotions, like everything else, are subject to change. The anger will dissipate. Second is that the anger is subject to judgments and thoughts. By not judging, the anger dissipates. Third is that if the anger dissipates by not judging, then it follows that judging may be connected to the arising of the anger. Fourth is the client has the power, based on making or not making judgments, to control the anger. Fifth is that although mindfulness will allow the client to control the anger, the environmental problem that the client is making judgments about is the immediate source of the anger and needs to be addressed. The sixth insight to be gained is that the environmental problem is perceived as a problem through the client's worldview.

Mindfulness will not make the presenting problem go away. It will be of significant benefit, however, in assisting the client and the counselor in exploring the adaptive problem in the environment and the worldview of the client.

Chinese Characters

[a] 無為

[b] 無事

Note

1. See Levant (2005, p. 5) for a discussion of the position of the American Psychological Association on mental illness and the prescribing of drugs by psychologists.

References

Levant, R. F. (2005). Serious mental illness, recovery and psychology. *Monitor on Psychology, 36*, 5.

Nesse, R. M., & Williams, G. C. (1996). *Why we get sick.* New York: Vintage Books.

Pert, C. B. (1999). *Molecules of emotion: The science behind mind-body medicine.* New York: Touchstone.

11

Behaving

William James (1842–1910) argued that behavior has a direct effect on feelings or emotions. By changing behavior, individuals are able to change their feelings or emotions. Thus if the individual is not happy and wants to be happy, then the individual should act happy. James noted:

> Action seems to follow feeling, but really action and feeling go together; and by regulating the action, which is under more direct control of the will, we can indirectly regulate the feeling, which is not. Thus the sovereign voluntary path to cheerfulness, if our spontaneous cheerfulness be lost, is to sit up cheerfully, to look round cheerfully, and to act and speak as if cheerfulness were already there. If such conduct does not make you soon feel cheerful, nothing else on that occasion can. So to feel brave, act as if we were brave, use all our will to that end, and a courage-fit, will likely replace the fit of fear. . . . To wrestle with a bad feeling only pins our attention on it, and keeps it still fastened in the mind: whereas, if we act as if from some better feeling, the old bad feeling soon folds its tent like an Arab, and silently steals away. (James, 2005/1899, p. 96)

Recent research in the area of social psychology and personality appears to support James's perspective regarding a link between behavioral change and change in feelings or emotions. Fleeson, Malanos, and Achille (2002) presented evidence suggesting that if an individual acts in an extraverted manner, then it is more likely that the individual will have a more positive affect and be happier. They found this link to be quite important for the area of clinical intervention. Regarding their results, they note:

> Every single individual was happier when he or she acted extraverted than when he or she acted introverted, and the extraversion–positive affect relationship was characteristic of the ongoing psychological

functioning of individuals. . . . The findings suggest that individuals have flexibility and opportunity to act in different ways and bring about personally desired consequences. That is, positive affect was predicted by what the individuals did regardless of what (traits) they had. Thus, individuals are not limited to a single, set personality or to the consequences of their long-standing traits. At a more specific level, the robust between-persons relationship between extraversion and positive affect has always promised a possible clinical intervention for increasing positive affect, that individuals can increase their positive affect by increasing their extraversion. The present studies show for the first time that a rather simple intervention of encouraging individuals to act more extraverted may be particularly successful. Before it can be established as clinically useful, the causality of this relationship and its applicability to the clinical context certainly needs to be established. But the first and critical step, showing this process does occur within individuals, has now been taken. (Fleeson, Malanos, & Achille, 2002, pp. 1413, 1418)

Integration and Application

Buddhism, Daoism, and Confucianism clearly view behavior as having a direct impact not only on feeling or emotions, but also on worldview. Behavior shapes, develops, and maintains worldview. Yet at the same time, worldview shapes, develops, and maintains behavior.

For Buddhism, Daoism, and Confucianism, chronic stress is eliminated by changing both worldview *and* behavior. The truth of the matter is, worldview and behavior are integrated and cannot be viewed as being separate. Changing behavior has an impact on worldview and changing worldview has an impact on behavior.

Fundamental to Buddhism, Daoism, and Confucianism are behaviors that are focused on establishing relationships with various environmental contexts. As alienated, individually focused behaviors are what contribute to chronic stress, the teachings of all three perspectives focus on behavior that is conducive to integrating with various environmental contexts.

Any behavior that is supportive of an individual, separate, distinct sense of the self is viewed as counterproductive and is not acceptable. Being self-centered, having a sense of entitlement, or being narcissistic are all viewed as problematic and contributing to an inability to functionally solve adaptive problems in the environment.

The Eightfold Path of Buddha is essentially a behavioral guide to eliminating *dukkha* or chronic stress. It specifically indicates that the practitioner should speak, act, and live in a manner that is conducive to doing no harm to others and to experiencing existence as being impermanent, nonsubstantial, and interdependent. It focuses on the behavioral practice of mindfulness guiding, through appropriate effort, how the individual thinks, views, acts, lives, speaks, and meditates. The individual must be consciously focused, in the present, on all behaviors. All behavior is oriented to being consistent with the impermanence, nonsubstantiality, and interdependence of the various environmental contexts.

For Buddhism, changing actions and behavior has a direct impact on the practitioner's worldview. Changing the worldview has a direct impact on the behavior and actions of the practitioner. Both are required for release from *dukkha* or chronic stress.

The behavioral component is quite clear in the practice of Daoism. Noninterference (*wu wei*[a]) and nonentanglement in the affairs of the world (*wu shi*[b]) guide the practitioner in all of his or her actions. The practitioner must be clearly and consciously aware, in the present, of not attempting to control the behavior of other people. At the same time the practitioner needs also to consciously monitor his own behavior, in the present, relative to being controlled by other individuals and various social affairs. Practitioners are quite well aware of how absolute, contrived, unchanging values, standards, and judgments can control and negatively impact their behavior.

Practitioners of Daoism engage in behavior that is conducive to their own growth and the growth of the individuals whom they encounter in their interactions in various environmental contexts. All of their behavior is ultimately oriented to be in harmony with the continually changing, integrated, interdependent, interrelated process that is called existence.

The behaviors of noninterfering and nonentanglement have a direct impact on and shape the worldview of the practitioner of Daoism. The worldview that is developed and reinforced through the behavioral practice of mind/heart fasting and sitting in forgetfulness has a direct impact on and shapes the behavior of the practitioner. They are not separate.

For Confucius, appropriate behavior (*li*[c]) is what holds society together. All individuals are expected to behave in a respectful, trusting, empathic, authentic manner with the focus being on positive, growth-producing relationships. Any behavior that is driven by and focused on self-benefit or self-gain is not acceptable. Only behavior that focuses on and positively reinforces positive interactions and relationships in the family, group, or social structure is considered appropriate and acceptable.

Individuals learn, through the family and the educational process, how to correctly choose and engage (*yi*[d]) in appropriate behaviors (*li*[c]) relative to specific contexts. The choosing of and engaging in (*yi*[d]) appropriate behaviors (*li*[c]) have a direct impact on and shapes the worldview. The worldview, in turn, has a direct impact on and shapes behaviors. They are not separate.

Example

Given the counseling context, assuming clearance by the client, the counselor, after having the client first perform the *Basic Breathing Exercise,* explores with the client, the worldview and the behaviors of the client that are contributing to and preventing the resolution of the adaptive problem. What are the client's expectations about how the world and the people who populate it ought to behave relative to the adaptive problem? How do these expectations shape the current behaviors of the client relative to the adaptive problem? How do the current behaviors of the client impact the expectations? Given the current behaviors, how does the client feel when engaging in these behaviors? How do these behaviors impact on the client's feelings?

To what extent are the behaviors of the client driven by a sense of self-centeredness or self-entitlement? How does this self-centeredness or self-entitlement prevent the client from acting in a manner that may resolve the adaptive problem? Does this self-centeredness or sense of self-entitlement alienate or disconnect the client from various environmental contexts?

Ask the client to consider the impact of his behavior on other people relative to the adaptive problem. Ask the client to explore the context or contexts wherein the adaptive problem occurs. What behaviors can the client change relative to functionally addressing and resolving the presenting problem? How would this change of behavior affect the worldview (sense of self-centeredness or self-entitlement) of the client and the subsequent behavior derived from it? How would the new behaviors affect the client's feelings? How would the change of behavior affect other people involved in the adaptive problem?

Having explored the relationship between the behaviors and the worldview, the counselor would have the client select one or more behaviors that he has identified as being in need of change. The client would replace these behaviors with more functional behaviors (to be determined by the client), and the client would practice the new behaviors with the counselor. The counselor would ask the client how he feels after trying the new behaviors. What impact do the new behaviors have on the client's feelings or emotions? What does the client notice? Do the new behaviors have any impact on how the client sees the world? The counselor would then provide feedback to the client regarding how the counselor felt after the interaction with the client. The counselor would practice with the client until the client felt comfortable with the new behaviors. The next step is the world of the client.

Chinese Characters

[a] 無為

[b] 無事

[c] 禮

[d] 義

References

Fleeson, W., Malanos, A. B., & Achille, N. M. (2002). An intraindividual approach to the relationship between extraversion and positive affect: Is acting extraverted as "good" as being extraverted? *Journal of Personality and Social Psychology, 83,* 1409–1422.

James, W. (2005/1899). *Talks to teachers on psychology; and to students on some of life's ideals.* Boston: IndyPublish.com

12

Interpersonal Relationships

Glasser (1998) raises significant problems regarding what he believes is a psychology that attempts to control the behavior of people. He sees this controlling type of behavior as problematic and conducive to distress for people involved in a relationship. In fact, this controlling behavior tends to destroy relationships. People become alienated and separate from each other. Glasser argues:

> All unhappy people have the same problem: they are unable to get along well with the people they want to get along well with. . . . We need a new psychology that can help us get closer to each other than most of us are able to do now. . . . Our present psychology has failed. We do not know how to get along with each other any better than we ever have. Indeed, the psychology we have embraced tends to drive us apart. . . . I call this universal psychology that destroys relationships because it destroys personal freedom external control psychology. . . . It is an attempt to force us to do what we may not want to do. . . . It is unfortunate that almost no one is aware that this controlling, coercing or forcing psychology is creating the widespread misery that, as much as we tried, we have not been able to reduce. It continues because when people do not do what we want them to do, coercion and control are all we think of using. . . . The belief in and use of external control harms everyone, both the controllers and the controlled. (Glasser, 1998, pp. 5–7)

Buddhism, Daoism, and Confucianism all understand the importance of interpersonal relationships and are all well aware of how behavior such as that described by Glasser compromises interpersonal interactions. All three teachings stress the importance of not engaging in any actions that may be harmful, physical and/or psychological, to another person. This includes both verbal and nonverbal behavior.

For Buddhism, Daoism, and Confucianism, a worldview that rests upon a self-centered, self-entitled, and narcissistic foundation fragments and disconnects people from each other and from the world around them. Interpersonal relationships are severely compromised, and all individuals in the relationship suffer. People are alienated from each other, their environment, and for all intents and purposes, themselves.

Glasser (1998) argues that these negative, coercive, and controlling behaviors that push people away from each other and destroy relationships need to be replaced by behaviors that draw people toward each other and establish relationships. For this to occur, people need to change their behavior. Glasser notes:

> To achieve and maintain the relationships we need, we must stop choosing to coerce, force, compel, punish, reward, manipulate, boss, motivate, criticize, blame, complain, nag, badger, rank, rate, and withdraw. We must replace these destructive behaviors with choosing to care, listen, support, negotiate, encourage, love, befriend, trust, accept, welcome, and esteem. (Glasser, 1998, p. 21)

Integration and Application

The Buddhist Perspective

The Eightfold Path of Buddha is about engaging in behavior that eliminates *dukkha* or chronic stress. Buddha is clear that harmful behavior, in any form, toward others or oneself, is *dukkha*. *Dukkha* or chronic stress is associated with an independent, distinct sense of self. This sense of self is not conducive to eliminating *dukkha* or establishing positive relationships.

For individuals to eliminate chronic stress, they must engage in behaviors that are selfless, compassionate—that is, teaching others about the Four Noble Truths—and do no harm to others. For example, Correct Speech, one of the components of the Eightfold Path, requires the individual to speak in a manner that is positive, does no harm, and is not self-centered. Correct Speech is not judgmental. There is no criticizing, complaining, whining, moaning, demeaning, or blaming. Correct Speech is about engaging others on a common journey toward the elimination of *dukkha* or chronic stress. In this sense, it is truly about positive, interpersonal relationships.

The Daoist Perspective

Of the three teachings, Daoism stands out as being most obviously consistent with Glasser's notion of not controlling the behaviors of others. *Wu wei*[a] or noninterference is about not controlling the behavior (physical and/or psychological) of other people. Not interfering in the lives of other people. Letting other people work out their own destinies. *Wu wei*[a] is oriented to creating an environment that is positive, supportive, nourishing, and conducive to growth.

Wu shi[b], or not getting entangled in the affairs of the world (physical and/or psychological), is about not getting so involved in the affairs of the world that you end up being controlled by others and by environmental contexts. Unfortunately this often happens.

For the Daoist, by practicing both *wu wei*[a] and *wu shi*[b], individuals will be able to have positive, supportive, and nourishing relationships. Individuals won't control or be controlled by others. The practice of *wu wei*[a] and *wu shi*[b] acknowledges and respects other people as part of an ongoing, continually changing, interrelated, integrated process.

The Confucian Perspective

It should be clear that of the three teachings, Confucianism has the strongest, most salient focus on interpersonal relationships. For Confucius, the reason that there is social disharmony is that people are unable to get along with each other. Poor interpersonal relationships maintain and are a manifestation of chronic stress.

Confucius's solution to social disharmony and thus chronic stress is to focus on, develop, and implement the components of positive, supportive, compassionate interpersonal relationships. Positive, supportive, compassionate, interpersonal relationships or *ren*[c] are the glue, if you will, that holds society together. *Ren*[c] refers to interpersonal relationships in which the individuals in the relationship understand the context of the relationship; know their status and role in the context; know, chose, and engage (*yi*[d]) in appropriate behaviors (*li*[e]) relative to the context, their role, and their status; understand the importance of correct interpersonal communication (*zheng ming*[f]); and are respectful (*xiao*[g]), trustworthy (*xin*[h]), empathic (*shu*[i]), and authentic/do their best (*zhong*[j]).

In one sense, *ren*[c] can be construed to mean sacred interpersonal relationships. Sacred in the sense that *ren*[c] is an acknowledging of, compassion toward, and engaging with another person as a living, breathing, contributing human being. Insofar as positive interpersonal relationships are what hold a society together and allow for growth and further development, these interpersonal relationships may be seen as being sacred.

The foundation, for Confucius, of interpersonal relationships is the family. The family is central to his teachings. In the family, individuals learn about their role and status relative to supporting and maintaining the family. For Confucius, the family structure is hierarchical. Every individual in the family, depending on the specific familial context, knows and acts from his or her interpersonal relationship position. Their sense of identity is directly related to their interpersonal relationship position and status within the family context.

Within the family structure, self-centered, self-entitled, and narcissistic behaviors are not acceptable. Everything in the family structure is oriented toward the family as a whole. While the members of the family obviously engage in individual behavior, that behavior is always seen in light of how it reflects, represents, and contributes to the family structure.

Within the interactions and interpersonal relationships of the family, the members learn to chose and engage (yi^d) in contextually appropriate behaviors (li^e) relative to developing and maintaining harmony (he^k) within the family context. The family is, if you will, the initial training ground for choosing, developing, practicing, and demonstrating appropriate behavior relative to maintaining a stable familial structure.

For Confucius, all individuals in the family need to be mutually respected. Although respect goes both ways, the hierarchical structure determines the degree. Respect is subject to the position, status, and role (li^e) of the various members of the family. The sons will always be in a deferential position relative to their father. It is not negotiable. This is what $xiao^g$ or filial piety is all about.

The skills, competencies, behaviors, and worldview developed in and practiced in the family relative to establishing contextually appropriate interpersonal relationships are then applied to the large social context. Having a firm foundation based on respect ($xiao^g$), trustworthiness (xin^h), empathy (shu^i), and authenticity/doing one's best ($zhong^j$), the individual is able to begin the journey of learning to choose and engage in (yi^d) contextually appropriate role and status specific behaviors (li^e) relative to establishing positive, harmonious, compassionate, supportive, nourishing interpersonal relationships (ren^c). The individual will not be motivated by self-gain or self-benefit. The success of the overall relationship and its positive impact on the social structure is the focus of the relationship. This being the case, the individual will not be chronically stressed.

Example

Given a family counseling context, some basic guidelines can be set. First, the focus is on establishing harmony in the family. The focal point is on relationships within the family, not on individuality. Self-centeredness, self-entitlement, and narcissism are not allowed. Second, every member of the family is treated with respect. Behavior, both verbal and nonverbal, should be supportive and nourishing toward all members in the family. Third, there is no blaming, whining, judging, complaining, criticizing, moaning, or excuse making. Fourth, do not interfere with others. Do not attempt to control or manipulate the behaviors of others in the family. Fifth, no defensive behavior is allowed. When someone talks about you or gives you feedback, simply listen and see what you can learn about yourself from it. Sixth, everybody participates. No excuses for not participating. Be authentic and do your best.

Seventh, stay in the present. Do not talk about the past and what has previously happened. Then focus in on finding a solution in the present.

Given the guidelines, the first exercise (assuming clearance is given by the clients) is to have all of the members of the family do the *Basic Breathing Exercise* together. If they faithfully practice the exercise, this will reduce some of the chronic stress that will obviously be present. Having finished the exercise, the counselor will ask for feedback from each member. The feedback, however, is not about the person's own individual feelings. The clients are to provide nonjudgmental feedback about how the other members of the family now feel to them. The counselor summarizes the responses.

The second exercise is to have each member describe, nonjudgmentally, the roles, status, and relationships of each member of the family from the perspective of each other member in the family. Answers must be within the boundaries of the guidelines. The counselor summarizes the responses.

The third exercise is to have each member describe, nonjudgmentally, what the adaptive problem is from the perspective of each other member in the family. Answers must be within the boundaries of the guidelines. The counselor summarizes the responses.

The fourth exercise is to have each member describe, nonjudgmentally, what the solution is for the adaptive problem from the perspective of each other member in the family. Answers must be within the boundaries of the guidelines. The counselor summarizes the responses.

The focus of the exercises is on exploring relationships and empathically understanding the perspectives and feelings of the other members of the family. When the clients move out of a self-centered, blaming perspective, a better understanding of the family process can develop relative to finding a solution to the adaptive problem.

Chinese Characters

a 無為	g 孝
b 無事	h 信
c 仁	i 恕
d 義	j 忠
e 禮	k 和
f 正名	

Reference

Glasser, W. (1998). *Choice theory: A new psychology of personal freedom.* New York: HarperPerennial.

13

Spirituality

The issue of spirituality is usually associated with a relationship between an individual and some higher state of being or existence. This can take such form as the Judeo-Christian-Islamic God or the Hindu's Brahman, or one of the many deities, spirits, and gods of the other religions throughout the world. This higher state of being or existence provides answers to the existential questions of what happens after death, what is the meaning of life, what is the purpose of life, and what is my relationship to the environment and the people that populate it. All of these questions are, ultimately, related to each other, with the fundamental focus being on some sense of immortality: an eternal, nonchanging, stress-free, absolute state of existence, a heaven if you will, that is beyond the stress-filled, continually changing world of everyday existence.

Given this dichotomy, there needs to be a commonality that links the spiritual world of the gods with the individual. It cannot be the "stuff" of the continually changing realm of everyday existence for the simple fact that the "stuff" changes, contributes to stress, and dies. There must be something else that links people to the gods and the heavens. This link is the immaterial soul or spirit in individuals. This immaterial soul or spirit is not subject to stress, change, or death.

Given the various religious traditions that operate from this dichotomy, the meaning of existence is to cultivate this spiritual component or soul for the purpose of living forever in the stress-free realm of some heaven or higher state of existence. The relationship of individuals to the environment and the people who populate it is guided by their focus on deities and life after death.

Research cited by Benson (1996), Myers (2000), and Corey (2005) clearly indicates that religion and spirituality, faith if you will, appears to have positive effects on both physical and psychological health. Benson suggests that incorporation of religious faith into the relaxation response (used in the word or phrase said during exhalation) enhances the experience and contributes to overall better health. He notes:

> I already knew that eliciting the relaxation response could "disconnect" everyday thoughts and worries, calming people's bodies and minds more quickly and to a degree otherwise unachievable. It appeared that beliefs added to the response transported the mind/body even more dramatically, quieting worries and fears significantly better than the relaxation response alone. And I speculated that religious faith was more influential than other affirmative beliefs. . . . Based on the survey responses we calculated "spirituality scores." But because virtually all of our survey respondents reported a "belief in god," this statement could not be used to differentiate people. It was the more amorphous feeling of spirituality that could be linked to better physical and psychological well-being. (Benson, 1996, pp. 155–156)

Questions about and solutions to the meaning of existence, the purpose of life, and what happens after death are an integral part of the worldview of people across all cultures. The solutions seem to involve, in one manner or the other, for many individuals, faith and some sense of spirituality or relationship with an eternal, absolute state of existence or being. These solutions appear to assist individuals in functionally adapting to their various environmental contexts.

From the perspective of Buddhism, Daoism, and Confucianism, concerns about life after death and the world of the deities and gods are not relevant to eliminating chronic stress and functionally adapting to the environment. In fact, concern with these issues may be a contributing factor to chronic stress, as they are grounded in a worldview that focuses on separation, fragmentation, certainty, absolutes, and nonchange; a worldview that is not consistent with the observed behavior of existence.

Integration and Application

The Buddhist Perspective

For Buddha, speculative questions about the meaning of life, the purpose of life, life after death, and the eternality of the world are simply not relevant to removing *dukkha*. These questions distract people from removing the toxicity or chronic stress that permeate their existence. Buddha was not concerned one way or the other with what happened after death. He was not concerned because what happened after death was not relevant to removing, in the present, *dukkha*.

In the sutra called *The Parable of the Arrow* (*Jian Yu Jing*) or the *Small Sutra of Moluojia* (*Moluojia Xiao Jing*), a disciple (Moluojia) asks the Buddha why he does not answer such questions as whether Buddha survives death, whether the world is eternal, whether fate is the same as the body, and whether the world has limits. The Buddha offers a parable. There is a battle going on. A warrior is shot with a poisonous arrow. The arrow is clearly covered with poison. The attendants run up to pull out the arrow. The warrior says do not pull it out. I do not want you to pull it out until I know the name of the man who shot it, his clan, his status, the color of his skin, the name of his village, the type of bow, bowstring, shaft, and so on. Buddha informs the disciple that if the attendants waited until they answered all of the questions before they pulled the arrow out, the warrior would die.

Moluojia, perhaps there is the view that the Tathagata [Buddha] after death either exists or does not exist. Or perhaps there is the view that the Tathagata [Buddha] after death neither exists nor does not exist. There *is* birth, there is growing old, there is sickness, there is death, there is worry, there is depression, there is suffering, there is anxiety, there is hostility. Therefore, my teachings are carried out to overcome all of these. Thus, Moluojia, that which I have not indicated accept as that which I have not indicated. In addition that which I have indicated accept as that which I have indicated. Moluojia, what is it that I have not indicated? I have not indicated that the world is eternal. I have not indicated that the world is not eternal. I have not indicated that the world has limits. I have not indicated that the world is without limits. I have not indicated that fate and the body are the same. I have not indicated that fate and the body are different. I have not indicated whether the Tathagata exists after death. I have not indicated whether the Tathagata does not exist after death. I have not indicated whether the Tathagata exists and does not exist after death. I have not indicated whether the Tathagata neither exists nor does not exist after death. Moluojia, for what reason have I not indicated this to you? Moluojia, they truly are not meaningful, beneficial or relevant. They are not the root of my practice, they do not lead to rejection, separation from desire, elimination, stillness, penetrating wisdom, real awakening, and Nirvana. Moluojia, what is it that I have indicated? I have indicated there is *dukkha*. I have indicated the cause of *dukkha*. I have indicated the cessation of dukkha. I have indicated the path leading to the cessation of *dukkha*. Moluojia, for what reason have I indicated this? Moluojia, they are truly meaningful and relevant. They are the foundation of my practice, they lead to rejection, separation from desires, elimination, stillness, penetrating wisdom, correct awakening and nirvana. Moluojia, that which I have not indicated accept as that which I have not indicated. In addition that which I have indicated accept as that which I have indicated. (*Small Sutra of Moluojia*)[1]

For Buddha, spirituality, if one is to use the word, meant elimination of *dukkha* or chronic stress. It means experiencing the self and the environment as impermanent, nonsubstantial, and interdependent. Spirituality means the end of separation.

The Daoist Perspective

For both the *Dao De Jing* and the *Zhuang Zi,* questions about the meaning of life, purpose of life, deities and gods, and life after death agitate the mind/heart and fill it with nonsense. If one stilled and emptied the mind/heart and fully embraced and experienced the present, these questions would simply fall away.

Death is clearly seen as a natural part of the ongoing, continually changing, integrated, interrelated process of existence. There is no fear about what happens after death.

> Life is the companion of death.[2] Death is the beginning of life. Who knows their arrangement? Human life is the gathering of breath [*qi*[a]]. It gathers and there is life. It disperses and there is death. If life and death are companions, why should I be fearful? Thus, the 10,000 things are one process. That which is taken to be beautiful is spiritual [*shen*[b]] and precious. That which is taken to be ugly is stinking and rotten. The stinking and rotten are transformed into spiritual and precious. The spiritual and precious are transformed into the stinking and rotten. Thus it is said, the world is a unified network of breath [*qi*[a]]. The naturally integrated person values this unified network. (57–58/22/10–13)[3]

For the *Dao De Jing* and the *Zhuang Zi,* spirituality is about being free from contrived, absolute, unchanging, restrictive standards, judgments, values, and worldviews. Spirituality is a selfless, full engagement, in the present, with the changing process of existence. There is no separation.

The Confucian Perspective

For Confucius, questions about life after death and the spirits are not helpful to understanding people and life. These types of questions draws one's attention from more pressing needs, such as teaching people how to establish positive supportive relationships, working together, and creating a harmonious life.

> Li Lu asked about the affairs of the spirits. The Master [Confucius] said, "You do not know of the affairs of people, how can you ask about the affairs of the spirits?" "May I venture to ask about death?" The Master said, "You do not know about life. How can you know about death?" (*Lun Yu,* XI-12)[4]

Spirituality for Confucius is about being fully attentive and committed in all interactions. It is about always being respectful (*xiao*[c]), trustworthy (*xin*[d]), empathic (*shu*[e]), and authentic/doing one's best (*zhong*[f]). Spirituality is about choosing and engaging (*yi*[g]) in appropriate contextual behavior (*li*[h]) while establishing positive harmonious, compassionate, supportive, nourishing interpersonal relationships (*ren*[i]). It is *about* relationships. There is no separation, self-centeredness, self-benefit, or self-gain. Spirituality is about people and society in harmony.

Example

On the surface, clients enter counseling to remove symptoms or the overall feeling of what Frank and Frank (1993) refer to as *demoralization*. There is a strong sense of a distinct, separate, fragmented self that has these symptoms and is unhappy. Unfortunately, at this level, the operating psychiatric paradigm is to clump the symptoms (which are real) together, reify them, and create artificial diseases such as generalized anxiety disorder, dysthymic disorder, social anxiety disorder, adjustment disorder, alcohol use disorders, substance use disorders, and so on. Given that these clumped symptoms are now considered to be diseases, they can be treated, by a select few, with medication.

Nesse and Williams (1996) argue that the psychiatric paradigm of studying symptoms without understanding their function is problematic. It is clearly a problem to take manifestations of chronic stress that are generated by an attempt to solve an adaptive problem in the environment, clump them together, and label them a disease such as anxiety. The absurdity of the clumping of symptoms into disorders, without determining what the symptoms are indicative of, is demonstrated by applying, according to Nesse and Williams, this procedure to a cough. The ability to cough is part of the evolutionary tool kit. It has an adaptive function. A cough is a defense; it helps to protect us. A cough, with rare exceptions, is not a disease or a disorder.

> To appreciate the problem this creates, imagine what would happen if doctors of internal medicine studied cough the same way modern psychiatrists study anxiety. First, internists would define "cough disorder" and create objective criteria for the diagnosis. Perhaps the criteria would say you have cough disorder if you cough more than twice per hour over a two-day period or have a coughing bout that lasts more than two minutes. Then researchers would look for subtypes of cough disorder based on factor-analytic studies of clinical characteristics, genetics, epidemiology, and response to treatment. They might then discover subtypes of cough disorders. . . . Next, they would investigate the causes of these subtypes . . . by studying abnormalities on neural mechanisms. . . . The knowledge that

codeine stops cough would lead other scientists to investigate the possibility that cough results from deficiencies in the body's codeine-like substances. (Nesse & Williams, 1996, pp. 230–231)

For those who are unable to provide drugs and/or do not accept the drug paradigm, the next level, believed to be the cause of the symptoms, is that of problems associated with interpersonal relationships. For Glasser (1998), the reason people are unhappy, the reason they have their symptoms, is that they do not know how to functionally interact with other people. They have a clear sense of being alienated from other people.

Underlying interpersonal relationships is the level of ultimate meaning, which is concerned with such existential questions such as death, meaning of life, and purpose of life. Yalom (1980) refers to these types of issues as ultimate concerns and argues that psychological symptoms can be traced back to the inability of the client to successfully cope with the fear of death or one of its many manifestations, such as uncertainty, loss, or change. The client feels isolated and alone in a vast universe. Clearly an entry point for spirituality!

Underlying this level is a stress response mechanism provided by the evolutionary process that has not been allowed to function in a normal manner. It is not being allowed to turn off. It is not being allowed to turn off because either an adaptive problem in the environment has not been solved or the stress response was inappropriately activated for a problem in the environment of which it would be of no benefit. Either way, the symptoms are indicators that something is wrong relative to the relationship between the individual and some aspect of his or her environmental (internal or external) contexts.

At its most extreme point, the stress response is responding to perceived (real or imagined) fears and threats. The fear of death is the most basic threat. It is a threat to individuality. It is on this fear that Western practices of religion and spirituality are based.

During the course of a counseling session, the client is asked if he or she would like to engage in a process that would explore the presenting problem on four levels: symptoms, relationships, existential, and that of chronic stress and adaptation to the environment. The client is informed that the presenting problem will be examined and explored by the client, on each level, from two different worldviews. The first worldview focuses on reason, independence, resistance to change, and the self as the center. The second worldview focuses on direct experience, interdependence, acceptance of change, and the relationship as the center. The two worldviews are explained to the client so the client has a functional understanding of applying them to the presenting problem on each level. The client is informed that the entire process may take a few sessions.

Assuming the client agrees, the first step is to do the *Basic Breathing Exercise* to center, focus, and relax the client. At this point the process begins with the client exploring and examining her problem, from both worldviews, at the level of symptoms. Such is the new beginning point of simplicity and commonality. The client and counselor will determine when it is time to move to the next level.

Chinese Characters

a	氣	f	忠
b	神	g	義
c	孝	h	禮
d	信	i	仁
e	恕		

Notes

1. The translation/interpretation, from the Chinese, of the Buddhist text in this chapter is my own. The Chinese text for *Small Sutra of Moluojia* (*Moluojia Xiao Jing*) can be found at Jie Zhuang Buddhist Educational Web site at http://www.jcedu.org/fxzd/ah/zb/8.htm#63. The Chinese *Agama* version of this text, *The Parable of the Arrow* (*Jian Yu Jing*), can be found in the *Madhyamagama*, number 221, [0804a23]. The *Madhyamagama* can be found at McRae (2003), the *Electronic Texts of the Chinese Buddhist Canon* Web site, T1, No. 26, located at http://www.indiana.edu/~asialink/canon.html. An English version, translated from the original Pali, can be found in Horner (1967), *The Collection of the Middle Length Sayings* (*Majhima-Nikaya*), *Vol. II,* No. 63, "Lesser Discourse to Malunkya (Putta)."

2. See Chapter 50 of the *Dao De Jing.*

3. The translation from the Chinese of this section from the *Zhuang Zi* is my own. The format of 58/22/10 indicates the page/chapter/lines in the *Harvard–Yenching Institute Sinological Index Series Supplement 20, A Concordance to Chuang Tzu* (1956). The text *Zhuang Zi Bai Hua Ju Jie* (1989) was used as a supplement for the translation/interpretation.

4. The translation translation/interpretation of this section of the *Lun Yu* is my own. The format of XI-12 refers to the Book (11) and Section (12) of the *Lun Yu*. The Chinese texts utilized for this translation can be found in Yang (1972) and Hong (1973).

References

Benson, H. (1996). *Timeless healing: The power and biology of belief*. New York: Scribner.

Corey, G. (2005). *Theory and practice of counseling and psychotherapy*. Belmont, CA: Brooks/Cole.

Frank, J. D., & Frank, J. B. (1993). *Persuasion and healing: A comparative study*. Baltimore: Johns Hopkins University Press.

Glasser, W. (1998). *Choice theory: A new psychology of personal freedom*. New York: HarperPerennial.

Harvard–Yenching Institute. (1956). *Harvard–Yenching Institute Sinological Index Series, Supplement 20. A Concordance to Chuang Tzu*. Cambridge, MA: Harvard University Press.

Hong, C. H. (Xiao Zhe). (1973). *Si shu shou ji, zhu xi shou ji*. Taibei: Hua Lian Chu Ban.

Horner, I. B. (Trans.). (1967). *The collection of the Middle Length Sayings (Majjhima-Nikaya), Vol. III: The final fifty discourses (Uparipannasa)*. London: Luzac and Company.

Jie Zhuang Buddhist Educational Web site. (n.d.). Available at http://www.jcedu .org/fxzd/ah/zb/8.htm#63

McRae, J. R. (2003). *Electronic texts of the Chinese Buddhist canon*. Retrieved December 21, 2005, from http://www.indiana.edu/~asialink/canon.html

Myers, D. G. (2000). The funds, friends and faith of happy people. *American Psychologist, 55*, 56–67.

Nesse, R. M., & Williams, G. C. (1996). *Why we get sick*. New York: Vintage Books.

Yalom, I. D. (1980). *Existential psychotherapy*. New York: Basic Books.

Yang, J. L. (Bian Ci). (1972). *Lun yu zhu shu bu zheng*. Taibei: Shi Jie Shu Ju.

Zhuang Zi. (1989). *Bai hua ju jie*. Hong Kong: Feng Hua Chu Ban Shi Ye Gong Se.

Index

Note: In page references, t indicates table, n indicates note.

About the Author

Robert G. Santee is professor of psychology at Chaminade University of Honolulu, in Hawaii, where he is the dean of behavioral sciences, the director of the Master of Science in Counseling Psychology Program, the coordinator for the Undergraduate Psychology Program, and the university assessment facilitator. He has been employed full time at Chaminade University for 12 years.

He has worked full time (16 years) as an operating room technician assisting in surgery and full time (5 years) as a psychological examiner administering IQ, achievement, and personality tests.

Dr. Santee has a PhD in philosophy (general focus in Asian philosophy, specific focus in Chinese philosophy, and a specialization in Daoism), a PhD in educational psychology (focus in assessment and psychometrics), a master's in counseling and guidance (community counseling), a master's in philosophy (specialization in Daoism), and a master's in educational foundations (focus on examining teaching methods of Kendo). Dr. Santee is a nationally certified counselor (N.C.C.).

He has developed and teaches Daoist Psychology, Buddhist Psychology, Psychology of T'ai Chi Ch'uan, Health and Stress Psychology, and Evolutionary Psychology in the undergraduate psychology department. He also has developed and teaches Introduction to Chinese Thought, Taoism (Daoism), and Confucianism for the religion department. At the graduate level, he teaches a class in Health, Stress Management, and Counseling and a class in Cross-Cultural Counseling. Tai Ji Quan (T'ai Chi Ch'uan) and Qi Gong (Ch'i Kung) are incorporated in both of the graduate classes, all three religion classes, and three of the undergraduate classes.

Dr. Santee's examination of the relationship among Western counseling, Chinese thought, evolutionary theory and evolutionary psychology, the stress response, and stress management has resulted in his writing and presenting papers at conferences in Taipei (Taiwan), Tiantai (China), Chengdu (China), and Honolulu, Hawaii. His exploration of the relationship between Western counseling and Chinese thought has been guided by training in Chinese martial arts. He is a student, practitioner, and teacher of Tai Ji Quan (T'ai Chi Ch'uan) and Qi Gong (Ch'i Kung). He is also a practitioner and student of Ba Gua Zhang (Pa Kua Chang).